ORGANIZING THE REVOLUTION

ORGANIZING THE REVOLUTION

SELECTIONS FROM AUGUSTIN COCHIN

Chronicles Press
Rockford, Illinois
2007

This book would not have been possible without the generosity of Linda and Harry Teasley.

The cover image is "The Execution of Queen Marie-Antoinette on October 16, 1793" (Danish School), which is held by the Musee de la Ville de Paris, Musee Carnavalet, Paris, France. (Photo Credit: Erich Lessing / Art Resource, NY.)

Library of Congress Cataloging-in-Publication Data

ISBN 978-0-9720616-7-4

CONTENTS

ORGANIZING THE REVOLUTION

PREFACE

by Claude Polin

Did you say Cochin? Who, except for a few specialists, has ever heard of him, even in France? Why read him? True enough, he is not the most famous, but there is a reason for that, and of such a nature as to be in itself good motivation for reading him. He has indeed dared lay a most incorrect hand upon the founding myth of contemporary France, the French Revolution.

1

American readers are probably aware that two centuries ago Frenchmen decided there were no such things as gods, but were seized with an epileptic fervor for the bare-breasted raving fury who most adamantly addressed them, as she is still doing from the face of the Arch of Triumph on the Champs-Elysées, and who is the apt symbol of both the Revolution and the French Republic. Every Bastille Day (July 14th) France is supposed to be moved to tears while reminiscing about the populace that rushed through the Bastille gate congenially opened by the twenty-odd veterans who served as the garrison, promptly slaughtered them with butcher knives, and kept dismembering their fellow citizens for the best part of ten years, before Bonaparte decided they had better massacre foreigners instead. It took a century for this new Sacred History to be officially validated as such—but from then on whoever criticized it was to be branded a traitor, a criminal, or a moron. Since 1789, the French, shining the dazzling lights of Revolutionary Reason over the centuries to come, have instituted themselves the pathfinders of mankind. Hail to the benevolent geniuses who fought over, planned, and implemented a new creation of man!

Well, said Cochin, the whole play was but a farce. A tragic one, which substituted tyranny for liberty, privilege for equality, and hatred for love. A badly acted one, whose stars were second-rate amateurs, and often misfits fleeing real life, all too willingly mistaking the applause of the rabble for the esteem of normal citizens. And an extravagantly bloody one, for its avowed purpose was to destroy minds and kill bodies in the name of freedom, justice, and love, for the sake of Humanity.

I can only surmise what urged Cochin to devote his life to making these points. Born to a typically bourgeois family; Catholic, but of liberal, and even democratic, leaning; conservative, but as people whose prominence might not have been possible without the Revolution; a brilliant and dedicated academic whose field was more the early Middle Ages than modern times, and who confronted the republican wrath of the Sorbonne's history professors turned watchdogs of the official dogma—Cochin, one is led to believe, must have answered to the appeal of something which he valued more than his career or even his life. Given the heroic way he died, it is difficult not to rest assured he wrote under the spell of a deep love for his country. But his was a love for what he perceived as true France, which meant for him an instant repulsion for seeing it defaced by obsessive, self-proclaimed humanitarians. In other words, Augustin Cochin was a true-blooded patriot, and he had to believe that a country in which ordinary citizens became murderers bent on systematic annihilation could not be his country, the one he gave his life for. It must therefore have been a country inoculated with a perverse disease. Cochin might have thought of himself as a political equivalent of Pasteur, had not the Revolutionary disease been of a kind that occurred only once, and had not his faith in his country's basic health been overpowering. I cannot help thinking this somewhat naive optimism induced the only real blind spot in his vision.

2

Cochin is not the only one to have spotted the weakest link in the usual apology for the French Revolution (Hyppolite Taine also did it in his irreplaceable *Origines de la France Contemporaine*), but he is probably the one to have derived from his observation the most surprising diagnosis of the nature of the event. The size of the upheaval was of such proportions that one may reasonably wonder if it could be of human making, but even barring that metaphysical vision, there is something about it that no unbiased observer can miss: the tremendous disproportion between the event and the ability of any of its acknowledged leaders to foment and control it.

Whatever one may think of them, the enlightened philosophers were men of words, not deeds. So who actually was at the helm? To name only a few of them: Danton was a flamboyant crook; Robespierre an obscure lawyer parroting Rousseau with typical eighteenth-century *emphase*, but also with the intellectual grasp of a myopic janitor; Marat was a rabid psychopath, a former hospital worker whose medical genius had been thwarted by society (along with his other talents, since there had been, as he stated bluntly, no musician, no mathematician, no biologist before he was born). Swarming around them were cohorts of semi-educated, bombastic agitators, echoing rather grotesquely the eminently controversial and eminently demagogical slogans of the Enlightenment. There were some hardened criminals or unstable adventurers amongst the troops, but not many; the bulk of them was comprised of extremely ordinary citizens, remarkable only as obscure, petty nobodies.

So the question arises very naturally how such mediocrity, often blended with personal corruption, could have bred such a gigantic earthquake—a fact that is all the more intriguing since almost all the main leaders ended up on the scaffold, having grown unpopular overnight. Such questioning was precisely Cochin's: what happened to a country that was supposed to be the flag-bearer of civilization, but that turned raving mad in a matter of months, tearing with uncontrollable fury at its own throat while embattling the whole of Europe, and after suffering twenty years of irretrievable demographic damage, finally surrendering out of exhaustion, saved only by the wise moderation of the European princes? French history between 1789 and 1815 is one of a slow descent into national chaos and European hell: what was its motor?

There are different types of answers, implicitly embodying three different types of philosophy.

Augustin Barruel, a Catholic priest, favors the conspiracy approach. Events of such magnitude, involving such great masses of men, cannot, says he, be spontaneous, self-ignited, or initiated overnight. The ground must have been tilled, the seeds sown. But it takes plowmen to do that, and here they had been indeed, thought the good priest, working throughout the century like worms eating away at a beam: the Freemasons. The rest of the theory is irrelevant to Cochin, who only appears to buy it; in fact he does not, and actually disagrees with the core of it. The point is quite delicate, but worth clarifying if one wants to assess accurately Cochin's definitive contribution to a classical historical riddle. Barruel's point of view is that the opinions entertained by the enlightened Revolutionaries were so unnatural that they must have been artificially planted in the Frenchmen's minds by some operation involving a certain degree of discreet and unconscious but forceful coercion. For a disease to take hold of a body that does not want to get sick, a microbe must be inoculated by some hidden hand. The good father could not know about the techniques of brainwashing, but that is obviously what he had in mind.

Cochin does not agree with this particular aspect of Barruel's hypothesis. He assumes—and rightly so—that such great numbers of men cannot be manipulated by so few. Whereas it is perfectly true that any mass movement must have leaders, it is plain common sense to realize that, beyond a certain number of people, these leaders can only lead toward a goal that already attracts the mass. Ironically, the standard twentieth-century political theorists have joined forces with Barruel, for the entirely opposite reason of defending democracy: inasmuch as nazism and bolshevism are tyrannies, these regimes cannot be the offspring of democracy, and therefore must be the tyranny of one man and his clique, using terror to subdue their fellow citizens and victims. Cochin sees through this politically-correct opinion. If he had lived long enough, he would have supported the view that at the height of their power Hitler or Stalin were immensely popular—just as Robespierre's popularity was such, when he was at the helm of France, that until his very last moments it did not suffer from the terror he was inflicting on the French population (and it has remained very high amongst historians).

That said, Cochin stops short of claiming those leaders essentially embodied the more or less conscious leanings of the vast majority of the population they led, that they were mere reflections of the population's inner impulses, passions, or drive. Cochin never adopted this entirely new conception of the real sources of tyrannical political power, though he may be credited with blazing the path leading to it, at least to the extent of debunking the conspiracy theory. In other words, Cochin cannot bear the idea that the French leaders of the Enlightenment and the Revolution were merely speaking the language the French masses wanted to hear. He wanted the French people to have been lured by the deceptive seduction of total freedom, but at the same time to have been deceived. Hence his idea that the whole process is a social mechanism: a sort of synthesis of the belief that the people must have been *induced* to thinking in such an unnatural way, and the fact that no tyranny, strictly speaking, was involved in their transformation.

As for the explanation of the French Revolution in socioeconomic terms (made famous by Marx), it is as if Cochin had never heard of it, or had never considered it worth even a critique. The received wisdom of our times will probably take this as a reprehensible loophole in Cochin's argument; yet one may not only excuse Cochin for bypassing the Marxist fad, but congratulate him for not getting snared in its fallacy. While it is true that poverty may lure people into revolt, it all depends on the way poverty is perceived by the underprivileged themselves. An idea that Cochin could easily have made his: poor harvests would not have triggered anything, if there had not already been a widespread belief that some wasted the bread others needed to survive, thanks to the poor not having their say in political life.

But Cochin has several more precise and amply justifiable reasons for rejecting Marxism. Cochin's concern is not to understand how the French Revolution may be considered as the inevitable result of men being subjected to some kind of determinism, but on the contrary—and this is much more fascinating—to understand how men can have been willingly, freely, drawn to such dire straits of tyranny. This particular line of questioning led Cochin to an assertion which counterbalances that of Marx: that leadership may have nothing to do with wealth and economic status (as we shall see later). All in all, it can be argued that Cochin goes beyond Marx: the latter thinks evil comes to men because they are not free or equal enough; the former presupposes this ideal state has actually been implemented and then proceeds to study what happens—which he shows to be tyranny and inequality. I could make a similar observation about Marx's famous claim that happiness will prevail amongst men once private property has been abolished. For Cochin this abolition is the logical outcome of the unnatural state of things that comes about when total freedom has supposedly prevailed—the monstrous flower that grows upon manure.

Now, there is a third theory about this ghastly episode in French history, one which is quite impressive though admittedly rather remote. The lofty genius of Count de Maistre gave it its most unforgettable hue. In his eyes, the atrocity of the event is of such magnitude as to exceed anything that human forces were able to beget. There was something supernatural in the amount of energy deployed by Frenchmen at the time to chop off one another's heads: the French Revolution is the result of a very conscious attempt to free mankind from the guidance of God (which pretty much sums up what the Enlightenment amounted to). Whoever wants to play the angel ends up acting the beast: men turning their backs on God results in men behaving as if they were out of their minds, literally possessed, hence their craving to hurt one another. This is undoubtedly a bizarre vision for contemporary eyes, though a rather fascinating one. But even though Cochin was a traditional Catholic, he does not allude to it (except perhaps when he finally confesses he is unable to discover the ultimate reason for such a lust for blood: "why do people kill? . . . This is where history fails us and can only ascertain the facts without understanding them"). For the archivist he was the truth must lie in tangible facts, recorded in documents.

Hence his most unfortunate reference to Durkheim's[1] sociology in order to describe his own approach: on Cochin's own confession, his approach was not to be a far-fetched spiritualistic one (too bad he did not realize how factual the latter can be), but a resolutely scientific one, according to which facts, and only facts, explain facts. But he did not understand his explanation had, in the last analysis, nothing to do with Durkheim's. Whereas the latter wanted to prove individuals are, in their behavior as well as their inner selves, exclusively a product of Society (with a capital letter, as in God), Cochin believed individuals during the French Revolution had been, though voluntarily and more or less consciously, somehow mechanically drawn into a type of societal bond (a Society) which actually deprived them of their natural ability to think and act by themselves, deprived them of their own nature as beings endowed with a personal liberty and consciousness which transcend their molding by society. In other words, Cochin endeavored to describe as a pathology what Durkheim insisted was normal—which resulted in Cochin's insights withering away under the imperial glare of the master of French sociology.

3

What then was Cochin's theory? Let us try to clarify some of his fascinating concepts, often rather severely obscured by his awkward style and constant reference to intricate facts he knows much more about than his readers do.

The gist of it is as follows.

The French Revolution basically replaced the monarchical system, traditional in France, with a democratic one of a very peculiar nature. To Cochin, the democracy the French picked for themselves was actually nothing but a new type of tyranny, a tyranny with willing victims and without tyrants, strictly speaking; for in this tyranny the people freely choose to be ruled by tyrants whom they freely appoint, without calling them tyrants or even acknowledging that they may behave as such. According to Cochin, French democracy is a tyranny that coincides with pure democracy.

What makes this possible is precisely a certain type of social organization (which is why Cochin claims to be a sociologist) invented and tested during the course of the eighteenth century, first on a very small scale (it was called a Philosophical Society), and then extended to the whole nation (and called democracy). Cochin's basic stroke of genius is to have understood how the fundamental requirements of perfect democracy (that no one yield to anyone, and therefore that every citizen's will be done) could be met if there were a way for decisions to be reached, policies to be implemented, without any particular will but the mechanics of society itself producing those decisions or policies—just as bales of hay are produced by the harvesting machine without the driver having anything to do with the shaping of the bales.

Let us consider the prototypical Philosophical Society. People gather together to exchange ideas, impressions, points of view; to think as they please on the basis of total and absolute freedom and express themselves at will. This is what democracy is all about, according to Jean Jacques Rousseau. One is entitled to suppose that, just as in real society, the reason for their gathering is to do something together which they would not be able to do if each was left to himself—elaborate a common opinion, for instance. They cannot reach a decision by compromise, which by definition implies that each has given up something, since perfect democracy means each person remains totally entitled to his own particular idea. But that is precisely the trick. Given a little more time, some sort of automatic ordering emerges from the chaos. The absence of any criterion for discriminating between the true and the false—between careful thinking and verbosity, reality and fantasy, meaningfulness and meaninglessness—makes for the continuous din of senseless discussions. Many lose interest in the meetings: those who have other things to do, duties to fulfil, a profession to tend to, talents to put to work. So they leave the premises, though remaining willing members of the club, and keen on its avowed purpose, though disappointed by its performance. Those who stay are people who have nothing else to do, the sheep, the dull-witted, the jobless, the ambitious, the incompetent.

Thus it happens that without terror, without coercion, without tyranny, the Society has managed to expel those who have a stake in real society and have an interest in making responsible decisions; those whose advice and judgment are sorely needed. Finally the Society is comprised almost exclusively of those who have no other objective than to keep the controlling position they have reached not through their talents, but mechanically, and which becomes for them a God-sent profession in itself, as well as a key to other advantageous, automatical-ly-opening doors. It must be noted that this process of elimination is in no way conscious or voluntary: it is rather a sort of built-in mechanism, the equivalent of a physical law (Cochin called it "purging"). The traditional comparison of society with a living organism has now lost its relevance; this new Society must be understood as a machine. It must also be noted that the mechanical character of the process is precisely what makes it so powerful: nobody is to blame, it is just that things work that way, because that is the way they are. Assume everyone's right to total freedom, let some time elapse, and what you get is the power of the few over the many.

At this point some may argue the situation cannot last: why should absentee members be loyal to, or even concerned with, whatever the more tenacious ones have decided; why should the former consider as their own whatever opinion the latter have agreed upon? Cochin does not evade this crucial issue, and addresses it with his usual inimitable mix of insight and   wording. The members of the Philosophical Society follow its self-proclaimed steering wheel because, says Cochin, each potential dissenter must feel profoundly and frighteningly alone when challenging the supposedly united others, and therefore naturally shrinks from opposing what he thinks is the general opinion. From whence comes this feeling? If he belongs to the group of those who have not had the time to participate in debates, the answer is simple: he is bound to believe their conclusion reflects the general opinion, and where would he get the courage to confront the majority? Things would be different if he had some inner conviction, if he had God's help. But that is impossible by definition: in a free society all citizens are entitled to think freely and entertain any notion that pleases them. So his own weighs no more than any other's. Which means his freedom is his own freedom's most effective shackles. On the other hand, let us suppose the potential dissenter has been more obdurate and has endured the debates throughout. It is not likely that his situation, though possibly trickier at first, will evolve in a significantly different way. For again, with everyone free to have opinions, all opinions being equal, and there being no truth to prevail over all of them and generate unanimity, the discussion would rage endlessly unless there happened to be a few people finally to unite and promote a resolution. Whatever this resolution may be, it still has the advantage of the small number over the single unit that the individual represents.

So the same principle holds: the freedom of all results in a minority taking an unassailable hold on the majority. The famous "tyranny of the majority" is actually that of the minority. And with that we have the second law of the dynamics that predominate in this type of Society, what could be called the law of inertia: the momentum gathered by a few amongst an amorphous mass of disjointed elements is irresistible. Cochin calls it the law of the *fait accompli* (once something has been done somewhere under certain conditions, it becomes a ruling principle elsewhere). I would ask anyone who doubts the human propensity to join the minority that shouts the loudest whether he usually buys a book because he has browsed for it in a bookshop, or because his favorite newspaper has told him it is a must.

Cochin may be considered as the real inventor of what modern psychologists call "group dynamics"—a field all political agitators have majored in since the blossoming of democracy in general and revolutionary assemblies in particular. Cochin would have been ecstatic, had he been able to observe the development of a student revolt in contemporary France. Once the red flag has been unfurled for a certain number to see, a marvelously spontaneous ordering of protests takes place, leaders emerge like rabbits out of a hat, coordinating authorities and bureaus sprout following illusory elections by raised hands (always showing admirable unanimity), and then the tide swells or subsides following a miraculous moon of its own.

If there be any reason to criticize Cochin's intuition, it is that he has not followed it far enough. I would argue that not only is the potentially dissenting individual *reluctant* to dissent, but he is actually *unwilling* to do so. For to dissent from any given opinion must be to dissent from the whole system that has produced it, and particularly the principle it is based on—the individual absolute freedom of thought—which was the very reason for joining it; so dissenting amounts both to reneging oneself, or one's vanity, as a being endowed with freedom, and to questioning a sacred belief, which no one can do without being branded an enemy of free thought, nay, of Thought. So however absurd the results the whole process leads to, there is little doubt in my mind that the appeal of such a glorified status, particularly upon mediocre minds, will easily supersede whatever inconvenience the actual loss of freedom might mean to them. It is true that the reluctance to acknowledge someone else's superior wisdom is not always groundless, and that trust-inspiring individuals are not to be found at will. But are these reasonable doubts not easily swept away by the feeling of self-importance that such a democracy must nurture in the average citizen's heart? In other words, it seems to me an indisputable truth that the moment free thinking means equality of opinions, the majority is bound to prefer the leadership of a supposedly—even if spuriously—elected citizen, even at the cost of his being tyrannical, to the most competent, benevolent king, if the latter is to be king on an hereditary basis. This psychological (or moral) tendency is, I think, the basis of the efficiency of Cochin's mechanical process. It eventually means the ultimate cause of this efficiency is the notion that the opinion formulated by the few is not only valid because it is a collective one, but also, and probably mostly, because somehow, in the last analysis (and maybe for no other reason than that the only other choice would be to rely on someone else's opinion), this opinion can be conceived by each citizen as being his own.

4

Cochin is now ready to take the next step and to move away from the Philosophical Societies towards real society, the political one. If such machinery is actually the hidden hand behind purely intellectual proceedings, could it not be at work just as well behind those of a political society, especially since it is based on the very same presumption that all men have an equal right to unlimited freedom? At this rate, the only difference is that free thinking must be translated into free willing, which again translates into free voting. The difference is negligible: the behavior of the voting citizen can be understood as a mere reflection of that of the thinking citizen, while society at large becomes a mere mirror image of the Philosophical Societies, except for its size, just as in a nest of wooden Russian dolls the biggest one reproduces the features of the smaller ones it contains.

At this point, two comments seem appropriate.

Why indeed should the difference in size have any bearing on the way the machine works? If anything, one could argue that its efficiency increases with the number of people it processes. For the smaller the society, the easier it is for everyone to know everyone else, and for absentees to catch up with the others or to require a reorganizing of the debates. Whereas the larger the society, the fewer people any given individual may know and the more isolated he is from the mass of his fellow citizens; and the more the society is bound to be comprised of people who need to earn their living, who fulfil a function, who do not have much time to waste. So it is easy to see that the purging process should be even faster in real society than in a Society whose members attend mostly in their leisure moments; the control of the few over the many all the more simple as the controlled do not know who is who; and finally, the propensity to yield all the more powerful as the individual feels more acutely his loneliness, i.e. his weakness relative to the momentum of masses who are seemingly united, if only by their mass itself. On top of all that, the lone individual must be aware that to howl or not with the pack of wolves is to play for high stakes: in real society, where strength lies, there also lies wealth and safety.

The size of the society has another noticeable side effect: as the mass of citizens to control grows, so must the number of their controllers, and the probability that there will be competing groups among the latter. Four people may control fifty, not millions: there arises the need for a much more complex apparatus, a sort of artificial nervous system, competing and progressively replacing the natural one, but aping it, with ganglions directing and receiving impulses to and from each limb, and eventually each cell. The Enlightenment nurtured such a system: falling prey to the lure of supposedly uninhibited intellectual freedom, the citizens spontaneously gathered into a myriad of Philosophical Societies whose inner mechanisms were the same, and purposes identical, and which readily ended up forming a spontaneously coordinated network. At first, they were all partners in the same movement; there was only one smaller Society inside the larger one, which, interestingly enough, called itself the Philosophical *Party*. It was only natural, indeed, considering the volume of potential clients, that competing networks should start blossoming, what with the ambitious realizing the fertility of the field. So it came about that the Philosophical Party became only the original blueprint for the democratic institution known later on as political parties.

Here Cochin undoubtedly owes a great deal to political scientists such as

Ostrogorski or Bryce whose studies he uses and cites repeatedly. Their descriptions of the functioning of English and American political parties at the end of the nineteenth century match to perfection Cochin's findings about the eighteenth-century French Philosophical Societies. They match to such perfection, indeed, that his chance encounter must have acted as a powerful enticement to follow up on his personal feelings, as a traditional Catholic, about democracy, and to adhere to these thinkers' pessimism about this regime (which becomes clearer as the pages are turned). If a club is to a party, and a party to a whole society, what one Russian doll is to the next one up, then Cochin, together with Ostrogorski and Bryce, are joint inventors of what Roberto Michels (who, surprisingly, refers to the latter but not to Cochin) will a little later call the "iron law of oligarchy," a law so universal that not even democracy is able to escape its hold. In other words, democracy is a sham, an ornate façade concealing slimy chambers. The sovereignty of the people is a front: "everywhere it was the small number, two or three citizens[,] who engineered the revolutions," said Camille Desmoulins, a French Revolutionary. Freedom is a front, hiding an autocracy of leaders that is all the more shocking as these leaders do not owe their leadership to their talents or virtues, but to their vices and obsequious enslavement to a purely mechanical process. Power without authority is their strength, but this is nothing but the definition of a tyrant's strength.

5

It is worth observing at this point that Cochin runs radically afoul of the standard vision of democracy as a regime constantly threatened by a tyranny of the majority. From the American founding fathers to Tocqueville or Constant, the basic concern seems to be the protection of minority rights—and today in the immigration-ridden Western countries this concern has turned into a self-inflicted obsession among the fashionably open-minded elites.

And so Cochin raises quite an issue.

To put it in a nutshell, Cochin's thinking definitely seems to revolve around Hume's famous assertion—the real wonder with political power is that the many always obey a few—and to be bent upon solving the paradox, at least in the case of the French Revolution. His central thesis is that there is such a thing as regular enslavement without coercion, once everyone is pronounced absolutely free: in this case the only alternative is general dissolution of every social bond, or yielding to a decision assumed to have been made by everyone, even if this entails everyone faking this assumption. Cochin's theory seems to have been vindicated by historical experience. It is a liberal commonplace that communism (or nazism, for that matter) is a political regime in which the vast majority of citizens obeys the small minority of communist apparatchiks, even though the latter acts tyrannically. Or, again, it is a plain fact that political parties, in Western democracies, have never stopped functioning exactly like the machines described by Cochin. He even seems to be supported in this respect by Jean-Jacques Rousseau, whom Cochin intensely disliked. For Rousseau was a fierce critic of political parties, which he called factions (subversive and subverting leagues), unduly confiscating the popular will ("will," he said, "cannot be delegated"). But then Cochin must be understood as going far beyond Rousseau: his is not a criticism of representative democracy only, but of direct democracy as well. Following his reasoning, one does not end up with the idea that all expressions of popular will—parties, to start with—are spurious, but with the idea that direct democracy is simply impossible once it is defined as a system whose basic principle is absence of any principle except that of pure freedom. Cochin actually never elaborated on these two conclusions—he was not a philosopher by training, and he died at age 40, before he could produce any finished work—but he should be credited with blazing the way toward that obviously momentous vision.

Yet this very outlook seems to me somehow questionable. Let us grant that he discovered the special role played, more or less behind the scenes, by a minority. This does not amount to the few being given a relatively free hand over the many (a truly despotic power). The few may be given utter control over the masses as long as nothing more is at stake than the phrasing of a resolution that will not be enforced anyway, or the utterance of an opinion that will not be taken into account in real life. But it remains to be seen whether this will still be the case when the power of the few weighs inescapably upon the average person's daily life, when the machinery of oppression, be it hidden as carefully as may be imagined, carves out his real existence. If Cochin was entirely right, why has no minority of recent times been able to restore monarchy in France? In real life it is arguable that masses are manipulated only when they agree. It is arguable that oppression will likely be resented all the more as those who appear to cause it—the parts of the machinery that cannot help but be exposed—are deemed to be the mere reflections of those who suffer from it. It is much more logical, because much more natural, for the masses to grow more impatient with any constraint as time passes, and eventually, as if exploding, to shrug it off all the quicker as the oppressors do not have any personal appeal. In a democracy it does not make sense that people will actually do, in the long run, what they do not want to do.

And here, as a spectacular reversal in this direction, comes Cochin's own confession: "though the oppression of the 'little people' in the Societies was endured for a while by the terrified country, the reign of the impersonal could not last. The 'great people' were too much alive to let themselves be thus subdued or reduced to inertia. The clubs were not the nation. The latter, which had reacted to every undertaking of communism,[2] started to straighten up after Thermidor. This was not the end of the crisis, but the specter was exorcised, and common sense gradually took possession of minds again. France could breathe [once more], as if awakened from a nightmare." Cochin suddenly and definitely takes sides with classical liberalism's optimistic wisdom: there is no tyranny except of the few over the many, but precisely because the tyrants qualify as such because they are few, tyrannies never last. This seems to imply that, inasmuch as there is a type of democracy whose real essence is to be the tyranny of the few, this type of democracy does not last. But if this is the case, why do representative democracies last, since they include as their essential components the institutions that are the very tools of tyranny, according to Cochin's own description? Isn't Madison right, and Tocqueville after him, when he fears democracy's resilience lies precisely in the ability it gives to majorities always to have the last say?

Here we face a central difficulty, which casts a considerable cloud over Cochin's thesis, or at least over its ultimate meaning. Hence my two final remarks.

6

First, this difficulty leads to a better understanding of the precise extent of Cochin's findings (at least in the unfinished state he left them in).

This much may be flatly stated: there is nothing he wrote that refutes the definition of a democracy as a potential tyranny of the majorities over the minorities. He does not even mention the notion. This blind spot in his vision is, I think, somehow natural, considering what he was as an individual, the way he lived and died. He died defending his country (returning to the battlefield several times after severe wounds), which means he fought with his fellow countrymen and for them. How could he not have believed in them? Therefore, whatever they (or their ancestors) did that was objectionable must have been the result of foreign inspiration; they must have fallen prey to fallacies that they would have seen through, after a few moments. While there were perverts amongst them, the French people at large were good and honorable men. They must have been infected with a disease; they could not possibly have been bent on inflicting it upon others. They were victims, not executioners. "A force reigned that was indeed a collective idea and will—hence an opinion and a people, not a faction or a party—but it was not [public] opinion. A [little] people took the place of the [common] people—the former more foreign to the instincts, interests, and genius of the latter than the English of York or the Prussians of Brunswick. Was it astonishing then that the legislation enacted to suit one was a straitjacket for the other, that the happiness of one was the Terror for the other, that the laws necessary for one were impossible for the other?" To put it succinctly: his whole thinking was geared toward finding an excuse for why the French people behaved as they did during the French Revolution. This is noble.

But this is also unrealistic: simple logic suggests the French people did what they did because they wanted to do it. Cochin himself said so: if the leading minority's power is experienced as tyrannical, it does not last. If it does last, that means the same power is experienced by the masses as an expression of their will ("I am their leader, therefore I must follow them.") He should have followed Hume's reasoning: if the many do what the few want them to do, it is because they are infused with the opinion they should do it. That the masses might have been inoculated with this opinion does not make much difference, because it only means they were receptive to it. Whence it follows that any leading minority is such because it happens to be—or is contrived to represent—exactly what the majority is itself bent on doing or thinking (this is what is usually called political flair). Not only is everything that occurs in a Rousseau-style democratic society supposed to be the will of the people, but it would be a severe mistake to believe the many do not know what they want. One of the mediocre nobodies who became minister twenty-five years ago in France declared bluntly, "We are morally right, because we are the political majority." In the naive expression of such a monstrous idea lies for all to see this certitude: majorities are entitled to define good and evil, because, better than minorities, they *know* what these are. The right of eminent domain is of the same vein: it may be put to questionable uses by minorities, but always in such a way as to appear to benefit the many. This is what demagoguery is all about—building private advantages and power upon policies that appeal to the majority.

Does this mean the bell tolls for Cochin's ideas? Not at all, for he has pointed out at least three crucial facts.

First, Cochin's observations have undoubtedly withstood time, as long as they are understood to describe how leaders are elected in democratic Western societies (at whatever level within the system). One cannot help referring to Cochin every time one wonders at the general mediocrity or interchangeability of these people, as if they could just as well have been selected on a random basis within the sphere of men who are endowed with what I would call a certain image (in the case of visible leaders, they can be tall or short, well-spoken or awkward, but what matters is that they offer a certain reassuring familiarity to most of the public). Since there are scores of people meeting the requirements, there must be a process of selection, and since the numbers of freely-opining citizens are staggering, this selective process must be essentially mechanical (though money is often a way to grease the squeaky wheels). If everything were not cut and dried, no leadership would emerge, and the whole system would collapse. In this sense, democracy in general is nothing but a vast artificial mechanism designed to give flesh to ghosts and produce supposedly popularly selected leaders.

The second worthy lesson of Cochin's is his assessment of the precise role that minorities play in the democratic process. While it seems to be demonstrable that they only lead inasmuch as they are led, it does not follow that their role is negligible. On the contrary, it is crucial, though in a rather surprising way which Cochin helps to delineate clearly. We can put it like this: there is no leader where there is no majority to produce its leader, but there is no majority where there is no leader to rally around, to embody its existence as a unified political force. This is a sort of vicious circle which makes the recourse to social mechanics so illuminating. Without a leader, the people constitute only an amorphous mass, or a crowd that is constantly on the verge of dissolution into a heap of disjointed members unable to act: there is no such thing as a spontaneous majority. But when the need is powerful enough, there is always some entrepreneur to sense it and answer to it.

Going a little beyond what Cochin wrote, this much can be argued: it is not that a majority does not know what to think or feel, but that it would not be able to express itself if not for the minority and its leaders, whose only talent is not to lead, but to perceive where the majority wants to be led. Then the need for the function breeds its organs. Nobody formulated this delicate but crucial balance of roles better than Cochin's private ghoul, Jean-Jacques Rousseau: "Spontaneously the people always want the good, but they cannot always see it spontaneously. The general will is always right, but the judgment that moves it is not always enlightened. This will needs to be shown things as they are, sometimes as they must appear to it. This will has to be shown the right way that it is seeking, be protected from the allure of individual wills . . . Individuals can see the good they reject; the public wants the good it cannot see. They all have the same need for *guides*."[3] This is a word that must be translated into a much clearer one: demagogues. There is no doubt in my mind that both Cochin and Rousseau had one famous disciple in the twentieth century: General de Gaulle, that supposed leader who liked so much to call himself a guide, and who knew so well how to follow his troops.

In other words, there are two different meanings for the word "minority":

there is the minority Cochin was concerned with, and which only expresses the wishes of the majority; and there is the minority in a more realistic sense, which is comprised of the people crushed by the majority, whom Cochin does not mention.

The third of Cochin's worthy—though not fully expressed—lessons is that the only real power that leading minorities are to be credited with is the power to accelerate the maturing of radical democracy, to precipitate its unveiling. Once it is understood that leaders lead only inasmuch as they go the way their followers are willing to go, it becomes obvious they will be all the more hailed as leaders as they see a step farther than their cheering constituencies. And in case of competition, the winner must always be the most demagogical. Some among the crowd will probably think their leaders go too far or too fast; but how could they rein in the horse's pace without showing some disapproval of the goal, i.e. without jumping out of the saddle and looking like renegades? Democracy—at least Rousseauist democracy, the one Cochin considers—cannot know any stability, only perpetual change encouraged by leaders steadily striving to stay one dream ahead of their troops' desires. The ultimate leaders of this sort of democracy will be found emerging from gutters to head street demonstrations—a conclusion that has met similar judgments, though made on other grounds, ever since Plato.

7

But there is more. The accumulated evidence of facts is such that Cochin himself, seemingly in spite of himself, hinted at the possible existence of an even more sinister kind of tyranny of the majority.

Confronting as an indisputable fact the unspeakable horrors through which the Revolutionaries waded periodically, Cochin's deep intellectual honesty forces him to confess at what a loss he is to understand their motives convincingly. In a crucial paragraph—a concluding one—he writes, "the Jacobin Fatherland was Rousseau's Society, which actually meant a federation of selfish interests. There was nothing beautiful or pleasant, nothing generous in it. Jacobin Patriotism was just one of the branches of this philosophical moral science, derived from Hume and Hobbes, and founded, as the pundits admitted themselves, on the great principle of 'self-respect.' 'Self-interest,' says the politician, 'Greed,' says the economist, 'Passions,' says the moralist, 'Nature,' chant the philosophers in unison: such were the wellsprings. The goal was a happier state, not a more perfect one, and the means [to attain it] was by destruction, not creation—and people do not die for all that.

"But then why do people kill? . . . *This is where history fails us and can only ascertain the facts without understanding them.* It can see the facts clearly. It can even acknowledge their logical connection to principles and the fact that this Humanity had to kill, this Liberty had to coerce. It does not see the origin, the nature of the feelings that can subjugate the heart of a man, an entire people, to this terrifying logic. Explaining '93 by Jacobin 'Patriotism' is like explaining a mystery by an enigma."[4]

The mystery is all the darker as the perpetrators of the crimes are by no means unusual monsters or psychopaths: Cochin knows and says so. "This was the only time small groups of men—republican authorities and patriotic clubs—accustomed enough to murder to practice individual and mass executions in cold blood, operated as though they were sweeping the streets. Yet these were not madmen, nor—at least not all—brutes; they were often *petits bourgeois* terrifyingly similar to their non-murderous peers."[5] Nevertheless, these normal citizens turned into bloodthirsty, pitiless, remorseless executioners, and not particularly gullible ones. Reading the memoirs of one of them, published recently, one learns how he used to walk to the Place de la Concorde after lunch, as a sort of digestive stroll, to watch a few beheadings, which spectacle filled him with ease and enabled him to enjoy a peaceful dinner, because he had seen enemies of the Republic die. The assassins—acting directly or indirectly, soiling their hands and eating the traitors' hearts or passing laws that made the murders legal—were all supposedly civilized, enlightened citizens.

If the only thing Cochin had ever done was to shed full light on this specter—the possibility of senseless, systematic, bureaucratized, moral mass murder, committed by the common man—he would deserve enshrining. Because this means questioning, for once, the fundamentals of one particular type of modern Western democracy. And not only for reasons of historical curiosity: for if it happened once, why couldn't it again? (For that matter, hasn't it?) What lies at the core of these democracies: unprecedented solicitude for Mankind, or sheer inhumanity? Whichever the answer, what does it stem from?

As Cochin himself wrote, he does not know—and (as he did not write) he is not that keen on knowing. But History—as he recounts himself—gives us a few hints. And first and foremost is the fact I find most *enlightening*: that the great mass of the victims was not comprised of what we could call the *logical* opposition (like priests or noblemen), nor of the more or less inevitable ones (former allies, disenfranchised competitors, federalists, moderates), but of the totally *unnatural* ones: average people. Cochin (and Taine before him) mentions babies, children, pregnant women, vagabonds, peasants, valets, stable boys, etc. mown down, bayoneted, shot, drowned, and of course beheaded, in cold blood, until the executioners stopped out of belated revulsion. As the Revolution proceeds, its propensity to devour its own children becomes more and more a conscious behavior. Three examples (quoted by Cochin himself) are particularly noteworthy.

In 1792, the Revolution invented universal conscription (*levée en masse*), which would provide it with plenty of cannon fodder. This gave all possible leeway to a new type of military strategy, using numbers (France was the most populous country in Europe at the time, with about three times the population of England), and obviously resulting in the heaviest conceivable casualties. From where would a majority of mediocre and self-centered individuals draw that ferocious will to send masses of their own countrymen to death, which at some point meant committing suicide?

Then there was the new economic policy initiated in 1793, which amounted to questioning the right to private property so cherished by the eighteenth-century Enlightenment that it was engraved in the sacred marble of the immortal Declaration of the Rights of Man. "The city is a people of equals, free by nature. But all those freedoms are swallowed up by the common will. If the person is not his own master, he can still less possess his own property. All possessions will become national property . . . The guillotine and the massacres concerned only the victims. *But the confiscation of all property concerns everyone.*"[6] That is certain, but that is the question, for at the same time the whole Revolution is, in Cochin's eyes, the product of selfishness. So why would a majority, who enthusiastically purchased national property (confiscated from the Church and noblemen, and put up for sale by the Revolutionary government), consent to its own spoliation, in the very name of the inalienable right of the citizen to private property? Where does what Cochin calls a "vast collectivist experiment," an attempt at "communism," come from? It does not make sense. Again, it is one thing to yield to an opinion one disagrees with, but which has no bearing on real life; it is a different thing altogether to surrender a piece of property one uses to support oneself and one's family, and also one's independence.

Lastly, under the influence of Robespierre, the Convention passed the famous law called the Law of Suspects, which can be summarized in these few words: henceforth everyone, Cochin says, becomes "the natural enemy of his neighbor," which is a new system, that of "government by hatred of one's neighbor . . . by mutual surveillance and mutual constraint."[7] Robespierre put it even more bluntly: from now on, terror becomes the law.[8]

These three facts tell the same story, that of *mutual tyranny*. And this is the real mystery, because it represents, as Cochin himself accidentally once phrased it, "a sacrifice of oneself for the sake of oneself."[9] Cochin would like this system to proceed from a necessity to do as the others do, but this bucket hardly holds water: why would anyone start doing to others what he must know others will do to him, especially when it might mean murder? Again, "Why do people kill?" asks Cochin. In other words, what emerges from the history of the Terror, like a snake whose head peeks out of murky waters, is a visceral drive, some sort of passion powerful enough to tear reason and even plain rationality or enlightened self-interest out of souls and hearts, blinding common sense enough to create a modern type of tyranny the world had not seen before. Cochin confesses that it boggles his mind, but acknowledges its existence and calls it "tyranny without tyrants"; I prefer to call it the tyranny of the majority over itself, or, ultimately, the *tyranny of all over all*.

Once the fact has been identified, it is up to everyone to imagine its cause. There are a few easy hypotheses. For instance, it is a common mistake to believe one can keep clear of the troubles one inflicts on others. But this amounts to saying stupidity and shortsightedness rule the world, and while this is probably true, since all thieves act in this way, thieves do not have to face everyone else as potential policemen. The passion we are seeking cannot be confused with a mere mistake in judgment; deliberate determination is, in this particular case, of the essence. The nice old gentleman is calmly satisfied to see his countrymen, whose crimes he is not even remotely aware of, die on the scaffold. Rousseau once said from the silence of the people, it must be presumed that the people consent. So they must be enthusiastic when they applaud, which indeed they did.

One may also claim that people are indoctrinated, subjected to continual harassing propaganda. Perhaps; but not to the point of millions of people endorsing massive, open, and glorified cruelty, wielded so indiscriminately and systematically as to make it nearly impossible not to feel threatened (one can fool some of the people some of the time, not all the people, all the time).

Or again, the mystery does not lie in masses despoiling minorities (the haveless robbing the have-more, or even the Parisians exterminating the inhabitants of Vendée, the first genocide of modern times), but with terror hovering over everyone's heads, or, as Cochin almost confesses he does not wish to understand, every French citizen hating every other French citizen.

Nor, finally, is envy a passion that may bear merely on everyone else — if only for the simple reason that not everyone else has something to be envied.

So my conclusion would be an alternative. One can either flatly deny the fact itself, pure and simple, declaring there has never been any such thing as *reciprocal terror*. Or, since all honest historians agree with the evidence (the latest being Alexander Solzhenitsyn), there must be a cause for it. As a student of communism, I have developed one hypothesis. In homage to Cochin, I shall mention it here in the briefest terms.

The gist is simply that the sort of man who can be like a wolf to any other man was not born before the sixteenth century. So it is one and the same thing to understand what men were before, what this new man is, and to determine the seed from which he originated. To me this seed must be seen primarily as of a metaphysical nature, that is to say a spiritual one, but true spiritual causes always translate into empirical, i.e. psychological or social terms. Now, it is logically obvious that the more a given individual takes himself as an ultimate standard of value, that is to say the more he loves himself, the more he must grow indifferent to others if their respective paths do not cross, and hostile to them if their paths collide. The more he loves himself, the more he feels entitled to whatever he may wish to be or do, and the more he must in the same measure grow aware of others entertaining the same self-love and therefore perceive them as so many threats to his being whatever he wishes to be (everything becomes a potential barrier to someone who wants to be able to go wherever he wants). Hence this creates a thirst for equality that nothing can quench, since it does not proceed from the recognition of other people's dignity, but from a wish not to be superseded in any way by others, who in their turn do not have any more reason to respect the individual than he has to respect them. So there comes a point when the only way Paul may feel safe from Peter, and Peter from Paul, is for each to annihilate the other (or at least that which makes him a different individual). This means that there comes a point when the individual's self-love drives him to make demands that are detrimental to himself; a point when a state of reciprocal surveillance and control prevails, which is a state of more or less explicit reciprocal terrorism. I think it is crazy logic that self-centered delirium should reach the point at which one's inflated ego cannot bear the sight or thought of another ego equally inflated; in any case it is an historical fact that Robespierre, in one of his most famous speeches (quoted above), demanded that "everything that provokes the passions of the human hearts to focus upon the *abject ego* should be rejected and suppressed." And it is another historical fact that the French Communist Party, some forty years ago, published the ravings of Babeuf, claiming that every human virtue, including intelligence, should be annihilated, because their unequal distribution prevented every single man from thinking of himself as a perfect being.[10]

That is precisely the situation that arises when men lose their belief both in the existence of a whole, of which they are parts, and in their own meaninglessness, once they try to live as self-sufficient gods; when men endeavor to live in a religionless society (and by "religion" I do not mean those tailor-made creeds or superstitions that fit this or that particular subjective need); when societies emerge that are devoted to the well-being and comfort of the individual, a well-being that is mostly determined not by any natural standard but by the individual's arbitrary whims. In other words, I am afraid that in spite of our technical achievements, our unashamedly atheistic and decidedly materialistic societies are the direct outgrowth of that lethal seed planted long ago in the hearts of men by some primeval evil-doer, which our blossoming Civilization tried for so long to prevent: the love of oneself over the love of God. (It is an odd fact that Marx, in his youth, wrote strange poems in which he exalted Satan together with his own self.)

It may be argued that these same civilizations are a long way from being so nightmarish. I think this is beside the point, which is that they may be on the way to this ultimate fate, both willingly and unwittingly, as is the case with every momentous historical event. Assuredly, no force except a purely physical one can overpower men and make them follow a path like pebbles carried downstream by the rushing torrent. But the short-sightedness of vast numbers of men similarly immersed in the love of their respective selves produces the equivalent of such a force. Individually, they think they act rationally; collectively, they do not know what they are doing, as blind to their coming mutual destruction as a mole to the trap ahead. As the French say, it only takes rivulets to make a river. In the present case, I am tempted to think that when our societies reach the point at which a majority of citizens will proudly choose never to do anything but for personal, subjective reasons; never to acknowledge the existence of objective norms they must obey, whether it pleases them or not—then at that moment our societies will suddenly founder under their citizens, and drag them down as if drawn by some mysterious and uncontrollable vortex.

At the risk of appearing presumptuous, I believe that Cochin would have agreed with this conclusion, had his patriotism not forbidden him to conceive of his country foundering in such sewage.

Claude Polin
April 2006

Translator's note: This translation represents about half of Cochin's published work. The chapters were selected by Claude Polin for their modern, universal interest. All the ellipses refer to omitted material. Unless otherwise noted, the footnotes in the translation are by Cochin or his publishers: Plon for the original edition of 1924, and Copernic for the second of 1978.

ENDNOTES

[1] Emile Durkheim (1858–1917), considered the father of the French school of sociology.

[2] This is Cochin's term in the text.

[3] *Le Contrat Social*, II, chap. 6, last paragraph. The italics are mine. Interested readers should also read chapter 7.

[4] "Humanitarian Patriotism," pp. 215–216, italics mine.

[5] "Humanitarian Patriotism," p. 213.

[6] Quotation from the original edition of Cochin's *The Revolution and Free Thought*, Plon, Paris, 1924, p. 228. It must be noted that Rousseau himself underwrites the abolition of real private property. In the *Social Contract*, Part I, chapter 7, he writes, "The right each individual has over his own property is always subordinated to the right the community has over all citizens."

[7] Part III, "Socialized Property, the Means," p. 212.

[8] Robespierre's speech: "*Sur les principes de morale politique qui doivent guider la Convention nationale dans l'administration intérieure de la République*," February 1794.

[9] Part III, "Introduction," p. 200.

[10] It should be mentioned here to American readers that, beyond a superficial resemblance, American societal culture is essentially different from its French counterpart—Cochin's exclusive concern—in one crucial respect: consciously or not, there is an ingrained realism about people in American minds. It does not prevent Americans from believing they have found the recipe for the least bad society, but keeps each citizen from self-idolatry.

THE PHILOSOPHICAL
SOCIETIES AND MODERN
DEMOCRACY

THE PRECURSORS OF THE REVOLUTION: THE PHILOSOPHERS[1]

I should like to speak to you about the "Philosophers" of the eighteenth cen-tury—but I mean their philosophy, and not, as you no doubt expected, their supper gatherings, witticisms, charming lady friends, quarrels, and triumphs. This is a thankless task, surely, for all the charm and interest—I was about to say the seriousness—of my subject lies in the minor details. What would Voltaire's metaphysics be without his mischief, the fame of so many thinkers without a few letters from women, and the editions of the *Encyclopedia* without their bind-ings? Yet we shall leave the binding aside, the pretty brown and gold back you can see from here, and talk about this book that you have never opened, for it would be useless, thank God, since you already know what it says. Everything has changed in one hundred and fifty years, except philosophy, whose name alone has changed—we call it Free Thought—and which varies as little from one man to another as it does from one era to another. Diderot, the conversationalist and scholar, no doubt had his own charm and physiognomy. [But] Diderot, the phi-losopher, is similar to all his "brothers." Enough said about him.

Yet if description is superfluous, explanation is very difficult. Just what is philosophy[2]? A sect, we usually say, and it does indeed possess all the external trappings of one.

Orthodoxy first: "Reason," writes Diderot in the *Encyclopedia*, "is to the phi-losopher what grace is to the Christian." It is the principle of our Free Thinkers: "We have faith in reason." Thus what is asked of the brothers is less to serve reason than to believe in it. This cult works the same way as any other: it is goodwill that saves. As Voltaire says, "There are philosophers even in our little shops," a phrase comparable to our "blind faith" in God. And d'Alembert writes to Frederick II in 1776: "We are doing what we can to fill the vacant positions in the Académie Française, in the same way as in the banquet of the master of the household in the Gospel: with the crippled and lame men of literature." The lame mind will be admitted, if he is a good philosopher, while the other, who is well-balanced but independent, will be excluded. The prejudice is obvi-ous and fosters, as you know, a quietism of reason that is even more harmful to the intelligence than the quietism of faith is to the will. Nothing is more damaging to the development of reason than its cult: one no longer makes use of what one worships.

Demanding in orthodoxy, the philosopher is no less so in discipline. Voltaire keeps preaching union to his brothers: "I wish the philosophers could form a corps of initiates, and I should die happy," he writes to d'Alembert, and again in 1758: "Band together and you will be the masters; I speak to you as a republican, but I mean the republic of letters, oh! poor republic [so much in need of assistance]!" The patriarch's wishes were granted in excess by 1770: the republic of letters was founded, organized, armed, and it intimidated the court. It had its legislators (the *Encyclopedia*), its parliament (two or three salons), its podium (the Académie Française), to which Duclos had philosophy admitted, while d'Alembert made it reign supreme, after fifteen years of strife and persistent lobbying. Most important, in all the provinces it had its colonies and trading posts: academies in the large towns, in which, as in the Palais Mazarin,[3] philosophers and independents came to grips and the latter were always defeated; and literary societies and reading rooms in the smaller towns. And from one end to the other of this vast network of societies there was a perpetual exchange of letters, addresses, wishes, motions; an immense and wonderfully harmonious concert of words. There was not a single jarring note. This army of philosophers scattered over the country—in which each town had its garrison of thinkers, its "seat of Enlightenment"—was training everywhere, in the same spirit and with the same methods, for the same verbal Work[4] of Platonic discussions. From time to time, at a signal from Paris, this army would gather for maneuvers—"affairs" as they were already called, political or judicial incidents. They joined forces against the clergy, the court, even against the impudent individual, such as Palissot or Pompignan or Linguet, who, imagining he was attacking an ordinary clique, was stunned to see, from Marseilles to Arras, from Rennes to Nancy, the entire band of philosophers rise up and swarm upon him.

For people were persecuted—another practice of sects. Before the bloody Terror of '93, in the republic of letters there was, from 1765 to 1780, a bloodless terror, for which the *Encyclopedia* was the Committee of Public Safety and d'Alembert the Robespierre. This terror swept away reputations just as the other chopped off heads. Its guillotine was slander, "infamy," as it was then called. The term, originating with Voltaire, was used in 1775 in the provincial societies with legal precision. "To brand with infamy" was a well-defined operation, an entire procedure comprised of investigation, discussion, judgment and finally execution, which meant the public sentence of [being held in] "contempt," another of those philosophical terms whose significance we no longer comprehend. And heads fell in great numbers: Fréron, Pompignan, Pallissot, Gilbert, Linguet, the Abbés de Voisenon and Barthélemy, Chabanon, Dorat, Sedaine, President de Brosses, Rousseau himself—and that is only to mention the men of letters, for the massacre was far greater in the world of politics.

Here we have all the apparent trappings of a vigorous, well-armed sect, enough to impress the enemy, and also arouse the curiosity of bystanders, such as we are this evening. For behind such high walls, we must expect to find a large town, and even a beautiful cathedral: one does not generally imagine fanaticism without faith, discipline without loyalty, excommunication without communion, opprobrium without strong, active convictions—no more than one imagines a body without a soul.

But this is the marvel: here, and only here, are we disappointed. This powerful defense mechanism defends nothing, nothing but a void and negations. Behind all of this there is nothing to love, nothing to grasp and become attached to. This dogmatic reason is just the negation of all faith; this tyrannical liberty the negation of all rules. I shall not dwell upon this reproach so often made of the philosophers, for they themselves admitted and glorified the nihilism of their ideal.

Indeed, what is oddest is that these two contradictory aspects were as readily admitted by the philosophers as by the uninitiated. Opinion, not fact, was the object of their discussion. "We are the human mind, reason itself," proclaimed the philosophers, and in the name of this reason they dogmatized and excommunicated, which they called emancipating. "You are the void," the uninitiated argued convincingly, "anarchy, negation, utopia; not only are you nothing, but you can be nothing but discord and dissolution," and the next minute they were screaming murder and calling up the guards against the specter they claimed did not even have the right to exist and yet was strangling them. This is the duel between Martine and M. Jourdain.[5] It began in Voltaire's time and is enduring still, as you know.

I can see only one way out of this dilemma: reverse this reasoning. Since in this strange church there is no Credo (nothing but negative dogmas), no soul (and yet such a robust body), let's turn the terms around and start with the body. Let's take philosophy not as a spirit, defined by its objective, not even as a tendency, explained by its end, but as a thing, an intellectual phenomenon, the necessary and unwitting result of certain material conditions of association.

This, I must admit, is an impertinent method. There is a certain irreverence in thus treating "modern thought," "free thought," like an inert and blind object. But the example comes from this thought itself. It is this same thought, after all, from Renan to M. Loisy, that has endowed us with a new theology and exegesis; that, by turning the individualistic attack of the sixteenth century around and catching faith between two fires, places the Church before Christ, Tradition before the Gospel, and explains morality by society. And I do not know why this Church should be the only one to escape the criticism it invented and applied to others without any indulgence.

So let's take the fact: the existence of this strange city that, despite all the rules to the contrary, was created and thrived on what killed others. How can we explain this miracle?

This is what I should like to discover with you. And do not imagine I am going to lead you in some lodge's mysterious sabbath, like Father Barruel, nor show you Louis XVI's head in the witches' caldron, like the good M. Cazotte. Not that Barruel and Cazotte were mistaken, but they did not explain anything—they began at the end. What bothers me, on the contrary, is having to reduce these appalling and diabolical consequences to the miniscule fact—so banal, so tiny—that accounted for them: talking. Yet this was the essential thing.

The republic of letters was a world in which people talked, but did nothing but talk; where every mind strove to obtain everyone else's agreement, [public] opinion, just as in real life the mind seeks achievement and results.

This, you will say, is quite a poor explanation for so great a consequence, and a severe judgment for the most innocent of games. But at least I am not the first culprit. The players had already begun—I am not speaking of the very first, the *bons vivants* of 1730, but the Encyclopedists of the following era. The latter were serious: how not to be so when one was certain that the awakening of the human mind dated from one's century, one's generation, oneself? Irony replaced gaiety, and politics pleasure. The game became a career, the salon a temple, the festivity a ceremony, the clique an empire whose broad horizon I have shown you: the republic of letters.

And what did one do in this country? Nothing other than what one did in Madame Geoffrin's salon: one talked. People were there to talk, not to act. All this intellectual agitation, this enormous exchange of speeches, articles, and letters did not lead to the slightest beginning of achievement, of real endeavor. It was only a matter of "cooperation of ideas," "union for the truth," "philosophical societies."

Now, it is not unimportant that such a world was constituted, organized, and lasted, for its inhabitants took by definition a different point of view, were on another bias, had other goals than those of real life. This point of view was that of [public] opinion, "the new queen of the world," said Voltaire, who saluted its arrival in the city of philosophy. Whereas in the real world the judge of any notion is its testing, and its goal is what it actually achieves, in this other world the judge was other people's opinions, and the goal was their consent. It was opinion that made the human being. Reality was what other people saw, truth what they said, the good what they approved of. Thus the natural order was reversed: there opinion was the cause, and not, as in real life, the effect. Appearing took the place of being, and saying of doing.

I cannot help recalling here the charming myth of Aristophanes. Many others have done so, but it always seems to me that they misinterpret it. When we speak of the city in the clouds, we are only thinking of the clouds, in order to mock those who wish to build a town there. Aristophanes, who lived in a century of philosophers and was very familiar with free thinking, does not interpret it thus. It is the city that he sees, built in the clouds no doubt, but with sturdy quarry stone, and populated with citizens of flesh and blood and feathers. The city in the clouds is the setting of a play and not the witticism of a pamphleteer. It is not utopia the Greek poet is stressing; it is reality.

Let us therefore do as he does. Let's ascertain the fact, the existence of this new world, however vain it may seem to us. Let's go up and into it. You shall see, the moment the threshold is crossed, their principles—these "dangerous fantasies"—become up there the most obvious and productive truths. You know these dogmas of philosophy. They are all reduced to a single one: nature is good; and all the rules are reduced to one: *laissez faire*. Man is self-contained; with his reason, his will, and his instincts, he can fend for himself. Faith, obedience, respect, these are the only dangers—which Voltaire designates by one word: infamous. He is wrong here below, but right up there, and you yourselves will agree—I am speaking to the "fanatics" and the "slaves" in the audience—if you are willing to enter the city of philosophers and put yourselves in their place, instead of yelling "utopia" without budging out of yours.

Is reason sufficient in itself? But this is quite clear. Oh, of course in the real world, the moralist without faith, the politician without tradition, the man without experience are pitiful people, doomed to every sort of failure. What can logic do by itself without the three craftsmen of any real product, this triple teaching: personal, social, and divine? But we are not in the real world, and there is no product to make, nothing but talk and talkers. Now what good is faith, respect for tradition, or acquired experience in such a world? These are things that are hard to express and useless in a discussion of principles. Necessary for judging honestly and justly, these advisers are simply bothersome when formulating an opinion. Indispensable for real work, in use they impede the verbal Work of expression.

Better still, while cumbersome for the speaker, they are disagreeable to the audience, for they cannot reveal themselves without becoming obnoxious or ridiculous. You know how difficult it is in mere conversation to mention faith or feeling. In our city of birds, irony and logic are right at home, and it takes real wit or talent to dispense with them. This is understandable: is there anything more obnoxious than preaching a faith devoid of sacrifice, extolling a patriotism devoid of danger, asserting a self-interest devoid of risk and work? Yet such is the position these three elements are placed in if they appear in a world where, by very definition, achievement and endeavor are out of the question. There they can only be called clericalism, chauvinism, egoism.

Is this prejudice? Ill will? No, these are self-evident truths to anyone observing from up there. One is certainly free not to enter the new city. [But] if one is there, one is not allowed to express an opinion otherwise than as a "philosopher" and "citizen."

You can see philosophy does well to assert the right of reason. There is no fantasy here: it is literally true that for each person reason[6] is sufficient. For the goal is displaced: henceforth the successful idea is the transparent one, the one that consists of words, not the productive idea that can be translated into action. Or rather it is discussion alone, verbal opinion, and no longer the testing that verifies and judges.

Thus a whole order of motives—those that go beyond the clear idea and serve real endeavor—are useless in that world, since there is nothing to do there. They are bothersome, since there is so much to say, and finally they are ridiculous and odious, the caricature of themselves. But then what happens to them? They are left outside. It is so simple. What can be wrong with that? Apostasy, treason, madness? Good Lord, no: this is only a game. Because one enjoys conversing as a philosopher for a few hours every evening does not mean one neglects God, the king, or one's business affairs—any more than it means one throws one's hat away in order to enter a salon. No, each man carefully deposits his hat behind the door to pick it up on the way out. The adherent may be a clergyman, a soldier, a banker—what difference does it make? There will be one day, an hour a week, when he will forget his flock, his men, or his business, to play philosopher and citizen, afterwards having no trouble returning to his real identity, his duties, and his interests.

But if this is very simple and natural, it is not without consequence, for the game lasts, and some are better at it: young men because of their age; men of law, letters, or discourse because of their status; the skeptics because of their convictions; the vain because of their temperament; the superficial because of their culture. These people take to it and profit by it, for it leads to a career that the world here below does not offer them, a world in which their deficiencies become strengths. On the other hand, true, sincere minds, with a penchant for the concrete, for efficacy rather than opinion, find themselves disoriented, and gradually drift away from a world they have nothing to do with. Thus the rebellious eliminate themselves—the ones the Philosophers call "dead weight," i.e. the people who produce something—in favor of the more qualified, the talkers. This is a mechanical selection, as fatal as the sorting of heavy and light weights on a vibrating plate. No need for a master to designate, nor a dogma to exclude: the weight of the objects suffices. The lighter will stay on top, while the heavier, laden with reality, will fall. This is a mere recipe, not a conscious selection.

And you can see the consequences of this automatic purging. Now our people are isolated from the uninitiated, sheltered from realistic objections and resistance, and at the same time closer to one another, and for both of these reasons subjected to training all the more intense as their environment is "purer." And this dual Social[7] law of sorting and training keeps working, pushing the reasoning, unwitting band of brothers in the opposite direction from real life, towards the advent of a certain intellectual and moral type that no one can foresee, everyone would reject, and all are preparing for. This is precisely what is called the "development of the Enlightenment."

You see, our hypothesis holds up: doctrines and personal convictions are nothing here, or are only results. Each stage of philosophical development produces its own doctrines and convictions, as each zone on a mountain slope produces its own plants. The secret of union and the law of development are elsewhere—in the fact of association itself. The body, the Philosophical Society, takes precedence; it accounts for the soul and the common convictions. Here it is indeed the Church that precedes and creates its Gospel; people are united *for*, not *by*, the truth. "Regeneration," the "development of the Enlightenment," is a Social phenomenon, not a moral or intellectual one.

Its primary characteristic is unawareness. The law of sorting we have described does not need to be recognized to function—on the contrary. Like any natural law it implies a force, but a blind and impulsive one. The subject enters the lodge,[8] opines, discusses, argues. And that is all there is to it. The Society will do the rest, all the more reliably even as the subject shows more passion and less clairvoyance. Work, to be sure; but this is still another of those words which our Masons of the eighteenth century write with a capital letter and no adjective, and which, as a result—like the words "philosophy," "justice," "truth," and so many others—takes on a special meaning, generally contrary to the commonly accepted one, in their city. Their Work must be understood in the passive, material meaning of fermentation, not in the human meaning of deliberate effort. Thought operates there like must in the vat or wood in the fire. It is by the action of its medium and position, by its starting point and not its goal, that this work is defined. The idea that comes to mind is one of orientation, which is opposed to the idea of direction, as a law one is subjected to is opposed to a law one acknowledges, or as servitude is opposed to obedience. The Philosophical Society is unaware of its law, and this is precisely what allows it to proclaim itself free: it is oriented unwittingly, not directed willingly. Such is the meaning of the name adopted in 1775 by the most accomplished of Philosophical Societies, the capital of the world in the clouds: the Grand Orient.

And the end of this passive work (I do not say its object) is destruction. In short, it consists of eliminating, reducing. The thought that submits to it first loses concern for reality, and then gradually the sense, the notion of reality. And it is precisely this loss that allows the thought to be free. Thought only gains in freedom, order, and clarity what it loses of its real content, its influence on the human being. It is not stronger. It bears less weight. This orientation of thought towards the void is a fundamental fact, and the brothers were right to speak of regeneration and a new era. Until their time, reason used to seek freedom only through an effort of conquest, a combat with reality, a whole deployment of sciences and systems. [But now] the Social Work passes from the offensive to the defensive: to emancipate thought, the Work isolates it from the real world and real life, instead of submitting the latter two to its contemplation. The Work eliminates the real world in the mind, instead of reducing the unintelligible in the object. It creates philosophers instead of producing philosophies. It is a mental exercise whose apparent goal is the search for truth, but whose actual interest is in training followers.

What, precisely, does this negative training consist of? This is as difficult to say as it is to show what a living being loses at the moment of his death. The life of the mind cannot be defined any more than the life of the body can be touched. But it is this life of the mind alone that we are discussing here, not such-and-such an organ, nor some apparent mental ability. No matter how intelligent the subject, how whole and perfect the organism in question, they have nevertheless lost the essential.

Nothing illustrates this odd phenomenon better than the conception of the savage or the ingenuous person that occupies such an important place in eighteenth-century literature. There is not an author, from the most playful to the most serious, who does not present you with his savage. Montesquieu began with his Persian prince. Voltaire immortalized the character with Candide. Buffon analyzed him in his awakening of Adam. Condillac examined his psychology in the myth of the statue. Rousseau created the role and spent his old age playing the savage in castle parks. Around 1770 there was no philosopher's apprentice who did not undertake a review of the laws and customs of his country, accompanied by his Chinaman and his trusty Iroquois, like the master's son who travels with his priest.

This philosophic savage is a very peculiar person. Imagine an eighteenth-century Frenchman who possesses all the material attainments of the civilization of his time—culture, education, knowledge, and taste—but without any of the real well-springs, the instincts and beliefs that have created and shaped all this, that have given their reason for these customs and their use for these resources. Drop him into this world of which he possesses everything except the essential, the spirit, and he will see and know everything but understand nothing. This is Voltaire's Huron.

The uninitiated protest this is absurd. They are mistaken. This savage exists, and they meet him every day. To tell the truth, he does not come from the forests of Ohio, but from much farther: the lodge across the street, the salon next door. It is the philosopher himself, such as the Work has made him: a paradoxical being, oriented towards the void just as others seek reality. His thought is without enthusiasm or real curiosity, more concerned with regulating than with acquiring, with defining than with inventing; he is always anxious to display his intellectual knowledge, and always impatient—in order to convert this knowledge into words—to break his ties to real life, within which he had been working and expanding thus far like invested capital or like a living plant, in the bedrock of experience, under the rays of faith.

Hence the tone, first, and the spirit of ironic surprise. For nothing is less explicable than this cut plant whose roots and life one does not want to recognize. "I don't understand," is our savage's refrain. Everything shocks him. Everything appears illogical and ridiculous to him. It is even by this incomprehension that intelligence is measured among savages. They call it wit, courage, sincerity. It is the motive and *raison d'être* for their erudition. Knowing is good; not understanding is better. It is by this standard that the philosopher is judged—nowadays the savages, who are Kantian, call it "the objective mind." It is by this standard that the philosopher is distinguished from the common compiler: here lies the soul of the Encyclopedia.

And now you can see why his body is so fat: there is no easier nor more flattering work. It is not that philosophical incomprehension is a common gift: it implies natural aptitudes, especially the Social training of the city in the clouds. Only this training can overcome the prejudices, faith, loyalty, etc. that logic can scarcely affect, for they are rooted in experience and life. One must oppose one city to another, one environment to another, one life to another, and replace the real man with a new man: the philosopher or the citizen. This is a work of regeneration that the individual would not be able to accomplish on his own and that can only be achieved by the law of Social selection: the Society is to the philosopher what grace is to the Christian. But still, when the Work functions, when the subject has really indulged in Social orientation, taken up residence in the city of clouds with its center over the void, and feels his philosopher's wings sprout, how intoxicating it is to leave the Earth and soar over fences and ramparts, over the cathedral spires! Nothing locks him out; everything is open in the sky. As a child loots a flowerbed to stick the blossoms into his sandbox, so he goes everywhere, reaping armloads of customs, beliefs, and laws. You know he did not give a second thought to picking so many old, majestic plants at random, and the bouquet was lovely the first evening, for flowers do not die immediately. But you also know what remained the next day of this huge pile of documents: the weight of the paper.

But though the condition of the philosopher savage has its comforts, it also has its burdens, the weightiest of which is Social bondage. The follower belongs body and soul to the Society that has formed him, and can no longer live the moment he leaves it. His logic, so well emancipated from reality, is destroyed on its first contact with experience, for it only owes its freedom to the isolation in which it lives, to the void in which the Work maintains it. It is a hothouse plant that can no longer bear fresh air. The philosophers always lose their aura when seen alone, at close quarters and at work: Voltaire discovered this at his expense with Frederick II, as did Diderot with Catherine II, and Madame Geoffrin with Stanislas.

Fortunately they have an instinct for danger, all the more acute as they are better trained and "deviate" more "towards the void," as the elder Mirabeau used to say of his son. With all their weakness and all their nothingness they prize this city of words, which alone gives them value and weight. Party spirit, fanaticism of a sect, people always say, but this is wrong. Party spirit is still a kind of faith in a platform and the leaders, and contradicts proportionately the instinct of self-defense. With the philosopher this instinct is all that remains. He acknowledges neither dogma nor master. But the Society loses nothing. Like the old owl of the fable, who cuts off his mice's feet, the Society holds the philosopher by his very freedom, this negative freedom, that would prevent him from living elsewhere. It is a stronger chain than all loyalties.

It is this bond that is called good citizenship, that used to be called patriotism in France during the Revolutionary years when the real country and the Social country happened to have the same borders and the same enemies—a short-lived alliance, as you know. The latter country has spread: since then it has become internationalism and shows no gratitude for its temporary host.

There is no more powerful bond than this citizenship, for it has both the brilliance of virtue, since one serves the community, and the primitiveness of selfishness, since one follows one's immediate interest. And here again is one of these actual situations that the Social Work creates and for which the subject's will has no responsibility. It is the Society that has oriented his mind contrary to reality, the Society that binds him to his brothers contrary to reality, the Society again that binds him to his brothers with all the force of its interest. Just as it has shaped his intelligence, it holds his will.

It is worth remembering, for it justifies the principle of the new morality, that self-interest determines what is good, and pure rationality what is true. It is literally true that there exists a city where selfishness binds individuals to one another, and individual good to the general good. From that moment, what need is there for masters, for authority? What necessity is there to impose authority on people it is so easy to convince? Why demand sacrifice when self-interest leads so directly to the [same] goal? And thus is achieved the second of the would-be philosophic utopias, that of self-interest, of course. There lies the secret of this strange brotherhood that unites these Epicureans and these skeptics, Voltaire and d'Argental, d'Alembert and Diderot, Grimm and d'Holbach, or rather that binds them all, by their very shortcomings, to the intellectual fatherland. The translation of this fact can be found in the famous philosophic myth of the origin of societies, which explains that the weakness of men brought them together for their mutual defense. Nothing is falser of real societies, born out of enthusiasm and force, among the lightning bolts of a Sinai, in the blood of martyrs and heroes. But nothing is truer of the intellectual Society, nothing more consistent with the law we have described. It is their own story the brothers are telling us, just as the aforementioned savage gave us their portrait. Such is the nature of the new Society that its union is founded on what would destroy it elsewhere: material forces, the weight of selfishness and inertia.

This is what the Masonic symbols—the temple of Solomon, the architecture and the rest—express so perfectly. The city in the clouds is an edifice and not a living body. Its materials are inert, balanced, assembled according to certain rules and objective laws. The eighteenth century still acknowledged the intervention of a great architect—Voltaire's clockmaker—and a legislator arranging human materials according to certain laws. Nowadays, Freemasonry does away with this person and does well: the Social law is a law of immanence. It is sufficient in itself, and this pastiche of God has no place here.

I need not tell you how this powerful union was revealed to the world, how the little city entered battle with the other, for this is not my subject. Here we reach the second phase of the development of the Enlightenment, the time when philosophy became a form of politics, the lodge a club, and the philosopher a citizen.

I shall only speak about one of the Enlightenment's effects, the one that disconcerts the most when one is not familiar with it: the conquest of lay opinion by philosophism.[9] For this purpose the latter possessed something better than arguments and preachers, which are the ordinary means of propaganda. Thanks to the union without masters or dogmas of the Societies, philosophism was able to set into motion a false opinion that was louder, more unanimous, and more universal than the true one—and that therefore was truer, concluded the public. Using the whole assembly of trained, hired clappers, not even resorting to the demagogical techniques of flashy scenery and skillful actors, it managed to make a success out of a bad play. These professional clappers, the personnel of the societies, were so well trained that they became sincere. They were so well scattered about the auditorium that they were unaware of one another, and each of the spectators would take them for the audience. They imitated the breadth and the unity of a great movement of [public] opinion, without losing the cohesion and conduct of a cabal.

Now, there is no argument or charm that can act upon [public] opinion better than this specter of itself. Each person acquiesces to what he believes is approved by all.

Opinion follows its counterfeit, and reality is born of illusion. Thus it was that without talent, without risk, without dangerous and crude intrigue, by virtue of its union alone, the little city made the opinion of the larger one express the former's wishes, determine reputations, and celebrate boring authors and poor books, if they were on its side. And the city had no qualms about doing this. It is difficult to understand today how Mably's ethics, Condorcet's politics, Raynal's history, Helvetius's philosophy, these deserts of insipid prose, could be brought to print and find a dozen readers. Well, everyone read them, or at least bought them and talked about them. A question of fashion, we are assured. That is easily said. But how can one comprehend this infatuation with pathos and ponderousness in the century of grace and taste?

I believe the explanation is elsewhere. All those authors were philosophers, and philosophy reigned over [public] opinion by right of conquest. [Public] opinion was its property, its natural slave. Philosophy made the opinion groan, applaud, or keep silent, in accordance with its views. There lay a source of illusions that neither historians nor contemporaries may have investigated enough. It makes us a bit skeptical about many philosophic glories—even the genius of certain "legislators," the minds of certain scholars, and the fame of the last salons.

I have spoken of the Encyclopedists as infidels, so you will be less surprised if I conclude with a blasphemy. I am not referring to the scaffold of Louis XVI or the destruction of France and religious faith, harmless old refrains. I shall be more audacious: I have sometimes gone so far as to wonder whether there was, after all, such a divergence between the spirit of the last salons and the grandiloquence of the first lodges; whether in the delightful little realm of taste more than one conceited republican pedant was not already enthroned; and whether, by 1770, people did not sometimes feel like yawning even in the homes of Madame Necker or Madame Geoffrin.

ENDNOTES

Translator's note: Cochin died on the battlefield in 1916. The articles and lectures of this book were collected and published posthumously by Plon, Paris, 1921. They are dated whenever possible.

[1] Lecture given at the Chateaubriand Lectures, May 15, 1912.

[2] Translator's note: Cochin means what was called "philosophy" in the 18th century.

[3] Translator's note: The seat of the Académie Française in Paris.

[4] Translator's note: "Work" (in French: *travail* or *travail social*) is used in its Masonic meaning, i.e. an endless verbal confrontation of ideas which are never tested.

[5] Translator's note: an approximate reference to Molière's *Bourgeois Gentilhomme*.

[6] Translator's note: By "reason" Cochin means a purely abstract notion which is not supported by experience.

[7] Translator's note: When Cochin uses the word "*social*" he is usually referring to the Masonic Philosophical Societies, as is the case here. For the sake of clarity, the adjective as well as the noun have been capitalized in the translation when they obviously refer to the Masonic Societies.

[8] Translator's note: In the Masonic sense of the term.

[9] Translator's note: a common term at the end of the nineteenth century, but which Cochin uses in a derogatory sense.

A CRITICAL PROBLEM IN THE ANALYSIS OF REVOLUTIONARY HISTORY, TAINE VERSUS AULARD (abridged)

CHAPTER 4: THE ARGUMENT OF CIRCUMSTANCES

It was not the Revolution that "commenced": it never acted but under the influence of external circumstances it could not foresee. So claim all the champions of this argument that tends to prove, firstly, that the ideas and sentiments of the men of '93 had nothing abnormal in themselves, and if their deeds shock us [today], it is because we forget their perils, the circumstances [of their time], and [we do not realize that] any man with common sense and a heart would have acted as they did, [had he been] in their place; and secondly [we forget] that such natural sentiments could only be widely shared, and terrorism was the act, not of a minority, but of the entire country of France. . . .

Mr. Aulard[1] has taken this argument of necessity farther than anyone else, extending it to the so-called circumstances of war, which allows this apology to include [and account for] even the very last acts of the Terror. Thus [according to Mr. Aulard] we see that the Prussian invasion caused the massacre of the priests of the Abbey, the victories of la Rochejacquelein caused the Girondins to be guillotined, the betrayal of Dumouriez caused denunciation to be sanctioned and committees of surveillance to be founded, etc. In short, to read Aulard, the Revolutionary government appears to be a mere makeshift rudder in a storm, "a wartime expedient."

It is, I think, disparaging to forget that this government had its principle just like the most legitimate monarchy or the most lawful parliament. In fact it was the regime of principles *par excellence*, and the least of its agents cited them at every turn like a good Muslim his Koran. Let us briefly sum up this Credo of freedom.

The Revolution was the emancipation, then the victory and the advent of the true sovereign, the people. Slaves under the *ancien régime*, the people cast off their irons on July 14, 1789. Then they became "enlightened" and aware of their rights, which were established first by declaration [of the rights of man], and then perverted by a bourgeois and monarchist constitution. Finally the people triumphed and reigned, in fact after August 10, 1792, and by right after October 10, 1793.[2] Then was officially established the so-called Revolutionary government, adjourning the "constituted" State, and maintaining the "constituent" State, i.e. the direct reign of the people over the people, until legal powers were constituted. The characteristic of this regime, Aulard rightly says, was the intermingling of the powers, and the reason for this confusion, he does not say, was that the powers remained in the hands of their common master, the people. Such was, in short, the principle of the Revolutionary government. As we see, it is the principle of a new regime, pure democracy—direct democracy—which keeps sovereignty in the hands of the people, as differentiated from the representative regime, which takes sovereignty from the people on loan, or the authoritarian regime, which takes it away from the people.

Here we have the principle of the Terror, which was a consequence of the first principle: so simple in theory, pure democracy is less simple in fact. For the people can neither administrate nor govern in detail. Something must be retained—at least the material armature, if not the spirit—of a constituted regime: representatives, civil servants to make the administrative machine work. But though they cannot dispense with rulers, the people can at least watch and direct them, keep the right to change them at will, and "terrorize" them unceasingly.

And such was the role of the popular Societies. They were "the eye of the people."[3] Their function was surveillance, and their means terror. From the moment of their creation the popular Societies watched the established authorities and the government itself. And it was this surveillance that constituted freedom: for the people, unable to be always gathered in primary assemblies, spread out into smaller Societies in order to keep an eye on the holders of power. This was the constituent characteristic of the "popular Societies,"[4] and the principle of the Terror.

In the eyes of the new regime's defenders, the Societies *were* the people. "The sovereign is directly in the popular Societies," said the Jacobins from Lyons[5]: "to attack yourselves *en masse* is to attack the sovereign itself," said those from Paris.[6] "In [the Societies] lies the constituent power" *par excellence....* [But] once it was admitted the people must reign on their own, how could they do so if they did not deliberate and vote unceasingly? And thus in place of temporary, electoral assemblies, standing, deliberative Societies were founded with what that entailed: correspondence to transmit opinions, and a center, the mother Society, to receive them. This was Jacobin organization, or if one prefers, the Birmingham "caucus," the American "machine," our Grand [Masonic] Lodge, our republican union clubs, our CGT [trade union], or some such similar Society of equals: a philosophical, political, or working man's Society applying the principles of pure democracy to the supporters within it, just as the Jacobin Society claimed to apply them throughout France in 1793. This was self-evident, and the organization resulted so naturally from the principle that one usually does not bother to describe it. Neither Taine nor Aulard thought of doing so. Direct sovereignty of the people, pure democracy, implies a network of standing Societies. One does not see how not [only] the reign, but the very existence of the sovereign would be possible without such Societies, how the sovereign could become aware of itself. There is no sovereign people, strictly speaking, except there [in Societies]. Pure democracy is the regime of Societies, just as parliamentary democracy is that of assemblies.

Such were the principles, independent, we see, of any circumstances, war or anything else. And it was from the principles, not the circumstances, that the appalling attributes of the new regime proceeded: the unlimited right over lives and property, the accumulation of all the powers in the same hands. We can see how this occurred: thanks to the Societies' active surveillance, the sovereign itself remained "standing"—this is the accepted term—behind its elected members, instead of abdicating into their hands under the protection of the law, as it does in a constituted regime. Hence the latter were no longer "representatives" with powers secured but limited by law; they were direct agents, "presidents of the people," watched step by step, fired tomorrow perhaps, but for this very reason gods today, strong in the right of the people, which had no bounds. Their power over others was without limit and without appeal, precisely because it was without guarantee for themselves, and could not be distinguished from the power of the people that held them on a leash. They remained in the master's hands, and from that moment, there were no laws, no principles to oppose their decrees, for these were the decrees of the people themselves. And the people were the law in person, the judge of justice.[7]

Hence the very precise meaning of the word Revolutionary. . . . Any act or decree that emanated directly from the sovereign was called Revolutionary, and all those of the Social regime had this characteristic. They were, by their very existence, above any law, any justice, any prevailing morality.

And thus there were Revolutionary laws in violation of the first rules of jurisprudence, on the retroactive effect, for example, [and in violation of] the most elementary rights and freedoms. Thenceforth Revolutionary massacres were legitimate. Armies, because they were Revolutionary, had the right to enter private homes, to do and take what they wished. Likewise Revolutionary police opened letters, ordered denunciation and paid for it; Revolutionary war overruled people's rights; Revolutionary justice dispensed with defense, witnesses, investigation, appeal. Why bother with all that? The people judged—or at least watched over the judges—so everything was fine. At first the sovereign worked alone. Then, after the September massacres, it took assistants. Hence the *raison d'être* of the Revolutionary Tribunal, which, according to its promoter Danton, was to "replace the supreme tribunal of the people's vengeance." Had it existed, the prison massacres would not have occurred.[8]

In sum, the Revolutionary government, i.e. the Social regime,[9] instituted the personal reign of the people-god. And the result of this incarnation was a new morality that did not question whether an act was good or bad, but whether it was Revolutionary or not, i.e. whether or not it was in conformity with the current, active will of the god. This was the Social orthodoxy that our Jacobins of '93 called "patriotism," the English "caucus men" "conformity," and the Americans "regularity."[10]

In 1793 and 1794 France thus had its several months of political theocracy, officially sanctioned by the decree of the Convention that put virtue on the agenda—meaning the new virtue, i.e. the cult of the general will, Social orthodoxy. But the public, being insufficiently "enlightened," did not understand. And nothing was stranger than the misunderstandings of the uninitiated where virtue was concerned, and the effort made by the doctors of the new law to reeducate their flock. As an example one must read Robespierre's indignant speech to the Jacobins, on July 9, 1794: could one believe that a Revolutionary committee [actually] used the Convention's decree to jail drunkards on a public holiday? A moral misconception whose effect easily proved its foolishness, for on that day good republicans were put in prison while bad ones remained at large. And thus, continued the orator, "scoundrels . . . see noblemen only as peaceful farmers and good husbands, and don't inquire whether they are friends of justice and the common people." As if these "private virtues," so highly praised by the reactionaries, had value in themselves! As if they could even exist without "public virtues"—i.e. Jacobin orthodoxy! "A man that lacks public virtues cannot have private virtues." And conversely, "crime cannot exist where love of the Republic is found." Thus the two moralities were perfectly contradictory. Whoever served the new god, the Jacobin people, was virtuous by the deed, and whoever combated it was a criminal.

Thermidor came along to shatter the new mystique in its stride, as was apparent the day Tallien dared utter this blasphemy: "What does it matter to me that a man be born noble, provided he behave well? What do I care for a plebeian, when he is a rogue?"[11] The two moralities, the Revolutionary one and the older one, came to grips in a strange way during the terrorists' trials. By which one should they be judged? A quandary for the judges. Sometimes the Social morality gained the upper hand, for example in Carrier's trial: all of his accomplices but two were acquitted. They had robbed, looted, assassinated—but Revolutionarily, therefore innocently. Fouquier himself almost had the same luck: though morally guilty, he was Revolutionarily innocent. But the audience rebelled, and the presiding judge Liger de Verdigny referred the matter to the Committee of Public Safety, who responded by speaking of "evil" intentions rather than "counterrevolutionary" ones—thus reinstating the rights of the old morality and signing the accused man's death sentence.[12]

Can we see now what a terrifying weapon the Social regime put into its agents' hands? This weapon was the product of principles alone. Is it true, as Aulard believes, that the circumstances justified all the Revolutionary laws and acts? This [reasoning] can be defended, but that is another question. What we assert here is that the very notion of Revolutionary law or act in the precise meaning of '93—i.e. of legitimate law or act, though violating all the most elementary rules of right and morality—would not have been born without the principle of direct sovereignty and the regime that derived from it: the Social regime. After all, the outcome proved this: the authorities of '93 were not the only ones [in history] who had had to deal with civil war and foreign war, [but] they were the only ones to put Terror on their agenda and keep the guillotine constantly in operation.

One cannot speak of "excess" here. Once the principle is admitted, terrorism is legitimate and normal, and the first illegal act of the Revolution was [the coup of] 9 Thermidor [1794, when Robespierre was overthrown]. Nor can one speak of "circumstances": circumstances account for an act or accident, not a dogma, a faith, or a new morality.

And we are indeed in the presence of a dogma: the advent of a new Messiah—the actual, tangible intervention in our contingent world of an absolute being, whose will was superior to any justice, whose defense justified any fraud or violence, [and this being was] the people, democracy, say our Freethinkers. This incarnation was neither an intellectual fantasy—as the reign of Terrorism has proved—nor a legal fiction, limited in practice by the law. It was an active, concrete reality, and it was on the very fact of this god's real presence that morality and the new law were founded. The powers were unlimited and intermingled in this regime, because the incarnation of the god was actual and total. And the incarnation was total because it was the standing Societies that governed.

Such is the preliminary question of principles and regime. Those who defend the argument of circumstances appear unaware of it. Perhaps this is because they themselves are citizens of the little city, followers of the Philosophical Societies, the new religion's seminary, where the principle of direct sovereignty exists and poses no problem for anyone. Like all believers, they take the foundations of their faith for granted and as necessary. . . .

CHAPTER 5: THE CONSPIRACY THEORY

There is, [however], a fact as certain as the principle is clear: as far back as one can go it is the distinction, then the divergence, then the conflict between the sovereign people in the Societies and the [real] people—between Aulard's Revolutionary France and France itself. The popular Societies, this essential instrument of pure democracy, were not the people. Such is the truth that broke out during Thermidor. Despite the clever ambiguities of the Jacobin Society, it came to be acknowledged as a separate power, a power that oppressed on the one hand the people's representatives in the Convention, and on the other, the people themselves.

As for the Convention, it repudiated the Terror. It had voted for it, but had not intended it: for fourteen months it had not been its own master, but obeyed the *Montagne*, i.e. the Jacobin minority, instead. The Terror was not the Convention's doing, nor were the violent purges, nor the dictatorship of the committees. Close to the Convention there was another power, another "center" as it was called then, through which everything was done in the Convention's name. This was the Social center, the keystone of the new regime. Thermidor was the Convention's act of despair, the struggle that followed its attempt to deliver itself. Thenceforth it was more and more openly fighting the enemy it had dared not name for months and which was the only enemy, the true one: the Social machine. "Long live the Convention" meant, in the streets as on the tribune,[13] "down with the Jacobins."[14] It became apparent to everyone that the loser of Thermidor was neither Robespierre, a name, nor the Commune of Paris, an instrument, and an instrument worn out ever since Hébert's fall; it was the Terror, a whole regime, that of the Societies, direct democracy.

For that matter, the mother Society soon saw another enemy arise: the Parisian sections themselves, delivered at last from their committees of surveillance (September 19). Indeed, for the preceding eighteen months the least of the communes, after the manner of the Convention, had been equipped with their own little Committees of Public Safety and General Security—Committees of Surveillance, created, sustained, and directed by the local Societies, as the larger committees were by the mother Society. The elimination of these committees was the Thermidor of the small communes, the signal for war on the Jacobin Societies.

Then a sacrilegious idea became manifest: the popular Societies—democracy itself—had tendencies, interests, an existence in themselves, that were not those of the [common] people. Where indeed were the people? In an electoral assembly where everyone enters and votes, or in the Societies, exclusive clubs that had always recruited among themselves from the first Philosophical Society, the first lodge, to the last Jacobin club? Had the Society not persecuted the assemblies from the start, under the pretext of excluding traitors that the Society alone designated? And in the end had it not spontaneously shut down the assemblies? Had it not criticized those who wanted to open them again and made the term "section member," in other words a voter, an indictment? Had it not made an appeal to the people a capital crime? And indeed the Girondin insurrection of June '93 was only a revolt of the section against the club, of the electoral assembly, still accessible to the public, against the Philosophical Society, purged and exclusive.

In truth the tyranny of the little people [the Society] over the great people had become so obvious that the Society no longer denied it. The "scarcity of subjects" was its great concern and the topic of its correspondence: Couthou wrote from Lyons to the Jacobins, requesting "40 good, wise, honest republicans," "a colony of patriots . . . in this foreign land" where patriots are "in such an appalling minority."[15] The same complaint came from Strasbourg, where there were not even four, wrote Lacoste—and there were 6000 aristocrats to be driven out;[16] from Troy, where an uncompromising member said there were not even twenty;[17] from Besançon, where Bernard de Saintes could not find enough for the positions to fill;[18] from Mâcon, Marseilles, Grenoble, etc.[19] There was not a town that its club did not depict as a Sodom and for which it did not appeal to the fires of heaven—the Revolutionary army and the guillotine. A whole village would be executed as if it were a single man. Legot, sent by Maignet to punish the village of Bedouin for letting its liberty tree be felled one night, wrote to his chief: "There does not exist a single spark of civic spirit in this town"—and consequently, the culprit not being found, the town paid *en masse*: 63 inhabitants were guillotined or shot, the rest driven out, and the village burnt to the ground.[20]

As a matter of fact, the pure [and uncompromising little people] would have been distressed to have the numbers on their side; they would have considered themselves less pure [and uncompromising]. One knows Robespierre's famous expression, "Virtue is in the minority on Earth," and what tempests he stirred up after Thermidor.[21] "Those who are not Jacobins are not entirely virtuous," Lanot explained. . . .[22] This doctrine of the small number of the elect was latent in every good Jacobin's mind and was openly declared in the spring of '94, after

Robespierre's great speech on virtue of February 5. In the Societies there was no talk but of purges and exclusions. Then it was that the mother Society, imitated as usual by most of her offspring, refused the affiliation of Societies founded since May 31. Jacobin nobility became exclusive; Jacobin piety went from external mission to internal effort on itself. This was the period of Jacobin Jansenism, as it would be called in Thermidor. At that time it was agreed in the little city that a Society of many members could not be a zealous Society. The agents from the Society in Tournan, sent to purge the club of Ozouer-la-Ferrière, in Brie, made no other reproach: the club members were too numerous for the club to be pure [and uncompromising].[23]

And in truth didn't the litany of praise the Jacobins bestowed upon themselves mean the same thing? They [said they] were the hussars, the mounted sentries, the grenadiers, the sappers, the columns, the boulevards of the Revolution, the vanguard of freedom, the sentinels of the people, the pedestal of the bronze statues of Freedom and Equality, the tribunal of public opinion—in short, by their own admission a reigning elite (a handful of tyrants, their subjects would say after their deliverance), the nobility of patriotism, an aristocracy, an aristocratic and monastic institution, a collection of men that resembled monks co-opting members from among themselves,[24] "the caste" of Society members.[25]

But then arose the clairvoyant witness, followed by the historian of the facts, who both discovered the usurpation by a minority and cried "fraud." Moreover this was easy after '92. The fiction gradually disappeared as the gap widened between the sovereign people and the [real] people. Indeed by then the oppression was too patent, the little people too "weeded out," i.e. too reduced in quantity and in quality, too obviously commanded and guided from the center. Hence the great hue and cry of Thermidor, which reverberated throughout the century, against the "conspirators" and "tyrants." This was the cry of all the little people's victims, which was quite natural: the victims could only see the hands that struck them, and put a name to each of the Jacobin machine's deeds and workings. [Thus] Danton was considered the man behind the prison massacres, Couthon those in Lyons, Maignet those in Orange. Fouquier paid for Revolutionary justice, Marat for the press, Robespierre for everyone.

Hence also the conspiracy theory. It has had many forms, from Father Barruel's naive one, in which the melodrama extends from Voltaire to Babeuf, to the erudite one that discusses the danger of parties attempting to outdo one another, and the threat to the balance of power among them. All these theories have this in common: they place men and personal calculations and talents at the forefront, and conclude that tyranny is made by tyrants.

Now after Taine's[26] investigation, these arguments are also to be dismissed. However, Taine does not take the nature of the new Social regime into consideration either, nor the new bonds it creates, in theory as in fact. Theoretically, under the direct rule of the people there is no longer any sort of authority, neither by right, like that of the lord, nor any actual and personal authority like that of the representative, which is still authority, still a "feudal" one as Rousseau so aptly says. Pure democracy goes one step further, and founds the rule of the "commissioner," or "delegate," as we would say, a mere spokesman of the people, who is to the representative what the latter was to the lord. Let's hear Robespierre: "Understand," he says, "I am not the people's defender: never have I claimed this ostentatious title. I am part of the people, I have never been anything else; I despise anyone who claims to be anything more."[27] This is the way a strict democrat talks. This idea does not come from the *ancien régime*, certainly, but not from ours, either. It is the cry of the English "caucus men": no man a savior![28]

We can see the new and precise meaning of the "war on tyrants" declared by the Revolution. It did not promise freedom in the common meaning of the term, which was independence, but in Rousseau's interpretation, which was anarchy, emancipation from any personal authority, from respect for the lord to the influence of the worst demagogue. If people obeyed, it would never be one man, but always an impersonal being, the general will.

And the fact agreed with the theory. The Revolution kept its word: true, it was a tyranny, but a tyranny without tyrants, "the regency of Algiers without the bey," Malouet used to say, "dictatorship without a dictator," said the Jacobins themselves.[29] How can one call tyrants—even leaders—people so incapable, I do not say of benefiting personally from the force that bore them along, but simply of understanding its secret? Was there a single Revolutionary team that did not attempt to halt this force, after using it against the preceding team, and that did not at that very moment find itself "purged" automatically, without either preventing or foreseeing a thing? Aulard talks about everything the king "did not understand" about the new ideas.[30] But what should we say about the champions themselves of those ideas? Did d'Espremesnil "understand" after the notables of 1788? Mounier after October? La Fayette after June 20? Brissot after January 21? Danton after returning from Arcis? It was always the same naive amazement when the tidal wave reached them: "But it's with me that the good Revolution stops! The people, that's me! Freedom here, anarchy beyond!" The same unconscious complaints against the proceedings and reasons by which they owed the very power they held, the same brief and piteous agony, then the plunge into the void—the guillotine or oblivion. A few—not many—died with dignity. Not one defended his power and his head like a man, not even the Girondin majority, not even the giant Danton. This was because there was not a single man who drew his force from within himself. These men were just temperaments, blind forces submitted to an unknown law. Michelet had the right word for it: marionettes, that nothing could fell so long as their wires bore them, but that collapsed the minute those snapped: it was not their legs that held them up.

This is the brute fact that should be accepted as the law of the regime rather than mocked as its vice. Was it not constant and asserted by the Jacobins themselves in their own way? Look at the last Jacobins, the "strictest," those who guillotined all the others; facing their judges, they had no other defense. "I had orders," Fouquier kept replying to each new accusation. "I was the ax, does one punish an ax?" said another. Poor frightened devils, these would-be Neros. They quibbled, haggled, and denounced their brothers, and then when finally cornered and overwhelmed, they murmured, "But I was not the only one! Why me?" That was the helpless cry of the unmasked Jacobin, and he was quite right, for a member of the Societies, a citizen of the little city, was never the only one: over him hovered the collective force, this mysterious sovereign, that only [in the city] assumed a face and a voice. We see we are far from narratives like Plutarch's that exalt the human character and make great men the kings of history. With the new regime men vanish, and there opens in morality itself the era of unconscious forces and human mechanics.

Thus people have been mistaken in their judgment of the Jacobins. There was, under the Social regime, oppression no doubt, and oppression of the majority, [but] there was no fraud, no misappropriation of the common force for the benefit of a man or a party. It is not true that every minority of oppressors was a faction or a conspiracy. The Terror was not the doing of "individual interest." The Jacobins were right when they denounced factions; they were not a faction. They ruled neither for nor by themselves, but by virtue of an impersonal force that they served without understanding, and that was to crush them as effortlessly as it had elevated them.

Such is the real truth, disconcerting [but] made evident by the facts. . . . Taine is the only person until quite recently who has confronted the problem with his reason and the science of his time, and made it the topic of a book. . . . He studies the reign of the crowd and observes the assistance of stooges. When he makes someone stand out (Danton, Marat), it is to describe his social type, not his personal character. When he speaks of the Jacobin party, it is because he cannot find the right terms, but the idea is there: he will also speak of "disease" and "virus," unconscious forces. . . .

He sees the real causes elsewhere than in external facts such as concerted wills or a combination of circumstances; he seeks them in a social development that has a law of its own. And this is how historians of societies will [now] proceed—methodically and synthetically. . . . . [For example,] Ostrogorski [does so] in his studies of English and American electoral societies. . . .

This new manner of presenting the problem is more accurate, but also more difficult to understand. The two generally accepted solutions [circumstances or conspiracy] reduced the problem in sum to well-known elements: external circumstances in one case, and ordinary passions and plots in the other. Taine's investigation dismisses them both to put a new and unfamiliar force in their place. The ideas, the history of the little people are not on the same plane as ours. The little city has its law, its own development, that even its citizens do not know. This is the main idea of the book.

And this law is disconcerting. In 1789 there appears a people that oppresses the many, a theoretical freedom that destroys actual freedoms, a "philosophy" that kills for opinions, a justice that kills without judgment. We see this miracle achieved: the despotism of freedom, the fanaticism of reason. Such is the Revolutionary paradox. Has Taine solved it? Has he unraveled the origin of these strange ideas? I think not. But he presents the paradox at last, accepts it as a necessary fact, a law of pure democracy, instead of heaving it once again at the democrats' heads as the honest liberals have never wearied of doing for more than a hundred years. He is the first to stop jeering in order to attempt to understand, the first to ask the law of the regime to account for the new religion, [rather than ask] the poor devils who serve the law one day, are annihilated by it the next, and never understand anything about it.

CHAPTER 6: THE SOCIOLOGY OF JACOBINISM

Taine's critique has allowed us, if not to solve, at least to see the Revolutionary problem most clearly. The humanity that kills is the sister of the freedom that imprisons, the fraternity that spies, the reason that excommunicates, and all of these joined together compose this strange Social phenomenon that is called Jacobinism. . . .

But to point out something is not to understand it, and though everyone has touched upon Jacobin fanaticism, no one really understands its means of rule and moral wellspring. It is a phenomenon of a peculiar order, removed from ordinary life and history. Taine has an instinct for it. . . .

And here enters into play the famous "psychological method" that Taine thinks so highly of, and with good reason. . . . [But] though Taine's psychology is excellent at extracting and highlighting the facts, it falters when trying to explain them. . . .

. . . Mr. Durkheim[31] mentions neither Taine nor Jacobinism. But his critique seems made for them. . . . The psychological school, Durkheim writes, puts too much emphasis on *intentions* when it wishes to account for social facts, and not enough on situations. It only sees men's calculations where a more powerful cause is acting: the slow, thorough work of institutions, of social relationships. And likewise Taine, who will say, for instance, that popular Societies were founded spontaneously in 1790 because people felt a need to unite in the face of anarchy—as if a fact of this importance could be the work of a single day and a single calculation, and as if, for thirty years and more, hundreds of literary, philosophical, and Masonic clubs had not been indoctrinating a whole class and a public in the political ways of the Societies and in the dogma of direct sovereignty.

Our sociologists, Durkheim continues, reduce great social facts to individual instincts—for example, religion to "a minimum of religiousness" innate in each person. And likewise Taine: in every abstract dreamer a Marat lies dormant, and all young men are Jacobins at eighteen years of age—as if there were some natural progression from a schoolboy's reasoning mind, or the dreams of an old crank, to the enormous and unambiguous fanaticism of a killer. One cannot help thinking here of the naive Darwinian, delighted to know a trunk is still a nose, a hoof a nail, a fin an arm, an ape a man.

And, says Durkheim, the psychologists often take the effect for the cause in their explanations of social facts, putting the conscious motive before the act. But things generally occur in the opposite way: it is the act that comes first, determined by unconscious causes, and reason that follows, to justify the act. Likewise, Taine constantly confuses Jacobin logic and the Jacobin frame of mind and does not see any more difficulty with one than with the other—as if feelings always followed principles; as if it sufficed to reveal the logic of the latter to account for the presence of the former; and as if revolutionary acts, in their very logic, did not imply unconscious indoctrination much more than a limpid theory.

And so forth. The mistake is always the same. It consists in crediting individual perversity with unprecedented acts and unnatural feelings that proceed from causes a great deal more powerful and profound. Reading Taine, one would think each Jacobin was responsible for his own fanaticism. Circumstances probably helped him, but indirectly, by removing obstacles, destroying moral authority, and substituting anarchy for the established order. [But] all the positive work would be done by the Jacobin. . . .

In Taine's analysis there is a flagrant lack of proportion between the causes — of a normal order, in sum — and the unprecedented effects. Taine the historian contradicts and disconcerts Taine the psychologist. If the latter's reasons are the only ones, there is only one hypothesis left for the former: the Jacobins were crazy. This is what Aulard repeats page after page in his book, and with good reason. He deduces that facts so poorly accounted for are impossible facts, and therefore false, despite all the evidence and all the texts; [but] this is to reason wrongly. It is possible to see well and [yet] to misunderstand, which is the case for Taine.

We now know why. His method is not false, not even vain, for it is certain the facts in question are of a psychological order: a Jacobin is a man, as a plant is a chemical composite. We can make a psychological analysis of one as we make a chemical analysis of the other. But this factual description will not enlighten us. . . . For an explanation we must have recourse to causes of another nature: Social training for the man, the generation of life for the plant.

. . . Have a closer look. Rats existed before cheese, and the Jacobins existed before the Revolution. Their manners and strange principles date not from 1789 but from 1770 and earlier still. Consider the great historical fact of the eighteenth century: the arrival of Philosophical Societies into the world and into power. Study, for example, the social crisis from which the Grand Lodge was born, between 1773 and 1780, and you will find the whole mechanism of a Revolutionary purge. The Work that eliminated the personnel from the Grand Lodge of France was the same that excluded the Feuillant majority in 1790, the Girondin majority in '93 — and this was automatic Work, whose formula and law can be explained. In the Philosophical Societies of 1785 one would discover the same moral and intellectual propensity, the same inextricable involvement, the same methods, the same political manners as in the popular Societies of 1794. No doubt the *mode* changed: the moral level, the quality of the personnel, the nature of the acts, the letters of doctrines. But the *law* remained the same, and the polite and powdered "brothers" of '89 obeyed it with the same strictness and unconsciousness as the crude and dirty "brothers" of '93. Better still, this same law of mechanical selection and training acts wherever the Social phenomenon occurs: in the Company of the Holy Sacrament of 1660, as in the royalist societies of 1815,[32] or the Birmingham "caucus" of 1880.

But Taine has not elucidated this law. In the Social relationships between "brothers and friends" he sees only a particular effect, not a general cause—and in Social fanaticism, only a case of individual psychology. This gives fanaticism a cause both too specific and too weak to account for its extension and its power. . . . [However,] the very improbability and rambling manner of Taine's descriptions serve the truth better than a smooth but conventional narrative, for at least they present the problem, and call for a solution. . . .

Without him, without his exploratory trip and his rather blunt clarification in his work *The Origins of Contemporary France*, we would not even suspect the existence of the little city. We would still be living with our "generous illusions" of '89, the "excesses" of '93, and this historical literature, restrained, sensible, liberal—ridiculous—that for the past hundred years has been gradually correcting, clothing, and attenuating the appalling memory; growing on the Revolution like moss on ruins.

The new school's task will be to take up the methodical study of the Social phenomenon Taine's genius has presented to History. The materials are available, classified for the past ten years by the patient, knowledgeable labor of our archivists, and already handled by three generations of historians. The object is in sight: the strange vision whose veil has been removed by Taine, without revealing the meaning. The tool is in hand: the method of a Bryce or an Ostrogorski. . . . The new school's work will be, on one hand, the natural history of the Philosophical Societies with their essential and constant laws and trends, and on the other, the details of the inevitable conflicts between these Societies and normal [public] opinion, between the little city and the large one. . . .

CHAPTER 7: THE HISTORY OF REPUBLICAN DEFENSE

Taine, we have said, has presented the Revolutionary problem without solving it. [But] Aulard[33] brings us a solution in his *Histoire politique de la Révolution française* [*A Political History of the French Revolution*]. . . .

When the acts of a popular power attain a certain degree of arbitrariness and become oppressive, they are always presented as acts of self-defense and public safety.[34] This is understandable, for the people will have to assume responsibility for these acts, though they neither desired nor accomplished them. This is what the regime requires. Any self-respecting popular power only acts in the name of the people; it is the people. But when the people do not ask for anything, one is obliged to refer to what they "cannot fail" to request, a popular phrase in '89, to their "presumed will," as our modern theoreticians say so admirably—i.e. their safety. Public safety is the necessary fiction in democracy, as divine right is under an authoritarian regime.

And this is justifiable. The first condition for saving the Republic—in '89 it was called the "Fatherland" with the same meaning—in other words, the cause of justice and freedom, is it not to defend its partisans, the good republicans, the good patriots, and to destroy its enemies, the reactionaries, the aristocrats? And against the enemies of the principles, are not all means justifiable, beginning with ignoring the principles? Is there justice for the enemies of justice, freedom for slaves? When the "statues of justice and freedom" were veiled in '94, it was the better to defend these divinities against the infidels who were attacking them.

Such is the argument for defense. It appeared with democracy itself. As early as July 28, 1789, one of the leaders of the freedom party, Duport, proposed to establish a search committee, later called "general safety," that would be able to violate the privacy of letters, and lock people up without hearing their defense. This was equivalent to reestablishing the King's mandates under his private seal [his infamous "*lettres de cachet*"], only a fortnight after the fall of the Bastille, but [now] in the name of public safety and against the enemies of freedom. Nothing was more natural in the eyes of the philosophers, who had been trained in such dialectics for thirty years. The proposal was voted into law and met with tremendous success, as we know. And thus it occurred that as soon as the oppression of authority was chased out the front door in the name of principle, the oppression of public safety returned through the back door, as a result of circumstances.

In short, it is in this difference of label and approach that lies the great development of the new arbitrariness over the old. The oppression of authority is *de jure* oppression, the oppression of public safety is *de facto*. The laws of defense (and all the Revolutionary laws have this characteristic) are, as their name suggests, laws of circumstance. . . . Anyway, as experience has shown, this theoretical difference is practically negligible: for while the despotism of principle is founded on the will of God, the despotism of circumstance is justified so long as one can find "wicked people," as they were called in '93, who threaten the principles. . . . This "despotism of freedom," as Marat called it—the hallowed term in '93 was "public freedom"—has destroyed more individual freedoms, locked up, dispossessed, and killed more innocent people than all the divine rights in the world. . . . [In the Convention, on August, 20, 1794,] the Jacobin Caraffe asked "whether it is for the patriots or the aristocrats that freedom of the press is demanded. . ." How can one reply to that? It was the decisive argument. . . . The Revolution was made on that argument. There was not a member of the Assembly who did not owe his career to it. It was an excuse for the acts of fraud that brought him to power and the acts of brutality that kept him there. And the deputies bowed their heads and continued [to examine] the items on the agenda, only to start all over again the next day. The famous Assembly, whose main quality was neither its subtlety of wit nor its sense of ridicule, wasted days on this argument without escaping from the dilemma.

And the dilemma is indeed vexing for patriots. It is the dilemma between two types of morals, personal or Social, which we have already discussed. . . . To give up the argument of defense, the emergency laws, the argument of public safety, would have been to give up the Revolution itself. Actual tyranny in the service of theoretical freedom: that was the whole Revolution. Give up the former, and the latter perishes immediately. This is because this freedom is theoretical. It is not of this world, and therefore can only rule by fraud and force. It was born in a separate world, the world of Philosophical Societies, lodges, clubs, popular Societies—the name matters little. It is the little city, a small, perfectly democratic republic, but isolated and exclusive, into which all the accumulated knowledge from real life—experience and beliefs, personal interests and obligations, everything directed towards action and effect—cannot enter, because it would have nothing to do there and would occupy space uselessly. People only go there, hypothetically, to "think," to "be enlightened," not to act and live. And that is precisely why Jean-Jacques [Rousseau's] fantasies, absolute equality and freedom, find themselves so much at home there. That is the country they come from. In the absence of the "people of gods" that Rousseau legislates for, these fantasies manage perfectly with an audience of ideologues. One needn't go looking for them in Corsica or Poland, Rome or Sparta, among the Hurons or the O'Taitians: they are in the city of philosophers, wherever a score of people assemble at fixed dates with presidents, secretaries, correspondence and affiliations, to talk and vote on the public good out of principle. That is the new fatherland.

However one day these fantasies happened to leave their native country, and the little people conquered and enslaved the great people, and imposed their laws. But straight away proscriptions, spoliation, and murders began, for the laws of the little city were not made for the large one. The human rights code was only suitable for the citizens of the world of thought, not the inhabitants of the real world. In the real world, the Jacobin fatherland would always be in danger, and consequently obliged to use violence to remain in place. At the first slackening of surveillance and coercion, the crowd would spontaneously return to its private interests, i.e. those of real life.

This was what all of the little people sensed, from the most popular of their orators to the most anonymous of their agents, and that is why they valued the argument of defense so highly. It was the very condition, the *raison d'être* of their rule. There was no petition, no pamphlet, no patriotic speech that was not inspired by it. It was the ordinary theme of all the Revolutionary literature.

CHAPTER 8: SOCIAL OPINION

Now, Mr. Aulard's sources—minutes of meetings, official reports, newspapers, patriotic pamphlets—are precisely authentic acts of this patriotism, written by patriots, and mostly for the public. He was to find the argument of defense highlighted throughout these documents. In his hands he had a ready-made history of the Revolution, presenting—beside each of the acts of "the people," from the September massacres to the law of Prairial—a ready-made explanation in accordance with the system of republican defense.

And it is this history he has written. . . .

The silence that covered up outrageous acts was not the least odd of the characteristics of this strange period. France may have suffered from the Terror, [but] one can say she was unaware of it; and Thermidor was first a deliverance, but next a discovery: during the months that followed, it was one surprise after the other. First there was the trial and acquittal, September 14, of the "132 inhabitants of Nantes," whose only crime was to have been notables of their town. They were arrested and for ten months dragged from one prison to another, causing 38 of them to die of misery. Then from the rostrum of the Convention Merlin de Thionville read the evidence revealing the drowning near Bourgneuf of 41 people: 2 men, one of whom was 78 and blind, 12 women, 12 girls, 15 children, 10 of whom were between six and ten years of age, and 5 still nursing. They were captured in insurrectionist territory, loaded one evening onto the ship *le Destin* (Destiny) commanded by Captain Macé, and thrown into the sea opposite Pierre-Moine by the order of Adjutant General Lefèbvre[35]—a new revelation for the public. And so forth. . . We know what surprises of this sort the trials of Carrier, Fouquier, Billaud, Lebon, Lacombe, etc., reserved for the public, with the revelation of these strange acts that could in no way be compared to the most famous massacres of past centuries, for the [Revolutionary] massacres were executed in cold blood, legally, throughout the country, for months. It was a "continuous Saint-Barthélemy massacre" [of Protestants, August 23, 1572].

And yet we can say [public] opinion knew nothing, as if it were anesthetized. Never, under any other regime, was this true to such an extent. The laws were known, not the acts. The arrest of the 132 inhabitants of Nantes had taken place nine months earlier, the drowning near Pierre-Moine ten, etc. [But no one knew] because, first, under penalty of denunciation and death, nothing was published, written, or spoken without the approval of the patriots, i.e. the Jacobins. Secondly, among the Jacobins themselves these facts were [suppressed], mechanically eliminated, through the operation of their correspondence.

On the other hand, the machine issued and exaggerated useful news, as surely as it covered up the other, and by the same means. One must not imagine the France of 1793 was like the Rome of Nero, *vasta silentio*. On the contrary, there was an opinion, and the noisiest that ever wearied a government's ears: the opinion of the Societies. Though not a word was uttered about the people drowned in Paris in May 1794, in July 1789 the tiniest of the villages knew from reliable sources—the "public rumor" kept repeating it everywhere—that the queen had had the Assembly's meeting hall undermined.[36] The villages also knew the nobility were throwing the cereal harvest into the sea to starve the Third Estate. The "anxiety about supplies," so useful to the democrats in 1789, was one of the "principles" professed by every good Jacobin in 1794.[37] Moreover, "anxiety" in general was the very sign of patriotism. The good patriot was an anxious man by definition; whoever felt reassured was suspicious. The Jacobins' circulars were just a series of alarms; it was by the degree of anxiety that they measured the vigor of the public mind. Here are a few lines from a report by Saint-Just that will give an idea of the prodigies accomplished in this domain: "In 1788, Louis XVI had 8000 people of every age and sex sacrificed in Paris, in the Rue Mêlée and on the Pont Neuf. The court repeated this drama on the Champs de Mars; the court hanged people in the prisons; the drowned people who were pulled out of the Seine were its victims; there were 4000 prisoners; 15,000 smugglers were hanged every year; 3000 men were thrashed; there were more prisoners in Paris than today." (February 26, 1794).[38] This was declared at the Convention, applauded, published, and sent to the smallest of towns. And the Societies commented on it and embellished it, and the brothers believed it all. And no one shrugged his shoulders—for fear of losing his head.

After Thermidor this permanent [state of] anxiety was what the Jacobins were reproached for first. "Where does the evil come from?" asked Clausel at the Convention on September 19, 1794. "It is because there have been men in this assembly whose feigned patriotism exaggerated all of our perils." We know the odd vitality of famous and outrageous calumnies like the pact of famine or the tortures in the Bastille, so powerfully launched that they are still alive, without a shadow of basis in reality. Never would a man, a party, or a newspaper have managed such feats, but it was mere child's play for the Social machine.

The most famous effect of anxiety was the "great fear" that caused all the towns of France to arm themselves in July 1789 in order to repel bandits that did not exist. Was this panic triggered and these lies produced wantonly by the center? No doubt; the nudge had to come from there. But the real marvel was the Societies' forced propulsion that kept their followers alert and at the orders of the center; these men were few, no doubt, but selected, eager, amenable to the slightest suggestion, gullible to the biggest lies, prepared for any act, and working in the same manner everywhere. The emissaries hired by the Duke of Orleans or anyone else to sow panic in the villages would have been wasting their effort, had they not found everywhere duly inflamed "patriots," ready to believe and rush to arms, as was expected of them.

There was another effect from the same causes: the famine of 1788, a mere phenomenon of [public] opinion. Its primary origin was neither shortages nor the threat of such, but just the abnormal persistence of false rumors, that finally troubled the markets and upset buyers and sellers in the midst of plenty.

But the reasons for the Jacobins' anxiety were flexible and impossible to evaluate: the power (ineffectual) and the plans (presumed) of the reaction; the people's anger with traitors, or when the people's anger was too obviously lacking; the impossibility of knowing where the people's real interest lay—all of this fed the famous fear of conspiracies. [And] we know what place the conspiracy theory held in the argument for [self-]defense.

Why were priests persecuted in Auch?[39] Because they were plotting, claimed the "public voice." Why were they not persecuted in Chartres? Because they behaved well there. What is the point? How many times does the argument not turn around? Why did people in Auch (the Jacobins, who controlled publicity) say the priests were plotting? It was because people (the Jacobins) were persecuting them. Why did no one say so in Chartres? Because [the priests] were left alone. In 1794 put a true Jacobin—Lebon, for example—in Caen, and a moderate, Lindet, in Arras, and you could be sure by the next day that the aristocracy of Caen, peaceable up till then, would have "raised their haughty heads," and in Arras they would go home. Where was the aristocracy a threat after Thermidor? Wherever there remained a terrorist Society.

Such was the Work of [self-]defense. It was not the product of a man or party, but the natural effect of the operation of Social correspondence, which had the virtue of producing popular opinion of a new kind: artificial, in that it was established by discussions of principles and set by voting, i.e. very differently from real [public] opinion, which is shaped slowly by contact with the facts. Hence its peculiar characteristics: precision, vigor, odd associations, enormous errors by omission or misrepresentation. It was natural and spontaneous in that it only obeyed its own laws, never individual guidance, and remained collective and impersonal like real [public] opinion, and from hence came its force—I was about to say its sincerity.

And thus it was that, without any impossible conspiracy or improbable perversity, by the operation of Social correspondence alone, the vast system of lies that the policy of defense needed for its support was elaborated in the heart of the little city.

. . . [Though the laws under this regime did a great deal to ease the task of the judges,] it still remained burdensome. It was a commonplace among the little people [of the little city] to mock the scruples and slowness of their judges. Indeed, what a difference there was between the wishes, the estimates, and the reality! Marat demanded 170,000 heads, Collot 12 to 15 million, Guffroy thought 5 million inhabitants would be enough to populate France,[40] etc.—journalistic exaggeration, of course, but the statesmen were nevertheless demanding: Maignet estimated 12 to 15 thousand people were arrested in Provence, his secretary Lavigne estimated 9 or 10 thousand [of them] were to be decapitated, and this was the reason they both gave the Committee of Public Safety for setting up a Revolutionary court of justice on site. [Otherwise] it would have necessitated an entire army, supplies, organized halting places, to conduct these 15,000 prisoners to Paris—a great and useless expenditure of men and money.[41]

The Committee concurred and appointed the commission of Orange. But then what! At most it only executed 40 people a day, 382 altogether, in its 44 sessions.[42] Even in Paris, Fouquier scarcely did better. He was delighted when he managed to behead 450 people within a ten-day period.[43]

Judges and jurors were no longer sufficient in number. Some were guillotined for being moderates, others went mad, others got intoxicated before the hearings. Fouquier himself lost his senses and [imagined he] saw the Seine running red [with blood]. And yet the labor of [self-]defense had to be sustained.

Odd practices were invented to help [the effort], *"moutonnage"* (spying), for example. The *"mouton"* [the spy or mole] was the agent living permanently amidst the prisoners to seize (or provoke, if necessary) the term or gesture that would send them to the scaffold. There was also "inoculation," which consisted of transferring a prisoner from a prison where there had already been a conspiracy to another: whereupon the least complaint, the slightest allusion, became a sign of revolt, a ramification of the conspiracy, and the smallest knife found on the prisoners became evidence. There were still other means, for example the zeal of a patriotic prison guard, like Verney of the Luxembourg, who by constant taunting would manage to exasperate the prisoners, and the *"mouton"* would take charge of the rest.

However, there still remained hopelessly patient prisons, such as Saint Lazare, that showed no signs of plotting. So the patriots took the initiative. The *"mouton"* sawed through a bar, imagined an escape route, and drew up a list of candidates. There may have been a few little improbabilities in his fiction: for example, he had the seventy-two-year-old abbess of Montmartre and Madame de Meursin, with two paralyzed legs, crossing a plank twenty-five feet above an alley. But never mind: they were both condemned and sent to the scaffold. That plot yielded three batches, of 25, 26, and 27 heads. Thus died Chénier and Roucher; Monsieur de Bérulle, the first president of the Parliament in Grenoble, and the wife of the one in Toulouse, Madame de Cambon, for refusing to tell where her husband was hiding; and a sixteen-year-old Maillé. "There are certainly eighty for this crime!" declared the president of the tribunal. The crime was throwing a rotten herring at the prison guard Verney's face.[44]

Such were the supreme efforts for [self-]defense, while the paradox was pushed to its extreme limits.

... Aulard has faithfully copied the panorama in [the painter] David's style that the Societies placed before their followers' eyes every day. One can see the people—a large nude figure, entirely impersonal and a bit banal—with sword in hand, confronting the wild furies of fanaticism and aristocracy. From one end of the Revolution to the other he restitutes for us the argument for defense, resulting from the immense and unconscious Work of Social correspondence. [He remains] silent concerning the embarrassing victories of Hondschoote and Wattignies; silence about the massacres and the universal oppression—not a word about the beheadings, the shootings, the drownings, the persecutions of all sorts. Did Lyons revolt? It was federalism, provincial jealousy of Paris—but Chalier had nothing to do with it. And in the Vendée? Fanaticism, monarchism, revolt against conscription—but not a word concerning the violent religious persecution of the preceding months. Were the famous committees of surveillance supplying people for the guillotine? I can see only one fact [in Aulard's work] that indicts them. Apparently there were village committees that the priests entered fraudulently, where they took tactless advantage of their situation to force people to attend mass.[45] And what about the [infamous] September days? The Prussians were rumored to be at the gates, or rather the people were said to have believed so and to have panicked. The little people [of the Societies] may have reacted thus, but it is doubtful that the masses did. No one said that half of those slaughtered were harmless women, children, and old men, and the murderers three hundred hired cutthroats. And thus [Aulard] reestablishes the balance in favor of [self-]defense.

Finally and most important [in Aulard's work], there is the personification of "the people." It appears at every turn: on October 5, the king refuses to sign the declaration of rights. "Then Paris intervened" (p. 58). On February 28, '91, "the people" become convinced the keep of the Vincennes [fortress] communicates with the Tuileries [palace] by an underground passage and the king is going to escape that way, so they go to demolish the keep. Fortunately Lafayette rushes after them and stops them on the way (p. 108). The king wants to go to Saint-Cloud on April 18, 1791. "The people prevent him" (p. 115)—and so forth. The epic of [the indefinite pronoun], the great "One" is admirably summed up in Aulard's book against Taine (pp. 169–177). In September 1792, "*One* saw the royalty powerless . . . *one* is indignant at this" . . . and *one* overthrows it. Six months later, again, "*one* gets worried, *one* fears the Girondins have not got the necessary energy," *one* ostracizes them.[46]

It is evident that criticism would stop the historian *of facts* at each of these "*ones*" to ask: who is *one*? How many? Assembled how? Represented how? Criticism knows what 500 or 2000 craftsmen or peasants or city dwellers are, but it does not understand *one*, "the people," or "Paris," or "the Nation." It cannot put up with the vague and the anonymous; as soon as the crowd gathers, it wants to see, count, and name. It asks who the good, anonymous patriot is who makes an opportune motion, and who the other is over there who applauds every single word, and the third who spontaneously makes himself the orator of "the people."

It is certain Aulard never asks any of these questions. Should we blame him? It would be as unfair as to blame him for the small number and the exclusive choice of his sources. Aulard is not an historian *of facts*. He is the historian of republican defense, i.e. the restorer of a fiction shaped to conform to special laws with a special intention: the laws of Social propaganda and the opinion of the little people.

CHAPTER 9: THE MYSTICISM OF THE PEOPLE

If what precedes has been properly understood, it is now possible to judge the influence and interest of such an achievement.

It is very easy—a bit childish, even—to criticize the argument for defense as an objective truth. . . .

But this argument, as we have already said, is not the intentional work of a plot or a man, but [rather] the natural and unconscious Work of the Jacobin machine, i.e. of a regime and a frame of mind. And this was obvious at first sight, for the power of one man would not have been able to produce effects of this dimension. It was a system, a fiction, blatant propaganda if you like, but let us not forget this system held up for years. It accredited outrageous lies, allowed unprecedented acts, was professed by thousands of people who did not know one another, and was admitted, willingly or not, by millions of others. Lastly it gave birth to a mysticism of a new order: this mysticism of the people, that Taine has described though not explained. An argument of this force, even an absurd one—mostly absurd—is no common lie. It is in itself an historic fact, a Social fact, as we have said, and deserves to be explained—and, to begin with, exposed. . . .

It is especially in our official history that this mystical idea prevails today.

I cannot better describe the place it occupies than to compare it to the one occupied by Providence in the textbooks of Jesuit schools during Rollin's time. In both cases, it is a question of notions and beings taken out of the context of history—one from theology, the other from abstract politics—humanized, although these are not men, and then introduced willfully and wantonly into the web of facts in the place of natural causes.

Providence has moreover this great superiority over the people of remaining, in sum, what it is, of a supernatural order: there is no false Providence. For example, if the historian feels like attributing the great king's setbacks . . . to the wrath from above, the reader can just shrug his shoulders and imagine whatever he likes. This is, in historical matters, a pious way of saying nothing; it is not a lie.

It is not the same thing with the people, for there exists a counterfeit copy of the people and [their] opinion: the people of the Philosophical Societies, the little city, and the latter, on the contrary, have direct, continuous, and tangible action. Attributing the acts of the false people to the true—the September massacres, for example, to the people of Paris—is more than an admission of ignorance. It is a misinterpretation of history, supporting a political mirage. This is not the omission of the true cause, but the replacement of it by a false one. And that is how the new anthropomorphism of the people-god is much more harmful to healthy criticism and, for education, much more dangerous for the minds of young people, than the old one. . . .

Can you now measure the enormity of Taine's crime? It is one that cannot be forgiven: it is a sacrilege. Taine knocked the idol down and tore the

Revolution's object of hero-worship, the people, to shreds. He did it bluntly and naively, more as a man of common sense than as a critic, without grasping either the depth or the extent of the cult, and without unraveling its origins. He is not the Renan of this religion; he is its Voltaire, a Voltaire with more knowledge, more honor, and less wit. And following Taine a crowd of erudite men have invaded the desecrated temple, picked up, examined, and described the god's shreds, with the same irreverence, but they have not understood, either.

Still, the idol has remained on the ground. The argument of [self-]defense manages to account for the unofficial acts of patriotism and still works for the official acts, at least under the patriots' rule. But what destroys this argument is the factual matters, the actual truth, those incidents and contingencies for which Aulard cannot muster enough scorn.

CHAPTER 10: THE DILEMMA

Thus the question remains open and the problem insoluble: on one hand there is an explanation that is valid only by omitting and attenuating, and on the other there are facts that are all the less explicable as they are well known. One has the choice between probability and truth. . . .

Shall we [ever] see the end of this critical period? I think so, but on two conditions. The first is that we preserve ourselves better from the scourge of all curiosity: indignation. . . . The acts of the Revolution are objects of scandal that some conceal respectfully, while others judge them sternly, but that no one thinks of examining [simply] with curiosity.

Now this is a pity, for they are worth the trouble. It is certain, for example, that if the last three months of the Terror, May, June and July, had not been unfortunately the most odious of our history, they would be the most interesting. For then a moral, political, and social experiment was attempted that was unique in the course of centuries. The mysterious depths of the human soul, under the action of causes still little known, then gave birth to unprecedented acts, sentiments, and types [of men]. For the seven thousand years that men have existed and fought and killed one another, I do not believe people have ever behaved in the same way. I am not speaking so much of the degree "the continuous Saint Barthélemy" reached—which was very high, of course—but of the manner. But to be astonished, one must keep one's sang-froid; and how can one not lose it when confronted with acts as vile as the trial of the Queen, as unnatural as the judiciary assassinations, the universal denunciation, and all the degrading practices of the rule of fear? Yet one will manage to keep it, once one understands that the laws of the Social machine were automatic, once one sees what [extensive] selection and forced disciplining the voting matter underwent on entering the machine, and how those inhuman beings, such as Chalier, Marat, or Carrier, were merely the mechanical products of the collective Work. Then one will not make the mistake of granting the Social product the same weight as the individual being. Then one will see there is more to understand than one thinks—more to deplore, too, and less to anathematize.

The second condition is that criticism rid us of the Revolutionary hero-worship of the people, that it put the people back in the realm of politics, like Providence in the realm of theology, and that it give the history of defense its place in the museum of religious myths that it should not have left. If our historians have not done this yet, it is because the anthropomorphism of the people is more recent and more plausible, too, than that of Providence. It still inspired respect at the time when one had trouble distinguishing, behind the principles, the operation of the Social machine and the laws of practical democracy. Taine and Aulard are historians of that time, historians from the *ancien régime*.

But our generation does not have the same excuse. For the past ten years we have been witnessing the founding of the new regime, *de facto* and *de jure*. With the reign of the "bloc," we have seen a Society's tyranny succeed party conflict and the political ways of the machine replace parliamentary ways. We have seen the Philosophical Societies' verbal morality in the press and on the parliamentary rostrum—justice, truth, conscience, etc.—in conflict with real morality. And now the [Masons'] great achievement is reaching its goal. In place of weakening moral forces, there remains only the Social mechanism to sustain the national body, encompassing it so that it will now have to submit to the mechanism's fatal law. We have one foot caught in the mesh. Already the first Social team—radical Masonry—appears contemptible, between the loyalty it is no longer allowed to appeal to and the extravagant promises of the next team—political trade unionism—that it no longer has the right to contradict. This is the first stage; there will be many others.

Let us at least hope this generation will benefit from an experience dearly acquired, to understand at last what it cannot prevent. . . . Then justice will be rendered to our two historians. . . .

We shall be grateful to Taine for the uncompromising sincerity that made him investigate and assert the improbable. . . . Certainly it required audacity to take such a risk alone, groping his way through the texts and facts, so far from the mainstream of acquired beliefs. But in the end Taine stuck to his position, and already he is no longer alone: an investigation like Ostrogorski's has come along as an important confirmation to Taine's. . . . Taine's effort will remain an example of freedom of the mind and intellectual probity, and his work a model of sincere history.

Aulard's merit will be just the opposite. We know how famous his work is for its radical orthodoxy—"purity of principles," a Jacobin of '93 would say. . . . He is a master of Jacobin orthodoxy. With him we are sure we have the "patriotic" version, which is not always so easy to grasp. . . . And this is why his work will no doubt remain useful and consulted.

ENDNOTES

[1] Translator's note: Alphonse Aulard (1849–1928), professor at the Sorbonne and historian, was an authority on the French Revolution and the author of *Histoire Politique de la Révolution Française* (1901). Aulard's main idea is that the history of the French Revolution must be understood as determined by the successive aggressions of the European monarchies in their attempt to thwart the democratic movement.

[2] *Histoire Politique*, pp. 313–314.

[3] *Moniteur*, Convention, Oct. 14, 1794.

[4] *Ibid.*, *Jacobins*, Oct. 16.

[5] *Ibid.*, Convention, Sept. 28, 1794, letters by Charlier and Pocholle.

[6] *Ibid.*, Jacobins, Oct. 2.

[7] *The Social Contract*, p. 289 in the Dreyfus edition. Cf. Taine, *Révolution*, II, pp. 26–27.

[8] *Moniteur*, Convention, March 10, 1793.

[9] Translator's note: i.e., the Society's regime.

[10] Cf. Ostrogorski, *Democracy*.

[11] *Moniteur*, Convention, August 19, 1794.

[12] Lenôtre, Revolutionary Tribunal, p. 350.

[13] Translator's note: The rostrum of the Chamber of Deputies.

[14] *Moniteur*, Convention, Sept. 19, '94.

[15] Melville-Glover, *Collection de jugements*, p. XI.

[16] Wallon, *Représentants en miss*, IV, p. 193.

[17] Bareau, *Histoire de Troyes*, II, p. 117.

[18] Lods, *Bernard de Saintes*, p. 17

[19] Taine, *Origines*, 1907 edition, VIII, p. 52 *et seq.*

[20] Bonnel, *Les 332 Victimes de la Commission d'Orange.*

[21] *Moniteur*, Convention, Sept. 14 and Oct. 3.

[22] *Ibid.*, Nov. 6.

[23] Archives of Seine-et-Marne, L 737, minutes of the Société d'Ozouer, Dec. 10, 1793.

[24] *Moniteur*, August-October '94.

[25] National Archives, Ad 91, Mailhe's report to the Convention.

[26] Translator's note: Hippolyte Taine (1828–1893), a French philosopher, critic, and historian, was the author of a monumental work in six volumes: *Les Origines de la France Contemporaine (The Origins of Contemporary France)*, 1875–1893.

[27] National Archives, AD XVI, 73, speech to the Jacobins, Jan. 2, 1792.

[28] Cf. Deherme, *Democratie Vivante*, article by Clémenceau, p. 5.

[29] *Moniteur*, Convention, August 25, 1794.

[30] Aulard, *Histoire Politique*, p. 115.

[31] Translator's note: Emile Durkheim (1858–1917), a French sociologist and professor at the Sorbonne, was considered the supreme authority on the science of sociology, invented by Auguste Comte in the 1830's.

[32] Strange information about these societies may be found in *the Mémoires d'Aimée de Coigny*, published by Lamy (p. 236 *et seq.*).

[33] Cf. translator's endnote no. 1.

[34] Translator's note: Historically, self-defense, which Cochin simply calls "defense," has been used by political regimes as an excuse to account for their acts. They claim they are merely defending themselves against threats, whether real or imagined, construed to justify their harsh domestic policies and aggressive behavior towards the outside world.

[35] *Moniteur*, Convention, Oct. 13, 1794.

[36] A. Young, translated by Lesage, I, p. 269.

[37] See, for example, in the *Moniteur*, Fayau's speech to the Jacobins (session of Oct. 8, 1794).

[38] *Œuvres de Saint-Just*, Vellay, 1908, II, p.231.

[39] Aulard, *Histoire Politique*, p. 473.

[40] Taine, *Révolution*, III, p. 393.

[41] Maignet's other reason was that "one must terrify, and the act is only truly frightening when it occurs before the eyes of those who have lived with the guilty ones." (Bonnel, *op. cit.*, I, p. 3. . . .) Here I correct a mistake in the first edition, for which I am very much obliged to Michel Jouve. . . .

[42] Bonnel, *op. cit.*

[43] Wallon, *Tribunal révolutionnaire*, IV, p. 122.

[44] Wallon, *op. cit.*, V, p. 101 *et seq.*

[45] Aulard, *Histoire politique*, p. 353.

[46] Translator's note: "One" in this case could be translated by the word "people" (in the plural).

THE REVOLUTIONARY GOVERNMENT

CHAPTER 1: THE PEOPLE

The purpose of this booklet[1] is to make all the revolutionary government's general acts (August 1793-August 1794) accessible to researchers. To justify the limits and the interest of this peculiar regime, we must explain its nature and spirit. This brief account, indispensable to the study of our sources, will be taken up again and completed in our last volume.

The initial date we have chosen, August 23, 1793, is that of the mass conscription decree, the *levée en masse* that made all French citizens, body and soul, subject to standing requisition for public safety. Thus was achieved the Social fiction of a single collective will substituted, no longer by law, but now in actual fact, for each individual will. This was the essential act of the new reign, an act of socialization[2] of which the Terror's laws would merely be the development, and the revolutionary government the means. It instituted a heretofore unparalleled political and economic experiment. In the political realm this is government of the people by the people, direct democracy. Serfs under the king in '89, legally emancipated in '91, the people become the masters in '93. And in governing themselves, they do away with the public freedoms that were merely guarantees for them to use against those who governed them. Hence the right to vote is suspended, since the people reign; the right to defend oneself, since the people judge; the freedom of the press, since the people write; and the freedom of expression, since the people speak. We shall not dwell upon this limpid doctrine, whose terrorist proclamations and laws provide one very long commentary.

Its economic counterpart is socialism. The collectivity thenceforth took business into its own hands and dispensed with individuals. By doing away with the grain trade (September 3–11, 1793), it socialized the agricultural stocks; by price controls (partial on September 29, 1793, and then general on February 24, 1794), it socialized commercial activity; by the universal requisition of labor and skills (April 16, 1794), it socialized the productive effort itself. This was the end of the personal regime for the people as for the prince—in the fields, workshops, and marketplaces, as in the Louvre [the prince's palace].

When the People are on the throne, the State becomes the shopkeeper.

This regime termed itself the "revolutionary order," the "dogmatism of reason," the "despotism of freedom." And one might add: the "agony of happiness." This regime was necessary to save France, said its proponents and apologists. Without such forceful remedies, foreign powers would capture Paris — a hypothesis we shall not discuss. But the French people of that time were apparently of a different opinion, since the system required such a prodigious deployment of coercive means that it was named the Terror. It is this quite obvious fact and the problem it presents that interests us — and thus the only fact that concerns us, if the role of history is to explain what was, rather than to guess what could have been. The reign of the impersonal is a hell. Democracy — the impersonal prince — governs backwards, and the State — the impersonal people — works at a loss. Such are the two great truths that the doctrine of the Revolution denies but that its history demonstrates. How could this paradox become established counter to common sense, first, and then to rights and interests; how could it last for ten months, and linger on for two years?

The reason is that it was not a paradox everywhere, not for everyone. It had its truth, without which nothing can be understood of the democratic phenomenon. If we look closely, the battle between two social orders, rather than two doctrines or parties, had begun by 1789, even by 1750. Before it became an ideal, democracy was a fact: the birth and development of a different type of association that used to be called "*sociétés philosophiques*" (philosophical societies), now aptly called *sociétés de pensée*" (literally, societies of thought), for their essence is verbal discussion, not real endeavor, and their goal is [control of public] opinion, not immediate action. From this inversion of principle the Society derives an inverted orientation whose essential laws we have pointed out elsewhere.[3] In our last volume we shall return to this peculiar phenomenon of the "philosophy" of "Free Thought," which deserves the attention of sociologists, for it may be the only fact in their domain that is devoid of any connotation, be it religious, economic, ethnic, etc. Free Thought is the same in Paris as in Peking, in 1750 as in 1914. And this similar nature in such diverse environments results from certain conditions of association and collective Work, for which Rousseau's [Social] Contract gives the formula, and the least of the lodges of 1780, or popular Societies of 1793, the example. Here we shall stress only the extreme consequences of the phenomenon: the [Society's] creation by intellectual training[4] and [its] selection of a certain moral state first, then a set of political trends, which, though by nature contradictory to the conditions of real life and society, are nevertheless the doing of a group, the outcome of collective

Work, as unconscious and objective as custom or folklore. Terrorist legislation was so little the product of isolated theoreticians, or united politicians, that the main decrees of the Convention often arrived merely to sanction the *fait accompli*. Such was the case for the law of suspects, enacted on September 17, 1793, but already administered by the Societies of Pontarlier on September 10th, Limoges the same day, Montpellier the 17th, and demanded by those of Valence the 3rd, Castres the 17th, etc.[5] This was also the case for the price controls decreed by all the Societies over a year earlier, but enforced before the letter by most of them, and again the case for the socialization of basic supplies for which the Convention in November 1793 copied the plan elaborated by the Societies of the Midi on October 9th, etc. For all the great problems of public interest, the Society's opinion had a ready response—equally spontaneous, equally natural, and much clearer and faster than the response of the real [public] opinion—and always its inversion, moreover, just as the conditions in which both opinions were shaped were inverted.

Thus, in short, the question is to know which of the two would make the law. But it was an unparalleled conflict, which must not be confused with competing doctrines or parties: it was not revolution against reaction, reason against dogma, freedom against authority. Here the question is not so much to know who would be the winner as to know what terrain would be the battlefield. The Philosophical Societies were not socialism, but the milieu in which socialism was certain to see the day, grow and reign, when nothing would seem to herald it, as in the lodges of 1750. Real society was not the Revolution, but the terrain where the Revolution would lose—where authority, hierarchies would win, once everything, men and laws, had become revolutionary, as in the France of Thermidor Year II—as soon as the Jacobin Society's yoke had been cast off.

It has often been acknowledged that opinion varies according to the conditions it is shaped in and the manner of questioning it. The same men, otherwise unchanged, will opine differently in a [Philosophical] Society—i.e. without contact with reality, with no other immediate goal than winning a vote or convincing an audience—from the way they will when taken individually, alone in their families, confronted with a specific task. It is merely a question of situation, not doctrine or conviction.

But ordinarily we stop at this banal observation, which means that despite collective terms (people, opinion, etc.), we only want to consider one moment and one man, never the group and the duration. No doubt this moment and this man are commonplace, so the fact is general. But they are nonetheless unique, isolated, so the fact is not collective. We must not confuse *everyone* with *anyone*, nor *always* with *any time*.

To catch a glimpse of the Society's law, one must realize that this unconscious factor of opinion—the speaker's situation—is lasting: the Society is standing. This factor dismisses any other: the Society is exclusive. This factor is reinforced: the Society recruits and purges, assimilates and eliminates men and ideas, always according to the same bias given by the factor of opinion. And then the imperceptible divergence in a single case, on one point, becomes an abyss; the point of view of one instant becomes an orientation, the law of a world and a milieu. A state of mind is developed, relations established, a moral and intellectual life created that are so many enigmas for the real world and are reduced, in short, to the original inversion between the Philosophical Society and real society. In the former what succeeds is only what is spoken and is communicated as such, though it may be nothing. What compels recognition in the latter, the world of achievement and endeavor, is only what *is* such, though it may be inexpressible.

Which of the two trends shall opinion follow? Or rather, which of the two opinions, the Society's or the real one, shall be recognized as sovereign and declared the people's and the Nation's? Such was the question asked in 1789 and finally decided in the autumn of 1793.

The great political fact of that autumn was the official advent of Social opinion. Secret in the lodges of '89, unofficial in the clubs of '92, the new force no longer allowed any divergences. There would be no people, no opinion other than this one. The Societies took possession of all the limited rights the new regime had just wrung from the mass of voters, and used them without any control. The people lost the right to elect their magistrates at the legally appointed time and in accordance with legal procedure; the Societies took the right to purge them unceasingly, with no respect for the rules.[6] The people were disarmed, systematically, down to the very last shotgun; the Societies took up arms. Better still, forming special regiments, the "revolutionary armies," the Societies purged, directed, and supervised them in the war on the "enemy within."[7] As a matter of fact, the Societies had never been so numerous—nearly 1900, according to the census of the Home Office [*Ministère de l'Intérieur*]—nor so disciplined, unified since the defeat of the Girondin schism; nor so well attended as since the "fear"[8] of September, during the arrests of suspects. People would take refuge in the Society as they used to in the church during the time of the right of asylum—everything else being constantly liable for requisition, confiscation, or imprisonment at whim.

Thus, before changing its government in January 1794, France changed its people in 1793. A force reigned that was indeed a collective idea and will—hence an opinion and a people, not a faction or a party—but it was not [public] opinion. A [little] people took the place of the masses—the former more foreign to the instincts, interests, and genius of the latter than the English of York or the Prussians of Brunswick. Was it astonishing then that the legislation enacted to suit one was a straitjacket for the other, that the happiness of one was the Terror for the other, that the laws necessary for one were impossible for the other?

CHAPTER 2: THE POWER

But then arose the real difficulty, the enforcement of these impossible laws—a formidable task imposed upon the little people of the Societies by the very conquest of these laws. For it was no longer, as in the lodges' golden age, a matter of soliciting the suffrage of the "republic of letters," the city of the clouds, by harmless moral constructions. Now one had to govern men, manage various interests—but the Society's opinion and its literature were not made for that. On first contact with reality, the legislators' reason was flatly contradicted, often within less than a week. For example:

The markets were not well supplied, so on September 11, 1793, the Convention decreed cereals could no longer be sold anywhere but there, and the markets emptied out on the spot. As produce was getting rare and expensive, on September 29th, the Convention lowered retail prices, thinking the wholesale would have to follow or not sell at all, but wholesale prices were maintained, and in less than a week the shops were empty and small businesses on their knees. The same law, by limiting the price of meat, limited the price of livestock: immediately the farmers slaughtered whole herds, even two-month-old calves, even the breeders, since feeding them was no longer worthwhile. Then the Convention hastily rescinded their decree (October 23rd) to save stockbreeding. But now the butchers, whose prices were still controlled, could no longer buy and stopped slaughtering. This led to shortages in the tanning trade, then in bark for tanning, then in shoemaking, then in clothing for the troops, not to mention the scarcity of meat, even more pronounced than that of bread (February 1794). On April 11, 1794, the Committee of Public Safety requisitioned throughout the land, for Paris and the armies, every eighth yearling pig, which was entrusted to its master until time to deliver it at the restricted price. This was quite an operation. It involved sorting, counting, branding, then organizing payment, rounding up the animals, delivering them to stockyards, slaughtering and salting them—all implemented by numerous circulars, inspectors, and agents. And when the commissioner finally arrived months later, the pig was dead or dying. Forced, but certain, to sell it at a low price, its master could only lose by feeding it, and obviously did not do so. The Republic only got skeletons, and too late to salt and cure them, as the hot weather had already arrived.

And so forth: all the socialistic types of endeavor led to impasses of this sort. If these endeavors had been applied to men, these brutal lessons would have made them think, but a Social phenomenon does not think. It plods on from one disaster to another, producing a forest of laws contrary to nature whose success in the Societies and whose enactment by the Convention were as fatal as their enforcement in the country was absurd or impossible.

The former ministerial government was not armed for such a task and succumbed to these two contrary necessities. This was the anarchistic crisis of the summer of 1798 during which each department,[9] each town, each interest took advantage of the situation and ignored a [central] power which was no longer the moral authority and not yet Social despotism.

But finally federalism was defeated, since the new city had its means of reigning, its government, as it had its people. This government was, moreover, as strange in its own way as the city itself, for the revolutionary order lived precisely on what would have destroyed the real order. The force that reigned in the Committee of Public Safety in the Year II was no more the prince than the force that revolted in '89 was the people.

Common opinion holds that chaos reigns in the same place as does anarchy in its literal meaning: the absence of all authority, either that of a man or a doctrine. This is a mistake. Anarchy can ally with order in its two forms, unity of direction and unity of opinion, and the least of the Philosophical Societies accomplished this miracle. The [Society's] law of selection and training we have already discussed acted gradually. The "development of the Enlightenment," the conquest of the real man by the Social man,[10] consisted of many steps and stages, from the intellectual socialization of the "philosopher" of '89, and the moral socialization of the patriot of '92, to the material socialization of the citizen of '93.

Of course, among the brothers there were differences in zeal and aptitude. For 100 registered members, there were less than 30 active ones, and less than 5 efficacious ones. The last ones were the masters of the Society. They were the ones who chose the new members, thus shifting the majority at will. They appointed the officers, made the motions, directed the votes smoothly, without affecting the principles or being reproached by their fellows, for the absent are supposed to agree, and are there not a hundred honest ways to ward off a troublemaker? A bit of mutual agreement was sufficient to discourage him. The worst an isolated independent could do was to withdraw with dignity.

Thus at the heart of the large Society took shape another smaller, more active and united one that would have no difficulty directing the larger unawares. It was made up of the most eager and most devoted, the most knowledgeable manipulators of voters. Every time the Society was to meet, they would meet first in the morning, see their friends, establish their plan of action, give their orders, stir up the less enthusiastic members, and bring their influence to bear on the timid. Since they had long been in perfect agreement, they held all the proper cards in their hands: they had subdued the board, dismissed the independents, set the date and the agenda. The discussion was free, of course, but this freedom remained limited and the sovereign's protests little to be feared: the general will was only as free as a locomotive on its tracks.

This system has a name. It is what the Freemasons of the eighteenth century called the system of inner orders, what the English politicians today call inner circles. It relies on that law of Social practice according to which every official vote is preceded and determined by an unofficial discussion, and every standing Social group, every people, is uninitiated in relation to a more restricted, more united, more clairvoyant group of "initiates."

Such is the origin of the new power and a whole set of political methods that have been inventoried in well-known books.[11] This is the "royal art" of our Freemasons, the science of electoral manipulations in American democracy, methods shared in common, in that they act upon the electoral matter in an unconscious, mechanical way. Hence the names "machine" and "machinism" given to the system and its recipes, and "wire-pullers" to the agents of the inner circles, the secretaries, the heads of correspondence, and the committees. Thanks to these methods this miracle is accomplished: Social order is ensured without affecting anarchistic principles, orthodoxy founded without faith, discipline established without loyalty.

To ensure unity of thought without dogma or credo, the rule is never to broach a subject except when a collective decision has already been made.

This is the English practitioners' method of the *"fait accompli,"* and the patriots' great trick during the upheavals of 1788. For example: to gain a province's approval of such-and-such a motion made by the machine, the towns were tackled one by one, starting with the towns one was sure of—and influencing the others by the approval of the first ones. The same snowballing method worked inside each town to win over, one after the other, the corporations and guilds that governed there. This method did everything for the elections of 1789, which, because of the complicated regulations, would have been impossible without the machine's propulsion. The method became institutionalized in the Year II, when a national agent sent sixty recalcitrant towns a circular informing each of them that they were the only ones to resist. Moreover, the very nature of impossible laws does not allow any other argument than this one, which cuts objections short.

This method founds a new type of orthodoxy, "conformity," "regularity," that is distinguished from the old orthodoxy (religious dogma, for example), in that it does not admit any divergence between the letter and the spirit, the rule and the fact. It is implicit, blunt acceptance of "cut-and-dried" formulas, as the English practitioners say, ready-to-use like cured meat, too numerous and precise to allow, and too topical to suffer, the least discussion. On the other hand, this rigorousness of form is without compensation, for the dogma is relative, changing, "evolving" with the votes. And it is literal, imposing an attitude, a language, in no way a conviction: "bound" outside, the brother is free inside. Such were the *cahiers* [lists of grievances] of '89, those masterpieces of cut-and-dried literature, identical even in their wording. Such were the "people's" hundreds of precise, unanimous initiatives during the struggle that followed, until the triumph of the system in '93. One recognizes the democratic idea of the *law*—a strictly formal conception, which we owe much more to the practice of the Societies than to the theories of Jean-Jacques [Rousseau]. This is the general will, the bill enacted, Social coercion, as such, without examination or content—dogma without faith.

Moreover, the argument of the *fait accompli* is the Social argument *par excellence*: the opinion of others is the only one that is unalloyed, devoid of personal conviction. Contradicted by personal motives, whatever they may be, from the upright man's conscience to the drunkard's glass of wine, it guarantees the inner circle all the unmotivated votes: the contribution of ignorance, stupidity, and fear.

The argument can only be productive, the contribution grow, under two conditions. First, in the inner circle, secrecy is essential. An opinion is acknowledged as everyone's only if it is believed to be held by anyone at all. To pull the wires, they must be hidden: the first rule for directing a group of voters *mechanically* is to mingle with them. The person who proposes a motion is a citizen, and the hired clappers are dispersed among the audience. When there was a desire to kill the life of the Societies in '91, signatures were required as a guarantee, which exposed the inner circle (decrees of May 10, 18, 22). On the contrary, when there was a desire to give the Societies an advantage over the official bodies, the bodies—and not the Societies—were forced to sign individually and to deliberate publicly (decree of September 2, 1792). With the signatures as a guarantee, there was no more secrecy, hence no possible manipulation of the machine. "The troublemakers, knowing they will have to sign, will then fear to be recognized,"[12] and "when the leaders of the revolt are known, the revolt stops instantly," for in every Society it is those "who hide behind the scenes"[13] who do everything.

Thus not only is the new power not the authority, and able to dispense with being acknowledged as the legitimate master, but it perishes if it is merely recognized. The fact in democracy agrees with the principle: there is no master in this regime, not even representatives or leaders. The people are free.

The second condition requisite for the operation of the machine is this sovereign's very freedom, even if it should exceed the restricted limits in which the sovereign is able to exercise it. Always, in the new republic—which abolished this limit on principle—the people as a whole [were supposed to] make decisions, on everything, unceasingly. But with time materially lacking for discussion—not to mention the necessary competence and also the leisure to think—it then became necessary for the action of the machine and the argument of the *fait accompli* to take the place of impossible debates. Thus the work of the inner circle was quite simple: it was to increase this theoretical freedom that was so useful to it. Everything that restricted this freedom upset it: the authority of a doctrine or a master, the strength of traditions or experience, legal limits, even physical limits to the right of discussion. If the people pretended to debate for real, it was because they were not free enough. So the agenda was overburdened and the debate raised to the philosophical clouds, then lowered to the latest administrative details (the Jacobins' major and minor agendas). The illiterate were invited to attend, even if it meant paying them (Danton's 40 pennies). The sessions were multiplied and lengthened: towards ten in the evening the hall was vacated; the most independent, competent, occupied, and conscientious members had left. This was the time for the machine.

Here we can observe the practical side of so-called "generous" ideas and democratic optimism that attributes all the virtues to the people and grants them all the rights. For a true democrat the best guarantee against the independence of man is still the freedom of the citizen. The secret of the new order resides in Gambetta's naive phrase, engraved on the Carrousel monument: "Now we know universal suffrage is us."

True: universal suffrage is them. However, it is not even necessary for them to know it and tell one another so. For they will always be there, due to the very existence of this regime, of which they are the necessary products, not the authors. Once freedom is conceived, the acknowledged authority has to disappear—which means the people deliberate constantly, with no master, no elected representative: this is the Philosophical Society. Once the Society is founded, an inner circle fatally takes shape to direct it unawares. Where freedom reigns, it is the machine that governs. Such is the revolutionary order, as irrefutable as logic, as indisputable as human weakness, which is all its strength. Indeed it asks nothing of its mass of followers except non-interference, nothing of the "wire-pullers" in the inner circles except to play unscrupulously on the *fait accompli* and maintain Social conformity by focusing the weight of passive consent obtained by the machine on each personal conviction, isolated by freedom. There is no task easier than this thought police, no leader of a lodge, club, or syndicate who does not manage this remarkably well. It is merely a question of unofficial connections, collecting information on index cards, and checking lists. The job requires neither the moral ascendancy of a chief, nor the technical knowledge of an administrator—not even the temperament of an orator. And the scrupulousness of a decent man would be troublesome. The basest, crudest activity, that of passion and fear, which was called "energy" in '93, is largely sufficient here. Gambetta was right, and faith in democracy is no vain word: "they" will not fail him and are there, certain to reign, under freedom.

Such is the principle of the new order.

It is evident that everything we have just said about a society of individuals applies to a society of Societies, to an "order," as our Freemasons say. The proportions change, not the relationships, and the bias is the same. The Societies of an order were equal and free in theory, like the brothers of a Society, but unequal in fact, just like the brothers. Like the latter the Societies united, federated themselves, and organized correspondence: thereupon a center took shape that acted on the circumference, like the inner circle on the Society, mechanically. No doubt this *de facto* power was not established immediately, nor without a struggle: it took seven years for the Grand Orient to get organized (1773–1780), four years for the mother Society of the Rue Saint-Honoré to kill its rivals and purge its daughters. It can even be said that every Social center was in constant conflict with the federalism of the circumference. But victory of the indivisible was assured against isolated dissidents.

Once the center ruled and unity was achieved, the machine was perfected. Such was the Grand Orient in 1785, with its 800 lodges; the Society of Jacobins in 1794, with its 800 daughters. This machine was surely the most formidable and far-reaching instrument of pressure there could be, for it had no limited motive force like real societies (a nation, a corps) that last only as long as does the moral reality (the idea, the tribal instinct) that creates and sustains them.

The more numerous and more distant the Societies, the more the inertia increased. The center's *de facto* action, which was exercised in the name and by means of the entire Society, grew with the Society, whereas the individuals' power of resistance did not increase. We see that the dream of humanitarian unity, which, moreover, was born in the Philosophical Societies, is not, in this case at least, so vain: such a power is not of a nature to impose itself on only one nation. If the government of mankind is ever to fall into the same hands, it will be those of Social manipulators.

CHAPTER 3: THE PRINCE

Thus, in the new city, order was ensured—and yet anarchistic principles were safe. Better still, order was augmented by anarchy itself. The same Social phenomenon that produced the impossible laws created the only power that could ensure their enforcement.

This power had always reigned among the little people of the [Philosophical] Societies. A lodge, a club, a popular Society are not governed in any other way. But this world has no contact with either the masses or realities. In the country as a whole, in business and real life, democracy was still acting only indirectly, by means of the people in place, its creatures, and the government, its instrument. The advent of the impossible laws and their consequences—the shortages of supplies and the anarchistic crisis of '93—disconcerted the people in place and broke up the government. It was clear that the former government's very carcass had become an obstacle to the new one, were it in the hands of humble servants of democracy like Bouchotte, Gohier, or Paré. The institutions themselves, even in the absence of men, interfered with the process of socialization. Methods had to be adapted to doctrines. The revolutionary impulse had to be placed in the government itself, which was a desperate course of action, a new revolution as profound as that of '89, but this time imposed by the law of democracy on the Jacobins themselves, who followed reluctantly without realizing where they were heading.

In this respect nothing is odder than the effort of the Convention to define the role of the Committee of Public Safety, particularly in their session of August 1, 1793. At first sight, Danton appeared to be the champion of reform. He lavished money and power on the Committee but did not join it: "I shall [thus] preserve the integrity of my thought," he said, "and the ability to keep prodding those who govern." He was still thinking in terms of the former game of '92 and the old ministerial dummy, which he clothed differently, to be sure, armored when necessary against the country, and then made flexible again in the hands of the democrats—but retained, in short, even in the wording itself.

Robespierre had the opposite attitude. He joined the Committee—he who had not wished to be a minister—but refused Danton's largess. No money: let the ministers keep it—under the watchful eye of the Committee, to be sure. Not even any power—at least not in the real, efficacious meaning of the term: nothing but the right of supervision. The Committee did not administrate—that was the principle of the new reign, continually violated and then reinstated again until Thermidor and as long as the spirit of the Revolution dominated—and it was a legitimate principle, certainly: the masters among the little people [from the Societies] were not made, any more than their laws, to reign over the vaster population. When they dominated in the world of Social opinion, it was for their talents and by means that in the real world were non-values or defects. Hence the concern to spare the phantom who was to reign from any burdening, any contact even, with affairs. Money, civil servants, and soldiers were the ministries' domain, as were work, accounts, and responsibilities, too—the Committee just supervised. But what did this mean? Is it possible to supervise without understanding? Command without knowing? Danton remained silent, the Convention understood little, and Robespierre made demands without explanation. Yet he was right, as is proved by what followed—and also by the study of the central and characteristic organ of the new regime, which at that very moment was taking shape inside the Committee of Public Safety. We are talking about the Office of Surveillance of Law Enforcement, established in July 1793. Omnipotent in February 1794, at the height of the Revolutionary government's power, paralyzed by the coup d'état of 9 Thermidor, on the 11th its correspondence ceased, and it was finally dismembered, i.e. destroyed, by the decree of the following 17 Fructidor.

Its origins were modest. The secretariat of the Committee—like those of all organs of execution—had three main functions: register the documents upon their arrival, distribute them to the competent services, and upon their departure record the reply and the procedure adopted. Taken by itself alone, and in a normal regime, this last function of supervision is the least of the three, a mere formality to prevent needless repetition and redundancy. But in the regime of impossible laws, at the height of the conflict against democracy and the people, between the Philosophical Society and real society, nothing was done any more except by terror. The natural laziness of bureaucracy would have become paralysis, if the ordinary means of government had been respected, but here the enforcement of the laws became the power's great concern—the "surveillance of enforcement" its weightiest task.

This new function produced a strange organ, the Office of Enforcement, whose most important specimen, of course, was found within the Committee of Public Safety—although other interesting examples could be found by December 1793 in the Commission of Provisions, in May 1794 in the Commission of Agriculture, and generally in the most socialized administrations. They were sorts of duplicates of the service in question; they reproduced subdivisions, but as a scale model copies the original: to be seen but not used. Their role was neither to conclude, nor study, nor even classify affairs. They had neither authority, nor competence—and were there only to determine, day by day, the results obtained, and also the constant revolts and failures in the unnatural labor of socialization. Their job, says a note of May 30, 1794,[14] "consists of following the enforcement step by step, not to learn how it was done, but only whether it was done." "This office," says a memorandum of May 1794,[15] "must consider itself the eye of the Commission, and must not allow itself any direct action. It will inform the Correspondence Office of orders not carried out, and the latter will propose letters for the Commission to use to prod the negligent parties." Thus the enforcement must not even correct the faults it detects. It neither commanded, nor administrated, nor even corresponded.

Its whole job consisted of establishing "states of enforcement," i.e. synoptic tables indicating, for every ten days, the degree of enforcement of a given operation in the various districts, when a general measure was concerned, or chronological tables with columns giving the date, the analysis, the follow-up, etc., of every decision, when specific decrees[16] were concerned. With a view to this continual itemizing, the "decadal[17] correspondence" was instituted in February 1794. This was the local authorities' reply, every ten days, to a uniform questionnaire on the enforcement of the laws. To fill in the gaps in this correspondence, on February 1st the [Office of] Enforcement started maintaining a special correspondence, all of whose letters had the same purpose, the same content, and soon the same format. These were the so-called "expeditious letters," written on triple-columned paper, the first for the date of the act to be executed, the second for its analysis, the third to report on its execution.[18] Such was the framework of this peculiar governing machine, that worked all by itself, like Vaucanson's[19] duck. There were no men inside, nor any handling of men, nor even any knowledge of the affairs. Everything was done mechanically and amounted to ruling paper. The reports of enforcement arrived in the central office, were classified, compared, detailed, and distributed by subject and region into ready-made slots. The "state of enforcement" was thus accomplished—and consequently the power's task was determined: to complete the picture and fill in the voids.

This barometer of social conformity is surely the most mechanical and passive instrument. None can be imagined less compatible with the time-honored attributes of power: the authority of the chief, the competence of the administrator. And yet this is indeed the principle mechanism of the machine, the center and bond of the indivisible. Better still, it is the methods of this Office that are the basis for understanding the spirit of the new powers. And each of them remains revolutionary only if, in its own domain, it imitates the Office of Enforcement and resists the natural propensity to go back to efficient administration.

Indeed, it was this Office's function to set the force of the new regime, and the socialized State, into play. This force was not the appeal of a doctrine, but the weight of a fact: the submission of other people. One recognizes here "the argument of the *fait accompli*," the Social argument *par excellence*, acting on the authority of common opinion, but without concern for the doctrines or interests that may have founded it. This argument addresses neither the heart, nor the intelligence, but only passive forces, from the herding instinct to fear. Those people who were won over obeyed because the crowd obeyed, or because they believed it did. And it was this mass of inertia that was channeled and focused to bring the argument to bear on isolated resistance.

The system is advantageous for the leaders, allowing them to dispense with rights, talent, even popularity. It is irresistible for the governed, under two conditions: first, that they be "emancipated" in the negative and democratic meaning of the term, i.e. perfectly separated, isolated from one another, therefore helpless against the argument of the *fait accompli*; and secondly that this disunited mass be homogeneous, equally distributed into uniform slots, so that the political arithmetic of surveillance works on units of the same type. Now, we know these two conditions, essential to the Philosophical Societies' Work, had been accomplished in the country by the first revolution, that of freedom. Thus the way was cleared for the second revolution, that of order, and the machine we have described could start running. For the function of its principal mechanism consisted in continually stressing, on every question, against all dissidence, the argument of the *fait accompli*. The tables and the itemizing had no other purpose. There lay the secret of the system—the only one that could ensure union without destroying freedom.

The socialist laws came along precisely to give the system a new force, and strengthen the constraints of the argument of conformity, which was already so powerful on isolated people. For these laws had this peculiar characteristic: that any violation of them not only benefited the culprit but visibly burdened the innocent. If price controls were not adequately respected in one district, where goods remained too high, they poured in from the more obedient neighboring districts, where shortages thus increased by as much. The same was true of general requisitions: everything one person did not give up had to be given up by another. With inventories, everything one person kept and hid was taken from another who had declared it; with rations, everything one person consumed in excess, was taken from another, etc. All the laws of socialization give rise to the same observation: materially binding the citizens to one another, these laws divided them morally. This was the principle of republican fraternity: a question of situation, much more than of morals and principles. The nature of things made each citizen the natural enemy, the overseer of his neighbor. During the ten months of the French Terror, the entire country, from district to district, town to town, man to man, acted out this spectacle of war between convicts on the same chain gang, which moreover, as we shall see, was as much the condition as the effect of the socialized order. Universal hatred has its equilibrium, as love has its harmony.

The unexpected consequence of this state of affairs was to spare the government the trouble of resorting to armed force—even when it seemed to need it most, when Terror was mounting. The revolutionary army, necessary in November to wrench grain from the peasants, became useless by March and was disbanded. This was due to the fact that each district, even each town, panicked by famine, organized the necessary raids against its neighbors to enforce the laws of provisions; the government's only role was to allow this and not interfere. To prevent the revolt of each, the misery of the others was henceforth sufficient. In March, following the same principle, the Committee of Public Safety had the grain of one district inventoried by the commissioners of another, and the representatives of one department[20] were sent to another, etc. Here was a whole system of government by self-interest, surveillance, hatred of others, whose examples were multiple and which could be summed up in a word: government by foreigners.

We can now see what facility and importance this new order gave to the surveillance of enforcement. Though the culprit no longer had to reckon with the masters of his conscience (his faith, his loyalty, God and the king), he had everything to fear from the witnesses of his conduct, and could no longer rely on his isolation and the indifference of others, since he caused them immediate and obvious harm. The power was thus assured in advance of the collectivity's actual and constant help. Surveillance and assistance were guaranteed against lack of good citizenship. And the power had only to observe and report [wrong-doing] to unleash the selfishness of all against the selfishness of each individual. This passion restrained by fear is precisely what is called virtue in Social democracy: one cannot say it is evil, since the guilty act does not occur. But it is something worse.

Such was the function, in its essence, of the Office of Surveillance of Enforcement, an unprecedented function peculiar to this regime. Once again, this office neither governed nor administered. It was the most worthless, but at the same time the most essential, of the machine's mechanisms. It was the Social organ *par excellence*, the center and the soul of the indivisible, its action growing with that of the regime itself. First it was domestic, restricted to the internal surveillance of the ministries; then national and universal in the spring of 1794, when the ministries disappeared and socialization was extended to all domains and into the least of the districts. In the last volume of our study we shall reveal the steps of this progression, which are the very history of the Terror. The information that precedes it will suffice to explain the purpose and the limits of our booklet.[21]

We first undertook this booklet for ourselves, during a local study, which we had to give up for lack of sufficient notions of the central power's framework and methods. We are [now] publishing it under the auspices and with the assistance of the Society of Contemporary History. We are convinced other people besides ourselves will sense its usefulness, which lies in the very nature of the object considered: the democratic phenomenon.

Local history is self-contained so long as it concerns the old order—a *personal* order for the subjects, still more than for the master; an order diverse in its essence that governed provinces, cities, and organized bodies, each according to its spirit, its past, and its law. This order included as many different constitutions as cities, and spoke of freedom and the people only in the plural. But democracy cannot allow this diversity: it is by nature the regime of uniformity and leveling.

For democracy, this necessity must come first, for since it no longer commands, it administrates more. But no administration is possible without uniformity. Uniformity is the first law of the work that began with the division of France into departments in 1790, and ended with the radical socialization of the Year II—this triumph of administration that substitutes the common rule for personal incentive and the legal formula for initiative, even in economic and private life. Submitted to this impersonal framework, the human crowd really appears as *matter*, i.e. an indeterminate and homogeneous driving force that only obtains its shape, direction, and use from the machine it sets in motion, somewhat like steam in a locomotive.

It is clear such a regime cannot afford the luxury of varying its measures and means according to people and places. The more complicated the mechanisms, the more the electoral or taxpaying matter must be disunited, malleable, and homogeneous. The great zeal for equality of the Year II was no doubt due less to the resentments of the crowd than the necessities of the power: from the day price controls and requisition placed the grain of the smallest villages, the accounts of the least of the retailers, in the hands of the Parisian offices, the leveling of '90 was felt to be insufficient and the leveling of the Year II took its place, reducing the administrative element by 80%. The "indivisible," by extending and complicating its action, had to compress its staff and framework proportionately.

And at the same time this is, for it, a necessity of a moral order, imposed on the democratic game from its philosophical origins, if it is true, as we have shown, that the great secret of the center, its only concern, is to use the argument of the *fait accompli* to maintain conformity by a constant effort of surveillance and pressure. It is obvious this job needs a leveled terrain, quite identical elements. Upon the thousand diverse countenances of the former France that the personal power knew individually by name, an administrative uniform had to be imposed to make regimentation possible in the Year II: towns had to be numbered, provinces subdivided, the nation chopped up.

But if this is so, the historian has a new task. He must bring out facts, establish this general plan that is henceforth so effective, this metric system of Jacobin action, which is everywhere determinant, everywhere similar to itself, although everywhere distorted and altered by inertia or revolt. Each democratic fact is a product of two factors: one constant, the impulse from the center, and the other variable, the local or personal reaction. To explain, it no longer suffices to relate exactly what happened. One must still evaluate each component's share, analyze the alloy. The same fact—for example the levy *en masse* of a village to treat ground with saltpeter in May 1794, or the "voluntary gift" of shirts by a people's association in March—attested by the same texts, in the same emphatic terms, can be as easily explained by terror, when the action of the center prevailed, as by enthusiasm, when it was due to personal initiative. Or it can even be explained, between these two extremes, by all the intermediate terms one wishes; all translations are proper, without changing a single comma in the text, and each historian selects the one that flatters his sentiments—hostile, favorable, or neutral. This is the triumph of political passion, which only in this case can afford precision, giving itself scientific airs without in any way diminishing its prejudices—the despair of sincere effort that piles detail upon detail, without approaching the truth.

To get out of this impasse and evaluate the fact, or resultant force, the two components must be separated. And the only way to separate them is to isolate the one that turns out to be the same everywhere, by taking a field of study broad enough to detect the characteristic in one point that may be concealed in another, and eliminate local circumstances. This task is simple enough if it concerns the official democracy of 1794, which printed and published its decisions, but more difficult for the unofficial action of 1791 or the secret one of 1788. However, the historian's task is always subject to the essential rule never to be satisfied, in the center, with the declaration of principle (be it speech, proclamation, or law), nor on the circumference with the brute fact. The former is merely a declared intention, which says nothing about what may follow, however clearly it is presented. The latter is merely a resultant, which, as we have just said, does not reveal its causes, however precisely it is defined. The tool for study that we are proposing is neither a compendium of laws, nor a series of local examples, but a plan of action, general like laws and real like local examples.

To tell the truth, this booklet only indicates a very broad outline of revolutionary action. To complete the edifice one will have to collect:

1. the circulars addressed to the various agents, whose every operation is presumed to have been ordered—from the removal of church bells to the cutting of alder trees, and from the draining of ponds to the levy of every eighth pig. This is a much more difficult task than ours, for the correspondence of this type was no more often placed in the department's files than that of civil servants today.
2. the circulars addressed to the local administrations by the officials of the various administrative subdivisions: the four regions of the police, the fourteen districts of provisions, the twenty-three military divisions, the eleven inspections of saltpeter, fodder, meat, etc.

Then would the architecture of the indivisible finally stand out in its unity and symmetry. Only then would the endeavor of actual history yield all its fruit. And, in each case, one could separate the action of the center and the local reaction with enough certainty to determine their relative strengths.

Our greatest hope is to be corrected, completed, i.e. continued—and to see the nature of things impose the outline for study that common sense seems to indicate. . . . All that is necessary is to abandon former methods that here are just old habits, study the Social regime otherwise than as a personal regime, and see in the Committee of Public Safety, not a king's counsel without the wigs and manners, but the center of gravity of an immense collectivist administration. . . .

ENDNOTES

[1] *The Acts of the Revolutionary Government (August 23, 1793-July 27, 1794)* by Augustin Cochin and Charles Charpentier, for which the following pages are the preface.

[2] Translator's note: Cochin uses this term to indicate socialism.

[3] *La Revue française,* Sept. 22, 1912.

[4] Translator's note: *Entrainement* (*coaching* or *training* in English) is the word Cochin uses to denote the Masonic Society's method of persuasion and mechanical indoctrination.

[5] Sauzay, *Persécution révolutionnaire dans le Doubs,* 1869, vol. V, p. 2 — Departmental Archives of Haute-Vienne, Hérault, Drôme and Tarn: series L. records of the societies.

[6] The investiture of this right was the main purpose of the summer missions, and the only one of the mission of December 29th — the role of the representatives generally being limited to presiding over the Society during the proceedings, and ratifying its choices afterwards. If they happened to purge the Society itself, especially in the Year II, it was not of their own doing but because of the will of a harder core approved by Paris.

[7] Archives of the war, subdivision of the West, carton of the Revolutionary Army, note included in the Minister of War's letter of October 20, 1793. Cf. letter from Paris on October 3 (for the purge of the general staff by the Jacobins of Paris).

Records of the Societies of Limoges, Valence, Montpellier, Lons le Saulnier, Castres, Dijon. This last record gives us every detail of the task: the formation of the "core" of the revolutionary army, the purge of the subjects presented by this core, etc. (Archives of Haute-Vienne, Drôme, Hérault, Jura, Tarn, Côte-d'or.)

[8] This term is used in a letter from the Society of Saint-Yrieux to the Society of Limoges, on February 5, 1794, Archives of Haute-Vienne, book 824.

[9] Translator's note: France is divided into 99 of these administrative districts.

[10] Translator's note: i.e. the man of the Societies.

[11] M. Ostrogorski, *La Démocratie et l'Organisation des Partis Politiques,* Calmann-Lévy, Paris, 1903. James Bryce, *The American Commonwealth,* the Macmillan Company, New York, London, 1907 (third edition).

[12] Bourdon de l'Oise at the Convention, Oct. 19, 1794.

[13] *Moniteur*, November 7, September 27, 1794, p. 205, 30.

[14] Archives Nationales, BB30 30.

[15] *Commission du commerce* — organization plan, Archives Nationales, DXLII 9.

[16] Archives Nationales, Justice, BB30 30.

[17] Translator's note: The Revolutionary calendar divided the month into three ten-day periods, called *décades*.

[18] Archives de l'Aube, L m 11/531.

[19] Translator's note: Vaucanson was a French mechanic (1709–1782), famous for his automatons.

[20] Translator's note: A French administrative district.

[21] Translator's note: the French publisher, Copernic, notes that in the original edition Cochin devoted thirty pages here to a minute detailing of archives whose interest is minimal for today's reader.

HOW THE DEPUTIES WERE ELECTED
TO THE ESTATES GENERAL[1] (abridged)

At this time when there is so much discussion about electoral reform, I should like to speak to you about the oldest of our election regulations, the ordinance of January 24, 1789, to which the Constituent Assembly owed its powers. Oddly enough, this is an entirely new subject, even though the text of this famous law has been published, its enforcement related, and its results analyzed with the greatest care. No one, however, has questioned its intrinsic value, its spirit, and its chances for success.

And yet it is worth examining, as you shall see, and this, our first electoral experiment, may have been the boldest and most thought-provoking of them all. . . .

To grasp the spirit of this ordinance, one must remember the royal government was then confronted with two very different conceptions of popular law: the old French freedoms of the [three] Estates,[2] and the new English freedom of the townships and the Parliament.

The French conception was positive, realistic, and organic. It was the entire nation that the king was addressing, but the nation with its established organization and framework, with its various hierarchies, its natural subdivisions, its current leaders. Moreover, the nature or origin of their authority was due to ancestry as well as popular suffrage, or to the orders of the Church, or the offices of the State; in a word, all the social values taken as they actually existed and functioned. To speak of elections here would be a misconception: it was only a summons. A Parliament is elected; Estates are summoned.

Democracy as unqualified Freedom was irrelevant here. We speak of freedoms as we speak of peoples: there were all kinds and forms of freedoms, each with its own history and titles, as numerous and diverse as the bodies they emanated from.

On the other hand, it was natural that this [French] nation, acting as an organized body, should behave differently from an inorganic mass of voters. The king acknowledged in the nation an active, positive role that our democracies [today] would not think of granting to the electoral masses. This nation was capable of initiative, wrote up its grievances by itself, designated its spokesmen when necessary, and followed them step by step: the deputy's mandate was strictly defined.[3] Representatives with general powers, men whose calling was to act as necessary intermediaries between the king and the nation, were unheard of. The relationship between the king and the nation was direct. The nation spoke for itself without a parliamentary go-between, and, in this way, the old popular law was far superior to our democracies [today].

Entirely different was the English and parliamentary conception of a people of electors. In this case it was the individual being that the power addressed, i.e. the capacity of the individual's conscience to form a judgment, regardless of his milieu, profession, actual duties and needs—or at least all of this retaining of its value and influence only what each person could or wished to save, which would not be very much. Hence the importance of the election, the vote, the only circumstance and act that allowed this new, abstract, unreal being—the citizen—to assert his existence. Hence the necessity, first, for a special terrain, politics, that allowed him to exhibit it; then for a special body, the Parliament, which was the depositary of his thoughts and powers; and finally for a dogma, freedom, that consecrated his superiority over the real being, the concrete man, involved in all the impediments of real life.

But by the very fact of their enfranchisement, this dust of political atoms could not sustain the active, positive role of an organized people. A people made up of electors is no longer capable of initiative, only assent, at most: it can choose between two or three platforms, two or three candidates, but it can no longer draft proposals, or appoint men. Professional politicians have to present the people with proposals and men. This is the role of the parties, an unofficial role no doubt, but indispensable in such a regime. Without this role, this extra-legal recourse, the sovereign [people] would remain free, but would fall silent.

In short, French freedom gave great consideration to popular sovereignty, by attributing an active, positive, direct role to it, provided the individual was ignored and only organized bodies were addressed; whereas English freedom isolated and enfranchised the individual, but left him only a negative and passive role, and relied for the rest on the party's organization. French freedom acknowledged the legal authority of organized bodies; English freedom required the *de facto* discipline of parties. One had to choose. Necker did not choose, and claimed he kept both: the French freedom that condemned any campaign of [public] opinion as a cabal, and the English freedom that rejected any social dogmatism as coercion. Hence the odd character of an electoral experiment that may be unparalleled in the history of democracy.

And first these were indeed English-style elections, with extensive, almost universal suffrage, since all the men who were registered for the poll-tax had a vote. But then, more importantly, this was a special consultation, a selection of political representatives appointed by a new manner of election that ignored the influences and notables that the older-style Estates would have made prominent. For example, the regulation deprived the town guilds and corporations of any chance of influence by summoning [instead] the various categories of inhabitants to the town assembly [to appoint delegates to the *baillage* assemblies]. And the villages were summoned directly to the *baillage* assemblies, thus even favoring the villages, since they appointed delegates to the *baillage* directly, whereas the inhabitants of the towns appointed them indirectly. Generally speaking, moreover, the resurrection of the *baillages*, an outmoded jurisdiction, was an indication of the same intention as the later creation of a new subdivision, the departments,[4] and tended to produce the same effect: to remove the administrative or professional notables, make room for special new political personnel, and widen the gap between the nation's political life and its real life.

This was a defensible course, although risky, for nothing had prepared for it, but at least one had to stick to it and sustain the individual's freedom with a party's discipline, supplying, at whatever the cost, this aimless crowd of electors with a ready-made structure, formulas, and men. This was what Malouet, the most intelligent of the politicians of the English school, requested.

But Necker refused. He intended to treat this corps of English-style electors (i.e. two million peasants and craftsmen) like French-style Estates (i.e. several hundred notables and established, experienced men), and preserve all the rights and prerogatives of direct sovereignty for them.

Then an extraordinary thing occurred: elections without candidates, without profession of faith, without the public conflict of men and ideas that allows people to elaborate an opinion in our democracies [today]. No candidates came forward to submit their characters and principles to public examination, as a peddler displays his wares for people to judge. And no one was shocked, for, on the contrary, a candidate would have been called a schemer, and a party a cabal.

Better still: it was the electors themselves whom the king asked to draw up the lists of grievances and appoint the men that the king would not allow himself to suggest to them; for this purpose he summoned them by small groups of one to two hundred voters at most—parishes, organized bodies, towns—that transmitted their powers and will to others, and the latter to still others. And at each stage, lists of grievances had to be drawn up, deputies chosen, the impossible work done over and over again. But it was agreed that the nation possessed every ability as well as every right. The [new] power thought only of defending its liberty, never of shoring up its weaknesses, and wantonly multiplied opportunities to upset or mislead the poor, helpless sovereign [people], without guide or advisor, disoriented by an excess of enfranchisement.

Thus the vote by assembly was preferred to the individual vote, the former being subject to every sort of mass demonstration, the latter still permitting a minimum of reflection and independence. Thus the numerous stages of elections, from two to five, and then the complication of some of these elections, in which not just one or two deputies were to be selected, but ten, twenty, or fifty. The assembly of the city of Rennes had sixteen names to give, that of Brest thirty, that of Nantes fifty, the *baillage* assembly of Nantes twenty-five, that of Rennes two hundred. This was what was called "reduction": every *baillage* assembly of over two hundred members had to be "reduced" to this number. No doubt, in this case, they split up and voted by fractions, but the lists of candidates were still long, from twenty-five to fifty names. And the effect was marvelous: imagine several hundred peasants, unknown to one another, some having traveled twenty or thirty leagues, confined in the nave of a church, and requested to draft a paper on the reform of the realm within the week, and to appoint two or three dozen deputies [from the group]. They were forbidden to write these names down in advance, for fear of a cabal; they had to pass one by one in front of the seneschal and say the chosen names aloud. Can you imagine such a procedure? Drawing up the lists, voting, counting the votes, the result? And what a degree of discernment such a job involved? There were ludicrous incidents, in Nantes, for example, where the peasants demanded that the names of the assembly's members be printed. Most of them could not have cited ten names in their assembly, and yet they had to appoint twenty-five deputies.

In short, thanks to the odd mixture of the two systems, the English, which broke up the established social framework, and the French, which excluded any personal influence, the regulation of January 24 placed the electors not in a situation of freedom, but in a void. Here extreme freedom joined despotism: by clearing the view too much, everything was put out of sight, and by severing all attachments, there was no support left. Under such conditions it was impossible for the voters to agree on a choice or an idea.

Now, what actually did happen? Everywhere the job was accomplished most easily. The lists of grievances were drafted and the deputies appointed, as if by enchantment. This was due to the fact that alongside the real people, who could not respond, there was another people who spoke and appointed for them—the people, few in number no doubt, but widespread and united, of the Philosophical Societies. At that time there was not a town of any significant size that did not have its club of Free Thought, its lodge, its literary association, its patriotic society, all federated and inspired by the same spirit, joining forces in the same "great achievement." I shall not describe this odd republic to you, but I must mention its political methods, so well adapted to the case in question.

This republic, it is often said, was the great school of democracy, and nothing is truer, for this ideal city was the only one that had found the secret of maintaining order and union without affecting freedom of thought—without recourse, I am not saying to respect for a master, but even to the popularity of a leader. This is because there are other means of governing men than by authority in principle, *de facto* ascendancy. There are the means of what is called in Masonic style the inner circles or orders, whose very name quite suggests their role. The inner circle had no power—not only no acknowledged power, like that of a legitimate master, but not even any well-known power, like that of a party's leadership. Its strength lay elsewhere: every time the brothers assembled, the inner circle had already met, elaborated its plan, given its orders, roused the lukewarm participants, and brought influence to bear on the timid. At the subsequent assembly, all the motions were ready, the clappers prepared, the troublemakers silenced, the officers subdued, the agenda set. The discussion was free—free indeed, since the very existence of the inner circle was unknown—but the risks of this type of freedom were much reduced, and impulsive acts on the part of the "sovereign" were little to be feared. The general will was free like a locomotive on its tracks.

This was, in short, the principle of the system. It relied on the essential rule that every official vote of the Society was preceded and determined by an unofficial deliberation of the inner circle. Every Social group was uninformed in relation to a more restricted group of initiates, who were more united, more active, more clairvoyant. Hence a whole set of procedures and recipes that the Masons used to call "the royal art," and that today's professionals call, with less grace, "the science of electoral manipulations." They all share this in common: they handle voters without the voters realizing it, influencing them by their weaknesses, foolishness, apathy, timidity, conforming instinct—their inertia, in a word. The force of inertia is the only one that secret leaders can use, since it has no master; also it is the only force, and for the same reason, whose use is in accordance with freedom in principle: it works unwittingly and without obeying. Such was the great recipe of the royal art: against the independent and the headstrong that threatened union, the inner circle held in reserve what then used to be called the "dead weight," i.e. the weight of the negative votes, due to the unconsciousness, the weakness of the voters—a mechanical, passive force. Hence these political slang terms: the party members spoke of the pack, whips, sheepdogs, voting cattle, while the inner circles spoke of wire-pullers, the machine, and machinism. Thus we descend a degree in the metaphors, moving from passions to inertia, from the animal to the automaton.

Hence in the city of thought and freedom, the condition for order was unconsciousness and inertia. Pure democracy needs inertia, as authority needs loyalty, and the power of the people needs passions. Now, what was required to develop this necessary factor? Nothing other than this very freedom, disintegrating and isolating, that the royal decree achieved above and beyond all hope. From this point of view, the instructions of this regulation, so absurd in appearance, acquired a meaning and practical significance, for, by defending the voters against any ostensible influence, the instructions facilitated the task of secret influences and served the operation of machinism, the resources of the brothers and [their] friends.

Let's have a look: was there an absence of candidates and platforms? But the machine had everything to fear from the presence of an interest, a man, a faith, that would have grouped the voters outside of the machine and given them their own will. And it had everything to gain from a balance of indifference in which a negative general will, so well defined by Rousseau, reigned in theory, while, in fact, it was the powers of machinism that reigned.

Did the voting take place in public, in assemblies, rather than individually? This was the easiest kind to direct, by motions and maneuvers during the sessions, and also the easiest kind to watch.

Were there many different stages in the voting process? But for the brothers each stage was an additional opportunity to levy the tithes of machinism on the ignorance, the inertia, the conforming spirit of the voters. Each stage provided a new toll for the benefit of the machine, which gained a share of the mandates and offices each time, and ended by diverting the great current of the people's powers entirely into the machine's channels, where these powers were submitted to the machine's men.

What about reduction? This was the machine's triumph, for only reduction was capable of carrying out such a difficult operation successfully, thanks to the union of the brothers, by combining their votes on a given list. Nothing was easier, even, and success was certain, no matter how numerous the outsiders, provided, of course, they remained dispersed, isolated from one another — in a word, "free."

Now we can see what role the electoral regulation was to play in the brothers' plan: it was the very role that the [Masonic] "principles," which in fact inspired this regulation, played in their great Social undertaking. It was a negative role, a work of isolation. It meant clearing the terrain, dissolving the voting matter and reducing it to the inorganic state of freedom, and the homogeneous state of equality, which were the conditions necessary for the machine to operate. The royal decree attained this goal, beyond all expectation, as if such were its aim. By the arbitrariness of electoral grouping that corresponded neither to a real sentiment nor real interest; by the abstract character of discussions doomed to remain universal; [by the abstract character] of choices that could only be concerned with professed principles, not well-known characteristics, and could only be determined by the logic of the electors, not by their experience; lastly, by the number and the complexity of the elections that repeated these vices each time, it can be said the decree forcibly imposed the [Freemasons'] Social orientation and philosophical point of view upon the electors.

But this was only the first half of the great electoral undertaking, the negative portion. Once the materials were collected and trimmed to size, the edifice had to rise. With the moral order dissolved, the mechanical order had to be imposed. In a Philosophical Society, this second stage occurred naturally, in the long run, thanks to an automatic and incessant process of selection and motive force, which eliminated the insubordinate people for the benefit of the hard core. But it was not the same thing in an assembly of electors. To orient a whole mob of uninitiated voters towards justice and the Enlightenment in several weeks, the brothers had to intervene consciously and actively, with an objective, a plan, a scheme. Now this was a huge job. Here the Societies found themselves in the condition of a small fire on which someone clumsily dumps a wagonload of wood. Though the wood is split, dry, and ready to burn, it is likely, by its mass alone, to smother the fire it is trying to revive. And this did not fail to occur in certain jurisdictions, such as Brest, for example, where the thirty elected representatives of the Societies were submerged by the flood tide of peasants, or again in Morlaix.

But the real obstacle was elsewhere. This positive, open intervention was not, as we have said, in the manner and spirit of the Societies. They were not allowed to make public appearances, to introduce their men. That was a party method, implying individual interests. It was as contrary to the spirit of the Society—which only recognized the universal—as it was to the interest of the machine, which would be undone if it showed itself. And even if the Society had wished to [show itself], it would not have been able to. The initiate, the agent of the inner circle, was not a leader, not a man to be brought forward to charm people and get them to follow him. Such [an agent, for example] was an attorney in Rennes[5] who never ceased fighting for the just cause for six months—publishing a score of pamphlets, drafting grievances, triggering riots, manipulating assemblies—and yet no one in Brittany knew his name.

But something had to be done. It was urgent. No doubt there was every reason to hope the sovereign people, being consulted in the manner we have explained, would forget their natural chiefs and their actual interests and situation, which was already a lot [to ask of them]. But they still had to be prevented from voting haphazardly. They had to be protected against personal intrigues, so that, in a word, the cabals would take shape "always . . . for the benefit of the enterprise," to quote a rector from the region of Retz who witnessed the work. Now this was a task the machine could not undertake, not directly, at least. It could not produce one influence against another, one platform against another.

Yet it managed to get out of this fix in the most elegant manner imaginable, thanks to the royal art's classic trick, similar to that used in every great crisis: the method of exclusion. Here is how it works:

The Society was not in a position to have its men nominated directly, so it had only one choice: have all the other possible candidates excluded. Such was the object of a campaign begun six months before. The argument set forth was in conformity with the strictest of principles: the people, it was said, had born enemies that they must not take as their defenders. These were the men who lost by the people's enfranchisement, i.e. the privileged men first, but also the ones who worked for them: officers of justice, tax collectors (tithes or property taxes), officials of any sort. This argument, advanced by November 1788, raised a public outcry, for what lawyer, prosecutor, or expert did not hold a public office or responsibility? How many tradesmen had been ennobled? And who besides these men would be in a position to represent the Third Estate, especially the countryside? One might as well refuse the people the right to vote as exclude all the candidates.

But the Society stood firm, and attained its goal, as was to be expected. As for the principles, the Society was on its own terrain. There was nothing here that was not in conformity with reason and liberty, and logically irrefutable. The campaign was led by the brothers with an enthusiasm that the common good required and individual good did not advise against. Even though the majority of the brothers should have been excluded, since they were almost all men of law and noblemen's officials, each brother knew the Society would give him credit for his virtue. Though it was natural for the Society to exclude outsiders, whose sentiments could not be guaranteed, it was equally just to except from exclusion the brothers, whose patriotism the Society knew. And the Society could afford to do this without being accused of partiality, for no one on the outside would have the desire, or even the means, to protest against these exceptions.

And thus it was accomplished. The law of exclusion, promulgated by the Society and enforced by the machine, acted—forgive me the trite comparison—

like a sieve, sifting the mass of candidates. Everyone was placed in it, in the name of freedom in principle, but the only ones let through were the brothers, those who offered the inner circles all the guarantees desirable. . . .

ENDNOTES

[1] 1912. Paper read at the 22nd General Assembly of the Society of Contemporary History, June 20, 1912.

[2] Translator's note: The three Estates were the nobility, the clergy, and the common people (or Third Estate).

[3] Translator's note: The deputy was appointed to carry out a specific order; he was allowed no personal initiative.

[4] Translator's note: These administrative districts, originally created by the Revolutionary assembly, have subsisted to the present time.

[5] Translator's note: the capital city of Brittany.

HUMANITARIAN PATRIOTISM

The [French] Revolution was neither caused by external circumstances, nor by the personal work of a few ambitious men. Thus there remains only one way to account for it. One must resort to those causes both internal and superior to man, that are deep-seated and yet dominate him: this is a phenomenon of a religious nature. Enthusiasm, "fanaticism," is the last possible explanation given by historians at a loss for means to account for revolutionary acts. And is not the most natural form of enthusiasm the love of one's country? Patriotism was the incentive for the Revolution. Failing to see this fact, seeing only the negative, "pathological" side of revolutionary effort is, in Mr. Albert Sorel's eyes, the short-coming of the Origines[1] [the Origins of Contemporary France, by Taine], while "exacerbated patriotism," in Mr. Aulard's words, should be interpreted merely as a reaction to "the circumstances of war."

However, one is generally wary of this Patriotism. It is disconcerting and upsetting. There is none more bloody and more brutal—enough to disgust even the most intrepid chauvinist. And yet it is well-received by the most squeamish of our pacifists, the most sensitive of our humanitarians. Why this exception? And since Danton is as much a patriot as the others, why not use the massacres in the Abbey [prison] in September 1792 as examples of "patriotic butchery?" They are much more evocative than the battles of the Empire.

The reason—Mr. Aulard himself tells us—is that Danton is not a patriot in the common meaning of the term:

> "The Revolution federated the various peoples who made up the realm of France into a single people, the French people, and melded these little countries into a single nation, the French nation, one and indivisible.
> "Scarcely had this new nation been founded when it got the idea of a federation of all the nations of the world into a single family of mankind in which each national group would preserve its personality. This was when the notion became popular that all peoples are brothers, and must love and assist one another, not hate and kill one another. That is what a Patriot was in 1789 and 1790."[2]

This is precisely what, in 1908, is called a humanitarian. We recognize this familiar silhouette, a bit stiff perhaps with a bourgeois dress coat like Jaurès.[3] But this is indeed the same silhouette—and the right idea.

The word *Patriotism* had two meanings at the end of the eighteenth century. There had existed since 1788, even since 1770, a Patriotism—of the Philosophical Societies precisely—that had nothing in common with ours[4] but the name. We need only to observe it at work to ascertain this. It was truly Patriotism in 1789 and '90 that killed "on principle," according to Rousseau's maxims, all the thriving organizations of the former France—from the provinces, the corporations, the public bodies, down to the lowliest trade associations; it was Patriotism that "removed the nation's spine," as Talleyrand said, that disintegrated the nation thoroughly enough to make it bear uncomplaining the enormous administrative yoke it has been dragging behind it for the past hundred years, and that has made it vulnerable to imperialistic or sectarian tyrannies. This Patriotism destroyed all the lesser patriotisms for the sake of the greater one, national unity, the only bond subsisting today of the many that used to attach a Frenchman to his country. And hence the term Patriotism, whose meaning is strictly negative here: it is much more a matter of killing the little countries than of supporting the larger one. The larger one gains nothing from this destruction, quite the contrary; it is superfluous to observe French unity was achieved before '89, too well achieved even, and was already detracting from the life of the provinces; and it is banal to repeat that, ever since, this unity has become a plague, the primary cause of congestion in the head and anemia in the appendages.

Indeed, this Patriotism was not concerned about France. Nothing is more enlightening than its short history. It was born in the Philosophical Societies around 1770, during the parliamentary unrest. It was then, and up to November 1788, mostly provincial. For it was in the individual provinces, among the States and Parliaments in rebellion, that the "correspondences" and "Pacts of union" were organized that made the "Nations" of Brittany, Dauphiné, or Provence "speak out" willy-nilly against ministerial "Despotism." Never had such ado been made about these little nations—to such an extent that in some the old provincial spirit that had been slumbering since the *Fronde*[5] awoke and mistook for renaissance a philosophical movement that was to administer its *coup de grace*. There was nothing odder, for example, than the alliance, in July 1788, between the nobility of Brittany and the philosophical lawyers of Rennes, between Duchess Anne's Contract and the *Social Contract*. For three months they fought side by side. In the fourth month Duchess Anne thought she was back on her throne. In the fifth she perished without a fight, strangled by her new soldiers. Patriotism had changed its denomination. From Parliamentary

Patriotism in '88 to enroll the towns, it became National Patriotism in '89 to dissolve the provinces and corporations. And this extended Patriotism did not stop there. As Mr. Aulard explains, it became European in '91 on the eve of war, for the Jacobins then imagined themselves at the head of a European republic. Though their patriotism was stopped half-way, restricting itself for a while to the French entity, it was for fortuitous reasons—because the provinces had yielded to Jacobin unity, while foreign nations resisted it. Patriotism defended the French borders, because they then happened to be the borders of the humanitarian Revolution; strictly a question of chance, moreover, judging by a perusal of the Jacobin speeches and circulars six months prior to the war.

There were two parties in the mother Society. One wanted war, because it was an unprecedented war, "the war of [all] the peoples against [all] the kings [of the universe]," [6] i.e. the war of "philosophy," "principles"—the doctrine and the sect—levying troops, commanding armies, forcefully settling among neighboring peoples [i.e. countries]. The other party did not want war, on precautionary grounds: "Do you consider of no account," says Robespierre on January 2, 1792, "the arbitrary right of life or death the law will grant our military patricians the moment the nation is at war? Do you consider of no account the power of the police that it will hand over to military leaders in all our border towns?" And if we win, "that is when we will wage a more serious war on the friends of liberty, and the perfidious system of selfishness and intrigue will triumph." [7] Beware of "militarism," and the awakening of the old discipline and the old sentiments when we are faced with the enemy! That, succinctly, was the objection. And the response was in the same vein. The advocates of war say they count on the "Patriotism" of the soldiers—do you see the new meaning of the term?—and to maintain patriotism they count on their union with the national guard. "In our armies there will reign a public opinion that traitors would have to yield to and that at least they would not dare contradict openly." Hence this interpretation: there will be societies, such as the national guard, to expose the heretics and prod the hesitant. Lastly, foreign brothers were counted on: "Believe, brothers and friends, the French Revolution has more partisans abroad than dare make themselves known." [8] Excellent reasons we see on either side, but where is the interest of France in all this? I can only see the interest of the sect. [9]

This Patriotism has since changed its name and horizons, but not its principles. Today it is called humanitarianism and is working to dissolve that France which served for a time as its instrument and refuge.

But did both Patriotisms, humanitarian and French, fight side by side in '92? Did the latter, in the service of the former, wage war on Europe? No doubt, and this was neither the first nor the last time the latter worked for someone else. In

1792, for the benefit of a humanitarian sect, it waged war as it had done a hundred years earlier for the pride of the great king, and as it would do fifteen years later for the folly of Napoleon, heroically, gloriously, idiotically.

Moreover, though circumstances happened to make allies of these two parties, they were never friends. They were suspicious of each other from the outset. The patriot of the Societies, who exposes, harangues, and does not fight, in no way resembles and can scarcely please the patriot in the field, who fights and does not guillotine. They worked on separate sides, one with phrases and pikes against poor French people piled into prisons, the other with gunshots at the Prussians and the English. And when the latter patriot had finished his task and returned home triumphant, he found his counterpart looking so unhealthy that he sent him off to Cayenne[10] to speechify.

Each party from the outset had its procedures and specific character, and attempts to merge failed. In '92 there was a desire to infuse the army with Jacobin ideals by using volunteers, military clubs, and organized, encouraged denunciation of the leaders—Camille Rousset demonstrated with what success. On the other hand, the Jacobins wanted to wage war in Vendée. We know the outcome, and how their generals, Léchelle, Rossignol, Ronsin and the "five hundred pound heroes" were routed by La Rochejaquelein's scythe-wielding peasants and sent home to their podiums and clubs. Professional soldiers had to be called upon.

From then on each side understood it best to remain in its own sphere. One waged war on the enemies of France as was its habit. The other invented a special war, a war on the enemies of mankind, a war without precedent. It had its weapons (pikes), its battles (Revolutionary street demonstrations), its battlefields (the prisons), its special corps (the Revolutionary army), its adversaries (the "enemies within," Fanaticism, Moderantism [moderate opinions], Federalism, Despotism, and other monsters in *–ism*). Strictly speaking this is what is called "war for freedom," "war on war," one which is to found universal peace and happiness. This would be the last war of all: "If blood is shed again," says Billaud, "at least this is the last time it will be used to validate human rights forever. This is the last murderous sacrifice man will have to moan about, since it is offered to reestablish on earth men's appreciation, the esteem they owe one another, the trust this esteem inspires . . . . and the civil harmony that binds all citizens together through the charm of such a lovely existence."

It would surely be interesting to study this new war closely, for it is the only one of its kind, and this was the only time this Humanitarian Patriotism could be seen at work in its natural state. It does not appear today except clothed in the frock coat of a lecturer seated behind a green table with a glass of sweetened water on it.

We shall observe only its most distinctive characteristic: ferocity. This was to be expected; one may be lenient with an enemy of one's country, even of one's own party, but what can be done with the enemies of the human race except destroy them? *Destroy* is the key word—by any means whatsoever. "It is less a question of punishing them than of annihilating them," says Couthon.[11] "None must be deported; the conspirators must be destroyed," says Collot.[12] There exists no law in such a war, nor justice, nor honor, nor mercy. To acknowledge one would be "to kill the Country and Mankind legally."[13] "What is there in common," says Robespierre, "between liberty and despotism, crime and virtue? It may be conceivable for soldiers fighting for a despot to lend a hand to beaten soldiers on their way to the hospital, but what is inconceivable, utterly impossible, is for a free man to compromise with a tyrant or his henchman, for courage to compromise with cowardice, or virtue with crime . . . There must be distance between the soldiers of freedom and the slaves of tyranny."[14]

And to make this distance clear, the prisoners were ordered to be shot. The new war, a Jacobin orator says, is a war "of the Nation against brigands"—*brigands*, the word was to stick as a designation for the enemies of mankind. Strictly speaking, these people were no longer men.

And they were treated accordingly. Hence the coarse insults, so shocking to true soldiers, and yet natural: the new war was brutal, less by instinct than on principle. The adversary's unworthiness was taken for granted, just as formerly his honor was considered worthy. The enemies were "monsters," "ferocious beasts seeking to devour the human race."[15] Pitt was declared "an enemy of mankind."[16]

Thus the contempt for people's rights, the massacres of parliamentarians and prisoners of war. And thus the destruction of men, women, even children— the children of Bicêtre in September '92, or the three hundred unfortunate little ones of the Nantes warehouse—so horrifying that its odd nature is seldom observed. Peasant uprisings, massacres under fire, proconsuls' cruelties had occurred in the past. But this was the only time small groups of men—republican authorities and patriotic clubs—accustomed enough to murder to practice individual and mass executions in cold blood, operated as though they were sweeping the streets.

Yet these were not madmen, nor—at least not all—brutes; they were often *petits bourgeois* terrifyingly similar to their non-murderous peers. But was this not wonderful training? In Nantes the hard core—about twenty following Carrier, as well as the eighty pike-wielders of "Marat's army"—were the people who stripped one hundred young women or girls between the ages of sixteen and thirty, several pregnant, several nursing, and attached them naked inside the infamous barges. Then, having opened the drain cocks, as the boats foundered, they slashed the beseeching hands that emerged from the portholes. In Nantes, Carrier announced calmly, one hundred and fifty to two hundred Vendean peasants were shot a day. As many as eight hundred at a time were drowned. In Lyons, the patriots had to stop gunning people down, because the dragoons in charge of finishing off the survivors with their swords mutinied in disgust—because the bodies were thrown into the Rhone River, for lack of manpower to bury them, and the people living downstream complained of the pollution. In the very first week one hundred and fifty corpses were found lying on the river gravel of Ivours. The same complaint in Arras, where blood flowing from the guillotine polluted the neighborhood. General Turreau in the Vendée gave the order "to bayonet men, women, and children and burn and set fire to everything,"[17] etc.

Such was the work of Humanitarian Patriotism. These blood baths revolt us, because we judge them as ordinary patriots would—which is a mistake. A humanitarian could reply they were legitimate: humanitarian war is the only one that kills for the sake of killing—it has the right to, and thus is it distinguished from national war. "Strike without mercy, citizen," the president of the Jacobins tells a young soldier, "at anything that is related to the monarchy. Don't lay down your gun until all our enemies are dead—*this is humanitarian advice.*"[18] It is because he is *humanitarian* that Marat demands 260,000 heads.[19] "What do I care if I am called bloodthirsty!" exclaims Marat. "Well, let's drink the blood of mankind's enemies if we must!"[20] Carrier writes to the Convention, "The defeat of the brigands is so complete that hundreds at a time are arriving at our outposts. I have decided to have them shot. Just as many are coming from Angers. I have reserved the same fate for them, and I ask Francastel to do likewise. . ."[21] Is this not appalling? And can we imagine Mr. Jaurès screaming [in protest] upon reading such a letter from General d'Amade?[22] However, the Convention applauded and published [Carrier's] letter, and, as far as I know, Mr. Jaurès did not scream in his *Socialist History.* Carrier's conclusion explains why: "It is on humanitarian principle that I purge the earth of these monsters' liberty." This is the answer. The Convention, Carrier and Mr. Jaurès were right. But General d'Amade could do no such thing, because he was only fighting for France. Carrier [on the other hand] was a humanitarian, who guillotined, shot, and drowned for the human race, Virtue, universal Happiness, the People, etc. Each of these men was just playing his role.

Let us therefore be careful to distinguish between the two Patriotisms, the humanitarian or Social one, and the national one—the former recognizable by its cruelty, the latter by the self-sacrifice it induces. To confuse them would be insulting to the latter, which does not massacre—and would do injustice to the former, which has the right to massacre. They were fortuitous allies in '93. But they have always been opposed in their principles.

Can we at least say these are two sentiments of the same family, two forms of political enthusiasm? I think not. Enthusiasm generally has two sides: sacrifice of oneself to an idea passionately embraced—this is faith; sacrifice of others to this idea—this is fanaticism.

Jacobin Patriotism had only the latter side. No political zeal had ever had such disregard for human lives—and yet faith did not increase proportionately. On the contrary, there was none. Just observe the great killers before their judges. Not one had the courage to look them in the eye and say, "Well, yes, I robbed, I tortured, and I killed lawlessly, recklessly, mercilessly for an idea I consider right. I regret nothing, I take nothing back, I deny nothing. Do as you like with me." Not one spoke thus—because not one possessed the positive side of fanaticism: faith. Not one loved, nor even knew, what he had served. They defended themselves like common assassins, lying, denying, and accusing brothers. Their main argument, legitimate but pitiful from the standpoint of common morality, was that they could not spare other people without destroying themselves; they acted under orders. Everyone spoke the same way then—in a word, they pleaded coercion, the contrary of free faith. How different from those thousands of priests and nuns who did not kill a single person for their faith—and gave their own lives rather than take the oath their faith forbade.

Were our patriots cowards? Certainly, and they owed it to themselves to behave differently: when one has shed other people's blood for an idea, one no longer has the right to be miserly with one's own. And yet there was a reason for this cowardice: their Patriotism was not a faith, it was negative. The Jacobin Fatherland was Rousseau's Society, which actually meant a federation of self-ish interests. There was nothing beautiful or pleasant, nothing generous in it. Jacobin Patriotism was just one of the branches of this philosophical moral science, derived from Hume and Hobbes, and founded, as the pundits admitted themselves, on the great principle of "self-respect." "Self-interest," says the politician, "Greed," says the economist, "Passions," says the moralist, "Nature," chant the philosophers in unison: such were the wellsprings. The goal was a happier state, not a more perfect one, and the way [to attain it] was by destruction, not creation—and people do not die for all that.

But then why do people kill? Where does this fanaticism *par excellence* come from? How can it be maintained when it only possesses the external shell of hatred without the core of love and self-sacrifice—when there are inquisitors without martyrs? This is where history fails us and can only ascertain the facts without understanding them. It can see the facts clearly. It can even acknowledge their logical connection to principles and the fact that this Humanity had to kill, this Liberty had to coerce. It does not see the origin, the nature of the feelings that can subjugate the heart of a man, an entire people, to this terrifying logic. Explaining '93 by Jacobin "Patriotism" is like explaining a mystery by an enigma.

ENDNOTES

[1] Cf. *Annales révolutionnaires*, April-June 1908, article by M. Mathiez.

[2] Speech given July 9, 1904 (Bibliothèque nationale, Lb 32/796).

[3] Translator's note: Jean Jaurès (1859–1914), a great political orator, was one of the founders (1901) and leaders of the French socialist movement.

[4] Translator's note: By "our" patriotism, Cochin means patriotism in the usual meaning of the term, love for one's country, i.e. France.

[5] Translator's note: 1648–1652, an uprising against the authority of Mazarin and the monarchy.

[6] "A crusade for individual liberty," says Brissot (speech of Dec. 30, 1791, Bibl. Nat., Lb 40/666; "an insurrection against all the kings of the universe," says Danton (Taine, *the Origins. . .*, 1907, vol. VI, p. 211).

[7] National Archives, ADXVI 73, speech of Jan. 2, 1792.

[8] National Archives, ADXVI 73, Jacobin circular of Jan. 17, 1792. Cf. Bibl. Nat., Lb 40/666, Brissot's speech to the Jacobins, Dec. 30, 1791.

[9] Translator's note: Cochin refers to the Freemasons and their revolutionary disciples as a "sect."

[10] Translator's note: An infamous penitentiary in French Guiana.

[11] *Moniteur*, June 11, 1794.

[12] *Ibid.,* Sept. 30, 1793.

[13] *Ibid.,* June 11, 1794.

[14] *Ibid.,* June 24, 1794.

[15] *Moniteur,* Oct. 15, 1793.

[16] *Ibid.,* Sept. 16, 1793.

[17] BRUAS, *Société populaire de Saumur,* p. 27.

[18] *Moniteur,* June 16, 1794.

[19] Marat, vol. II, p. 261.

[20] *Moniteur,* March 13, 1793.

[21] *Moniteur,* Dec. 20, 1794. This is a summary of the letter read by Réal at the trial.

[22] Translator's note: Cochin was writing at the time of the conquest of Morocco, in which Amade played a key role.

THE REVOLUTION AND FREE THOUGHT

INTRODUCTION

1. THE HISTORICAL PROBLEM

When one first looks at the convulsions of the French Revolution, what is most surprising is that in these combats of Titans—if one may judge by the ruins they made—no man stands out of the crowd. There is no dominant figure. The France of 1789 did not have its Cromwell, a man capable of containing the flood once he broke the dike. The sovereign people never had masters; they never ceased to proclaim that their leaders were only their valets. And taking a closer look, one is tempted to take them at their word, for the men of law drawn out of their offices by the Revolution, who lectured the king as long as the rising tide carried them, fell back into proportion the moment the tide abandoned them. And a mediocre proportion it was. So imposing from afar, they are disappointing close up. They are neither heroes nor monsters, but common, ordinary men, with ordinary souls and talents—all of them generally inferior to their roles. They lose their judgment in success, their self-control in ordeals, and their dignity in setbacks. Mirabeau does not measure up to his glory, nor Robespierre to his power, nor Fouquier to his crimes. The drama is somber and poignant, but performed by a provincial troupe, and the situations are greater than the men.

Today the men of the Revolution are studied with less passion and in more detail, and it must be admitted this is not to their advantage.

What is more wretched, ridiculous, and vulgar than a session of the Convention in 1794? Yet these men defeated the Girondins, who defeated the constitutionalists, who defeated the deputies of the Estates General.

This is really the quintessence of the Revolution: nothing illegal was done, or at least the principles and procedures were the same as those that put these men into power. It is impossible to draw a dividing line [between legality and illegality] before their time: to condemn them would be to condemn the Revolution itself. They are indeed its orthodox representatives.

What is outrageous are the crimes and destruction, which darken men's characters and lend them some sort of interest—but these characters are mediocrity, triviality itself, devoid of psychology or human feelings; just big effects.

However, what remains are their deeds, outrageous deeds, whose effects not a single one of them understood. What they destroyed was great, which makes one uneasy about judging them.

The same observation applies to the fights that shook Brittany in 1788 and 1789. The people's army, and even the army of the privileged, had no officers, just a few file-closers. The "Third Estate" and the "nobility" were the only antagonists. They were no longer willing to put up with protectors and chiefs; they attacked each other unmasked, using their real names. The heroes of these battles were not the men behind the scenes . . . The hero was the master of them all, the one whose valets they claimed to be, as they were indeed: the Third Estate.

What were the men behind the scenes? Legal experts, but what more?

And how can one explain that these honorable bourgeois managed to demolish something so great, and defeated that which men like Retz, Condé, and others had fought unsuccessfully, and men like Fénelon, Vauban, and d'Aguesseau had criticized to no avail—and served? It was a victory without conviction, since they humbled themselves to much worse.

It is neither the force of genius, nor the force of conviction that demolished the *ancien régime*.

And yet these armies without officers were not without discipline. They even relied on discipline and were as attached to it as to their rights. They respected it better than did the regular, regimented army of the government. But this discipline was as abstract as its leadership was impersonal. Discipline was based neither on a man's popularity, like the discipline of a faction, nor on the necessity for reform, like a party's discipline. Chiefs, orders, plans of action changed every day, but not the real object of all discipline: *union*. Union, this was the one and only catchword, the magic word repeated daily in the pamphlets and speeches, the only argument offered to the hesitant, the only reason given for victories.

Before considering the details of the struggle, we should become familiar with the combatants. We must draw the portrait of our hero, the Third Estate, before we tell its story and seek the far-reaching significance of this word, union—a word which was then uttered with a sort of religious respect inside the Revolutionary party, and was declared to be its only concern and its true force.

This necessity takes us back to general considerations applicable to all the periods of this particular Revolution and many others.

Indeed, it has often been observed that the offensive of 1789 was conducted in the same way everywhere. The force that finally achieved the leveling of the orders [the nobility, the clergy, and the Third Estate] and the provinces, as if it were cutting up France into identical squares, already contained something of the monotony of its achievement in this very action that obliterated, first in the law, and then by means of the law in actual fact, the different types, customs, and appearances of the people and the towns. This force worked the same way everywhere, in Quimper [in the northwest] as in Marseilles [in the south]. Revolution has no local differences.

The union of the Third Estate in 1788 may be studied from two points of view. It is founded on ideas, and expressed in acts. It has a *principle* and an *organization*.

The ideas of 1789 are quite well-known and have been explained by cleverer people. We shall only mention them with reference to the union that concerns us, to show that it could be established not only in fact, as we shall see below, but also, in a way, in [public] opinion. It has quite often been denied that this intellectual consensus was real, or even possible.

For the peculiar characteristic of this union is this: it is precisely between tomorrow's relentless enemies that today's union is most solid. The first victims of the brothers' hatred are always yesterday's brothers.

We know the history of all the purges in the Revolution's different stages. The victims were not old adversaries, not even recent acquaintances, but precisely the leaders and saviors of the preceding week. "The Revolution eats its children," but it would be more correct to say "its creators." The parliamentarians in November 1788 and the Girondins in May 1793 were firsthand witnesses to the fact. So people have concluded that appetites, not ideas, were the only well-spring of the Revolution, that the Revolution constituted a vast looting operation from which the leaders withdrew first because they helped themselves first, while the soldiers continued because they wanted to make their fortunes, and thus there were quarrels, constantly renewed and always the same, between the satisfied and the voracious.

But how can such a strong union and then such furious hatred be explained by personal interest alone? How too can this enthusiasm, this profusion of noble words, this display of principles, these bursts of generosity or fits of rage be accounted for? Could all that be only lies and play-acting?

And could the Revolutionary party be reduced merely to an enormous plot in which each person would only be thinking of himself when behaving virtuously, and would only be acting for himself when accepting iron discipline? Personal interest has neither such perseverance nor such abnegation. Nevertheless, this is the explanation given by the authors of extreme opinions: Father Barruel, on one hand, and several historians of Freemasonry on the other.

Throughout history there have been schemers and egoists, but there have only been revolutionaries for the past one hundred and fifty years. What is the origin of the unknown force and also the dignity in which well-known vices clothe themselves?

The truth seems simpler. We forget the Revolution was the triumph of *philosophy*, and not of a specific doctrine, the triumph of *freedom of thought* in general and not of one liberal idea or the other. The force of the ideas of 1789 lies in the *method* and not in the *system*.

It is from this point of view that we shall try to study it. We shall show that:

1. the doctrines are mutually dependent;
2. one faction necessarily follows another.[1]

We do not mean a clearly defined doctrine, i.e. positive knowledge and specific requirements, but rather an intellectual method and a moral trend.

To go further, this means, as a rule, the systematic and radical substitution of method for doctrine and trend for stable condition. We mean and shall show that the method begets the doctrine and the trend ends in a specific social condition.

It would be improper to credit individual perversity with outrageous acts and unnatural sentiments that are, in fact, due to *social* causes of a much more powerful and profound nature.

Historians of Republican Defense[2] make the Revolution the work of the people. Historians who analyze the details see it as a plot instigated by a few ambitious men. These are equally false notions. The mistaken interpretation always stems from the same source: one makes a psychological problem of what is a social problem; one ascribes what results from a situation, from the nature of things, to personal action.

It is not the Jacobin's psychology that will be the last word of the Revolutionary enigma. It will be the *sociology of the democratic phenomenon*.

The Societies

Shortly before the Revolution there appeared a still little-known phenomenon whose causes, conclusion, and ultimate effects are not clearly discernible: the Societies.

"The Societies," plain and simple: the term was not qualified. It was said, in October 1788, that the parliamentarians were defeated in advance because they were "excluded from all the Societies." The words the prominent man of the moment uttered in a "Society" were reported. People talked about "the opinion of the Societies." *Society*, not Club, was the correct term to designate Revolutionary Societies. In 1792, people spoke of the "Society" of such and such a town.

There was a reason for this [new] term. These were no longer the literary salons of the seventeenth century. These were Societies of philosophers.

With the decline of the reign of Louis XV the phenomenon spread throughout France. The Grand Lodge of France was formed in 1773. Secret societies and various orders (the Scottish rite, the Illuminati, the Swedenborgians, the Martinists, the Egyptians, the *Amis Réunis*) vied for followers and epistolary networks. And lastly, between 1769 and 1780, there arose hundreds of little, only partially visible Societies, theoretically independent like lodges, but acting in unison, like lodges too; established like them, driven by the same "patriotic" and "philosophical" spirit, and barely dissimulating similar political aims behind official pretenses of knowledge, charity, or pleasure. These were academic, literary, and patriotic Societies; museums, schools, even agricultural Societies.

"The republic of letters," a mere allegory in 1720, became a very tangible reality around 1770, thanks to Voltaire and the Encyclopedists. The reign of the salons and elegant ridicule was over. The reign of the Philosophical Societies had begun. The *"Cacouacs"*[3] followed their old master's advice. They formed a "corps of initiates," a "pack" to hunt down the vile "Beast" with a relentlessness which somewhat troubled the majesty of the French Parnassus. Monsieur Roustan, in his book on *The Philosophers and French Society in the Eighteenth Century*, has quite rightly pointed out the formation of the philosophic "sect" around 1760, and what he calls the "lay clergy." This sect reigned in the *Académie [française]* under d'Alembert, exercised censorship with Malesherbes, had its adversaries' books banned and the authors imprisoned at the Bastille or Vincennes, and cast a sort of bloodless terror over [public] opinion and the world of letters. Lord Chesterfield's letters, and the mishaps of President de Brosses, Palissot, Gilbert, Roussseau, Fréron, Linguet, to name only the most famous, showed what independent or heroic people risked.

The object of the Academies was to create a public opinion. They were not only news agencies, but Societies of encouragement for patriotism, forums of public spirit. To attain their goal they created an ideal republic alongside and in the image of the real one, with its own constitution, its magistrates, its people, its honors, and its battles. There they studied the same problems—political, economic, etc.—and there they discussed agriculture, art, ethics, law, etc. There they debated the issues of the day and judged the officeholders. In short, this little State was the exact image of the larger one, with only one difference: it was not large, and it was not real. Its citizens had neither direct interest nor responsible involvement in the affairs they discussed. Their decrees were only wishes, their battles conversations, their studies games. In this city of the clouds, ethics were discussed far removed from action, and politics far removed from real affairs. It was the city of *thought*. That was its essential characteristic, the one both initiates and outsiders forgot first—because they took it for granted—but the one we must examine first in order to evaluate this association's value, and account for its laws and fatal inclination. For it is of no little significance that a public spirit should awake and take shape in this manner, *socially*, nor that a society should be founded, *theoretically*.

In the eighteenth century, this was a novelty. We had already seen philosophers as builders of metaphysical political systems, but they were isolated and enemies of one another, each man erecting his own entire intellectual edifice, finished and distinct. We had seen religious sects, professional corps, commercial societies, but never before associations constituted for the single goal of bringing its "enlightened thinkers" together, thinking in common for thinking's sake without any practical goal, seeking speculative truth together for its own sake.

This is a general fact that must be studied in itself, if we wish to understand its effects at the beginning of the Revolution.

All of these Societies have the same characteristic: they are *egalitarian* in form and *philosophical* in purpose, what we would call Societies of Free Thought today. They formed the material framework of the "Republic of Letters" and gave philosophy an unprecedented consistency, vigor, and empire over [public] opinion.

Indeed, though only an ideal, the new State, the "republic of letters" grew prodigiously between 1760 and the Revolution. The Societies scattered about the Realm were all more or less connected to one another and associated with those in Paris. Constant debates, elections, delegations, correspondence, and intrigue took place in their midst, and a veritable public life developed through them. Now, is this not a major—but too often ignored—fact concerning the end of this [eighteenth] century?

This state of affairs—the very existence of Philosophical Societies, the type of opinion that developed in them, and the particular conditions in which the Societies placed authors and the public—had very serious consequences on the exchange of ideas, for it imposed, in advance and with no appeal possible, the intellectual, unreal point of view on the authors and the public.

Never perhaps was the mainstream of ideas and literature more remote from the world of reality, from contact with things, than at the end of this century. [To understand this] we need only name political philosophers like Rousseau and Mably, an historian like Raynal, economists like Turgot, Gournay and the school of *laissez-faire*, men of letters like La Harpe, Marmontel, Diderot.

It is thus that philosophism[4] was born.

The training, the motive force, of free thought had serious consequences, in the intellectual realm first. As a result of its influence, the privileged forgot their privileges. We could likewise cite the learned men who forgot experience, or the clerics who forgot faith. Experience and religious dogma are two orders of facts brutally imposed on our intelligence from the outside, halting the development of "philosophy" or, as we say today, free thought. [But the] "Philosophy" [of the eighteenth century] was to upset these obstacles to freedom: *experience, tradition,* and *faith.*

One must distinguish between *artificial* union founded on theories and principles and *real* union founded on facts. I am not saying that in the movement of 1789 there was only artificial union—there were real causes for the Revolution, [such as] a bad fiscal regime, that exacted very little, but in the most irritating and unfair manner—I am just saying these real causes are not my subject. Moreover, though they may have contributed to the Revolution of 1789, they did not contribute to the Revolutions of August 10 or May 31, and in any case artificial union did exist.

Now, such a union does not reside in an actual situation: the connection must be found elsewhere. Nor can it reside in ideas alone. Ideas need a framework to support them, and action requires one all the more so. This framework was the *organization* of the Societies.

Documents of that period designate this necessary organization by a vague word: "The Societies." We must familiarize ourselves with these Societies, find out how they were formed and maintained, and what effect they had on the men and the political customs of the time. The instinct of contemporaries did not mislead them: the *form* itself of these associations mattered still more than the personalities of their members or their real or imaginary goals. And it is this general character, however simple and banal it may appear, that must be our first concern.

If we consult the statutes and the spirit of the Societies, from the literary Societies to the Jacobins, we see this word [Society] is always taken in the strictest, most general meaning.

What is a Society? What is a Society in the strict and general meaning of the term? It can be defined as a group of men joined together *by their will alone and for their good alone*. It is active, it is standing and durable, it is free, its only object is the good of its members, and this word "good" is taken in its most general meaning, without restrictions or specifications.

Thus a corps of the State, such as the army or the magistracy, is not a Society: its members are freely joined, but not for their own good. The army is not independent and the magistracy is not active. A deliberative assembly is not a Society: it is neither active nor united. Families or clans are not Societies: they are not freely formed. A nation is not a Society: it is the community in its origins and not in its goal, the bond of blood before the alliance of interests, and nature before will that unites compatriots. A guild is not a Society, at least not so long as it remains professional. A professional corps or an administrative body is not a Society, for its members' positions are due to their jobs, not their will alone. A "community," i.e. the inhabitants of a village or town, is not a Society: the inhabitants belong to it because of their residence, and not by their free choice.

But all these groups can become Societies, in different ways: organized bodies when the spirit of the body prevails over duty to State and honor, representative assemblies when the parties in them become associations of electors, guilds when they broaden their goals and give up professional interests, towns when they admit strangers and the natural bond loses its value, and lastly churches or religious orders. By indulging in free enquiry, the Protestant churches constantly come close to this danger and often yield to it when they make an immediate reality of their ideal, bringing it back to this world either in fact, by laxity and politics, or by law, through free enquiry and what is called broad-mindedness. And particularly through social systems.

All of these different routes lead these groups to the same point, "the Society." And let us make note of this first point: in a Society the participants appear free, freed from all attachments, all obligations, all social functions.

From these free and egalitarian eighteenth-century Societies, a new conception of laws, power, and rights would emerge. Rousseau made the theory of this regime. Secret societies had always practiced it within their closed walls. The Jacobins attempted to apply it to the government of a nation. This regime was none other than *pure democracy*, the personal and direct government of the people by themselves. It was [public] opinion submitted to this regime that was called "the people" in 1793. The *Philosophical Societies* were the artificial environment in which the new moral and political conception would germinate.

Now we see the Republic of Jean-Jacques [Rousseau]. Indeed, this is the first thing that strikes us when examining a system of Societies, an order. It is not in antiquity, nor in a tiny state that the blueprint must be sought, but in the lodges and the literary Societies.

Thus the Social Contract,[5] in a sense, was no fantasy, it was achieved. It had been before Rousseau, in the republic of letters, and it attempted to become the regime of France under the Terror.

Such a new regime produces and implies new political customs. These customs and procedures are not attributable to an era, or to a country, but to the regime itself and to the new relationships it establishes between men. There exists a type of good associate and a code of social practice. We shall describe them to show how this type emerges from the social *form* itself.

The social development of Rousseau's idea therefore coincides with the political development of the *Philosophical Societies* which will be the object of our study.

The phenomenon of free thought merits the attention of sociologists, for it may be the only fact in their domain that is unalloyed with religious, economic, or ethnic factors. Free thought is the same in Paris as in Peking, in 1750 as in 1914. Its identical nature in such diverse environments shows we are observing a mental process as unconscious as custom and folklore. It is a secular, historical phenomenon that has its laws and phases.

Rousseau, along with the other philosophers of his time, assumes the Philosophical Society to be the only regular form of human societies.[6]

Now, in the history of a society two types of rules can be distinguished: the ones that correspond to its preservation, to reasons for order and discipline, to social practice; and the others that correspond to its object, to reasons for justice and freedom, to social theory.

Rousseau restricted himself to the second point of view: he set the rules for the contract from the point of view of ideas, starting with his ideal *principle* of liberty and equality.

One can do the complementary work: examine the reality to see whether the development of the Societies was not submitted to certain laws, their existence subordinated to certain conditions. Instead of taking the Society's ideal goal as a principle, one can take its being, its actual existence as a starting point. This second method leads one to establish the Social Contract's counterpart [i.e. the customary laws of this particular type of Society], just as the first method established its rational code of law. And we shall see that the second method is as coherent and necessary as the first, but practical instead of theoretical.

Rousseau asks: What must a society whose aim is the common good do, to be founded lawfully? We may ask: What must Rousseau's society be, to live and last?

The historical facts that allow us to answer this question are numerous. In our documentation we shall try to show the effects and conditions of the Societies' activities in 1789 and in Brittany,[7] and throughout France in 1793.[8] But these are individual cases. The action of the Societies has necessary, general laws inherent in *the very nature of the union*, and not in the men or the circumstances. We must give a brief idea of these laws in order to understand the Revolutionary phenomenon properly.

To help us make our point we shall take the most striking examples supplied by the history of the Societies over the past two centuries. In France these are either secret Societies, such as the Congregation, the royalist Masonry of the Directoire and the Empire, and the Grand Lodge; or partially visible Societies, like the Revolutionary Societies, the Friends of the Constitution, and the Jacobins. Outside France we have the examples of the large, standing electoral associations, the "Machine" or the "Caucus," that have reigned in America since Washington's time, and in England since 1880, and that a first-rate critical study has recently described.[9]

These illustrative models are not the only ones, and without looking so far, we shall also find some in our subject itself.

To prevent confusion we shall define the meaning of the terms and distinguish the difference between the customs of "pure democracy" and the political customs of the parties, i.e. the "parliamentary regime," with which the "Social regime"[10] is often confused because of their common principles and common name: democracy.

In *pure democracy*, or direct democracy, the *current* will of the community, at each instant, is law. Thus the personal government of the people cannot be imagined otherwise than in the form of continuous consultation—therefore *standing Societies* of free discussion.

In the *parliamentary regime*, the democratic theory is not pure, nor is the government of the people direct. Indeed, in the representative regime, either the elector votes for a man more than for the platform and thus makes scarcely any discussion, or if he does discuss, it is only general questions, every four years for a period of six weeks. In these conditions, parties and candidates can accept debate and offer themselves the luxury of enlightening the voters and answering their objections, for mutual agreement does not suffer much, and the dignity of both sides gains by it. This is the time for serious meetings, prepared conferences, sincere professions, "lectures," as the English say—but lectures have ceased in England since the establishment of "standing associations" that have replaced periodic campaigns.

The parliamentary regime of periodic electoral associations is just an intermittent form of democracy. Thus has it always been judged by strict democrats, such as our Jacobins of 1793, for whom the people, the will of the people, resided essentially in popular Societies; or such as the English and American democrats who transformed the formerly authoritarian and feudal organization of the *parties* in the same spirit, the deputy becoming the spokesman—and no longer the master and leader—of an electoral district where the people would remain assembled continuously, organized and "standing," instead of dispersing once the election was over and the power granted. [Thus] the districts became standing, deliberative constituencies, a situation that already existed in Revolutionary times.

Pure democracy does not acknowledge either doctrine or doctor. Everything is consigned to free discussion, and this discussion is extended to all questions, all the people, all the time, rather than being limited to general questions, certain electors, and certain periods as in parliamentary or *constitutional democracy.*

The parliamentary regime is a [type of] freedom regulated by a Constitution.

We must stress the difference, because pure democracy is always confused with parliamentary democracy. Direct democracy has never yet been exercised steadily except in Philosophical Societies. It is so exercised, however, with the Jacobins, the Grand Lodge, and the C.G.T.[11] All of these standing organizations are as different from representative democracy as the latter is from divine right.

2. OUR PROPOSED STUDY AND ITS ARTICULATIONS

We propose to study the progressive development of the democratic phenomenon from its innocuous form in the Philosophical Societies of 1750 to its terrifying form in the Revolutionary government of 1793.

This is a drama in which the *individualized* and moral man is gradually eliminated by the *socialized* man, who in the end will be nothing but a number, an abstract supernumerary.

The study of the facts will lead us to this observation which might seem paradoxical: "There cannot be any more possibility of freedom, any real sovereignty,

for the masses in a strictly democratic society than in an authoritarian one."
[Popular sovereignty is but] an ideal that remains at the end of the evolution.
[But] in fact, the power is in the hands of the few — in the reign of freedom as in
the reign of authority — and the masses follow, obey, and believe.

We can distinguish three stages in the "Development of the Enlightenment,"
accomplishing three different states in the Philosophical Societies:

> the philosophic state
> the political state
> the Revolutionary state.

These are the three stages of logical evolution that correspond to the three
historical periods of the Revolution.

The first, "the philosophic state," is that of the Philosophical Societies,
strictly speaking, a period of Platonic speculation in the eighteenth century. It is
the intellectual revolt of Free Thought preparing the Revolution (1750–1789).

The second, "the political state," corresponds to the second phase of development, the passage from pure speculation to political action. [Public] opinion
then becomes a *party*. It has clubs and it strives for real results, for certain decisions from the authorities of the time, for laws. This is the first period of the
Revolution from 1789 to 1793.

The third is "the Revolutionary state," [when] the unadulterated idea, fettered until then by social realities, surges forward triumphant and fulfills all its
promise. This is direct government by the sovereign people: the twelve months
of the Terror (1793–1794). Being unnatural, it could not last.

Now, in each of these three states, in the guise of enfranchisement and
emancipation, we meet a new subjection of man to society.

Indeed, the reign of the people, the standing, absolute reign of [public]
opinion presupposes "guidance," i.e. the existence of standing Societies whose
only object is to shape this opinion. These Societies are the instrument of the
people. But the instrument will prove to have its own laws, different from those
of living people, since it can only last by means of a triple restraint that corresponds precisely to the three stages of democracy.

In the philosophic state, the secrecy of the lodges stifles the public thinking
they claim to represent (1750–1789).

In the political state, the unofficial, extra-legal pressure of the clubs hampers, then tyrannizes, the action of the official powers (1789–1793).

In the Revolutionary state, the official tyranny of the popular Societies finishes confiscating individual will and property, (1793–1794).

Thus democracy is not the people.

What, then, are these laws of the instrument reduced to its function as an instrument? We shall follow their development, both logical and historical.

In these three stages, three goals are proposed as a triple enfranchisement:

Truth, Freedom, Justice.

But they correspond to three types of oppression:

Free Thought, Individualism, Socialism.

And this bondage is asserted:

In the intellectual domain, by secrecy.
In the moral domain, by corruption and blackmail.
In the material domain, by force.

And always in the form the most radically opposed to freedom.
We shall study successively:

1. Free thought which, in the name of *truth*, introduces us to *intellectual bondage* through the secrecy of the lodges. The outsider does not know where he is being led; he must go there blindfolded. The particular form of restraint required for the elite to reign over the greater number is *ignorance* such as it is manifested in the Masonic Societies. For the ignorant this will be called the "Development of the Enlightenment."
2. *Individualism* which, in the name of *freedom*, achieves *moral bondage* through corruption, blackmail, and fear. The individual is freed, which means isolated, all the better to enslave him. In the political domain, as in the religious one, association is presented as a means of emancipation, moral purification. Does it not place the least of the citizens in a position to discuss political acts and follow his leaders with his eyes open, freely, and not out of personal interest? Actually, it is just the opposite: corruption becomes dominant when the Society moves into this second phase of its development, shifting from the intellectual to the political mode.

Organizing [public] opinion by external pressure has always, and everywhere, resulted in the lowering of moral standards.

3. *Socialism* which, in the name of *justice*, implements the official tyranny of the popular Societies: the *material bondage of property* follows and is added to the moral bondage of wills. This justice is called equality and is the violent plundering of all property through despotism, in the universal silence of terror and hatred. This is the communism of the Revolutionary government.

This is what the rising enfranchisement of the people accomplished.

First it was done gently in the lodges and political Societies. And finally with a heavy hand in the Committee of Public Safety.

And the personal result would be *the progressive socialization of man*, substituting an *imaginary Social being* for a *real, individual being*.

The emancipation of the spirit would be *socialized thought*, the intellectual socialization of the philosopher of 1789.

The emancipation of the citizen would be *socialized public life*, the moral socialization of the patriot of 1792.

The emancipation of property would be economic life and *socialized private life*, the material socialization of the citizen of 1793.

An impersonal fiction replaced the human personality.

Let us not imagine this is the past. The dream has not vanished; the idea is with us still. Rousseau deified the people, and Durkheim socialized God: God, the unalloyed symbol of the Social order, and the Social order, the only reality.

Reflection (1909)

The three forms of oppression that correspond to the three states of the Philosophical Societies are not the product of individual temperaments or chance, but the [necessary] condition for the very existence of societies that make absolute freedom a principle in the intellectual, moral, and tangible order.

Every Philosophical Society is intellectual oppression in the very fact that it denounces on principle any dogma as oppression. For the Society cannot renounce its unity of opinion without ceasing to exist. Now, an intellectual discipline without a corresponding object, without an idea, is the very definition of intellectual oppression.

Every society of equals is privilege in the very fact that it renounces any personal distinctions on principle, for it cannot dispense with unity of direction.

Now, direction without responsibility, power without authority, i.e. obedience without respect, is the very definition of moral oppression.

Every society of brothers is combat and hatred in that it denounces any personal independence as selfishness, for it has to attach the members to one another and maintain social cohesion. And union without love is the very definition of hatred.

ENDNOTES

Translator's note: Cochin died on the battlefield in 1916. This unfinished book was first published by Plon, Paris, in 1924.

[1] Cf. *The Revolution and Free Thought*, Part I, chapter 3, no. 4, "The Development of the Enlightenment."

[2] For example, Monsieur Aulard, cf. *The Philosophical Societies and Modern Democracy*, "A Critical Problem in the Analysis of Revolutionary History."

[3] Translator's note: A term of Voltaire's invention.

[4] Translator's note: this term, which first appeared in the eighteenth century, was used by Cochin with a derogatory meaning.

[5] Translator's note: Proposed by Rousseau.

[6] Moreover, all the historians who were Masons have said the Revolution was made in the lodges before it was made in the nation.

[7] For the origins of the Revolutionary movement, see: *Les Sociétés de Pensée et la Révolution en Bretagne*, 1788–1789.

[8] Cf. Augustin Cochin and Charles Charpentier, *Les Actes du gouvernement révolutionnaires* (August 23, 1793-July 27, 1794).

[9] Ostrogorski.

[10] Translator's note: Cochin means the regime of the Societies.

[11] Translator's note: The *Confédération Générale du Travail*. In Cochin's time this was a socialist trade union. Today it has been taken over by the communists.

PART ONE: TRUTH OR SOCIALIZED THOUGHT

(abridged)

CHAPTER 1: THE PHILOSOPHICAL SOCIETIES

INTRODUCTION

In our century of universal curiosity it is singular that no one has undertaken a study of the Philosophical Societies. Yet this is a political phenomenon worthy of interest for several reasons: their distinct character and, oddly, their well-known existence, at least for the past one hundred and fifty years, and then a certain influence—several times decisive, and today dominant—in the destiny of our country. If we look closely, they are the democratic phenomenon itself, in its principle and purity.

But thus far, in the lives of these Societies, people have only sought the melodrama of secret societies—rites, mystery, disguises, and plots—which means they have strayed into a labyrinth of obscure anecdotes, to the detriment of the true history, which is very clear. Indeed the interest of the phenomenon in question is not in the Masonic bric-a-brac, but in the fact that in the bosom of the nation the Masons instituted a small State governed by its own laws, which to this day have not managed to be applied elsewhere. These are laws of pure democracy, of a perfect republic, in which the people remain constantly standing in order to govern, in which the power remains so impersonal as to be secret—in short, in which opinion is sovereign, in the strictest sense of the term.

What is the opinion that reigns? Is it the same, except for its power, as the one that does not reign? And if not, what are its particular laws and propensities?

For opinion to govern, in the precise meaning of the word, for democracy to exist, opinion must command, i.e. speak, and I mean distinctly and continually. For opinion to speak in this way, it must be "organized," i.e. fixed, expressed, centralized, a task that is inconceivable without a network of Societies unceasingly elaborating the "Sovereign's" decrees, by means of discussion and correspondence. Either this sovereign is only a legal fiction, good for any tyranny, or, to exist in itself, it needs a social framework that gives it cohesion, conscience, and speech.

But is it certain the people (I mean everybody) thus organized, will remain themselves? The fact the people speak [as one] presumes they are organized, but can they get organized without being submitted, by that very fact, to fatal and unforeseen selection, motive force, and orientation? When [public] opinion gives itself a social organ—and its reign depends on this—who must be asked for the laws of this reign, the opinion or its organ? Opinion, the democrats never fail to reply: the organ is nothing, adds nothing, no more than the word adds to the idea. And the theoretician can reply in this way, because he is reasoning about an organization without conflict, and thought without any weakness. The adherent [to this system] must reply in this way, he for whom the word *people* means the "hard core" minority, *freedom* means the minority's tyranny, *equality* its privileges, and *truth* its opinion: it is even in this reversal of the meaning of the words that the adherent's initiation consists. But the theoretician is considering another object, the adherent speaking another language. For the historian who is neither a theoretician, nor an adherent, such a reply is worthless. At a glance he sees democracy and the people, free thought and [public] opinion, the organ and the being, in perpetual conflict—either because he is thinking of philosophical Masonry's intellectual experience with its very reduced "center" of initiates, and its immense "circumference" of outsiders, or because he is thinking of the political experience of organized parties, "blocs" or "machines," with their general staff of "wire-pullers" and their "voting cattle," or the Social experience of trade union or Jacobin terrorism with its committees of effective "militants" and its herds of passive members. Unity, certainly, and conscience, and a voice—the Social organ gives all of this to the popular sovereign, but at what price? If their intelligence, their "enlightenment," is at stake, the people will have to submit to the secret impulse of masters they do not know; if it is their freedom, their "emancipation," to the unofficial pressure of politicians they despise; or lastly if it is their lives themselves, their "happiness," to the Jacobin yoke. Secrecy, blackmail, violence, such are the three resources of the Social organ; ignorance, weakness, terror, its three instruments, to ensure the collective being's conscience, autonomy, and happiness. These are the three postulates of democracy, the three stages of new "regeneration."

To tell the truth, the first of these three resources is secret and must not be seen. The second is unofficial and can always be denied. The third is temporary and never fails to cite circumstances as its excuse. Thus the principles are preserved. But in fact, all three coerce, and it is this fact of coercion that we wish to emphasize.

We say *fact* without evaluating it, and coercion without intending to blame or praise it. Should one blame the organ that exceeds its function, or the people who fail in their duty, who are not "up to it," according to the hallowed expression? Should one curse the tyrants who set up their own judgment as dogma, their personal ambition as the public good? Or should one exalt the virtuous, conscious elite who manage to raise individual interest to the level of the general interest, and ensure the triumph of civic will over natural selfishness by reasoning and force? Should one take the circumstances—revolts, plots, famine—as an effect of the principles, or an excuse for the procedures? One can make many value judgments that add nothing to the material account of the facts, and are not our domain. It is not our place to curse any more than to praise democratic coercion: we need only determine its existence.

And this observation is possible today, for though democratic doctrine remains the same, experience and the facts speak louder and louder. The intellectual work is no longer so secret that outsiders cannot be informed enough to understand it. Nor is Social pressure still so general that witnesses do not remain free enough to pass judgment. Democracy is not the people. Philosophical Societies are not [public] opinion. The organ has other laws, other tendencies than the being. This is the obvious fact that a century of democratic experience no longer allows us to deny. And it is the only fact that interests us, for if the organ is not the being, and contradicts the being, then what exactly is it? What is this truth that tells lies, this freedom that binds, this happiness that burdens, this temporary [status] that lasts? The purpose of this present study is to seek the organ. Its object is not the people, but the democratic organ that speaks for the people: the Philosophical Societies. What is a Philosophical Society? Nothing more than what is indicated by its name, recently but appropriately chosen: it is a society formed without any preoccupation with achievement—to opine, not to act—a "cooperative of ideas," a "union for truth." The Society can be defined: an association founded without any other object than to elicit through discussion, to set by vote, to spread by correspondence—in a word, merely to *express*— the common opinion of its members. It is the organ of opinion reduced to its function as an organ, and constituted, designated as such.

This definition suffices. It would be a mistake to lengthen it by mentioning doctrines and rites, but also a mistake to consider it banal, for it contradicts prevailing notions about the Societies, which are generally expected to strive for a goal, and about the expression of thought, an essentially personal task. We must study what a philosophical association can be—a collective work of expression. The task is well-defined today, if not easy, for these paradoxes, long denied or concealed, are now achieved and appear in broad daylight at last. They have a proper identity, first in their hallowed names: free thought, individualism, socialism. They even have their patrons: they invoke three entities of ambiguous meaning and recent origin, despite their ancient names: Truth, Freedom,

Justice. Let's start with Truth.

The Truth in Philosophical Societies

I. COLLECTIVE WORK AND THE LAW OF REDUCTION

1. Real Opinion

It is not an indifferent matter for an association to be constituted with the single goal of establishing in common the collective opinion of its members, through discussion and voting. For this opinion will thus be found on the outside—and will be shaped in reverse—of its normal conditions of formation.

Indeed, in real life the communion of all appears to be the effect of each person's convictions. Is that a mere illusion? Perhaps, and Durkheim's school of sociology thinks so. But this illusion itself is a fact, the only one that interests us. And we stick to the appearance, true or false, that the truth is given first—truth of faith, fact, or reason—and that afterwards comes union, based on truth, in which we share communion. This is the moral fact of agreement, which precedes and determines the social fact of mutual understanding or contract, if it is still worth making a contract when harmony [already] exists, or talking when one [already] agrees.

Everything happens the opposite way in a Philosophical Society, for it is precisely to shape collective opinion, by discussion and voting—therefore outside of any common convictions—that the association has been made. Here mutual understanding is the means, and no longer the effect or the sign, of agreement. It is the Social fact that takes precedence. People are united *for* and not *by* the truth. And in this way thought can be said to be freer here than elsewhere: it is the only world that theoretically does not exclude any opinion—in which all opinions can enter and have a voice.

Here are two opposite conceptions of collective opinion. We shall call the first *real*, since it expresses an actual agreement, whatever the unconscious causes may be, and the second *Social*, since it results from a mutual understanding elaborated collectively. The first is born spontaneously, without any special organ of information, discussion, or propaganda. The second is elaborated "consciously," as our democrats would say today, i.e. by discussion, voting, and correspondence, in a Philosophical Society.

The external effect, the sign, of these two opinions is the same: it is expressed consent, unanimity. [But] the meaning and value of these signs are very different.

In the case of real opinion, this value is sovereign, for there is no organ here that speaks for the group and solicits individuals in the name of union for union's sake, and without reference to the truth on which the union is based. Consequently there is no generally recognized opinion that is not actually each person's opinion. Of course, the conviction must be quite strong to make so many people talk about it and testify to it—and quite profound for all to be in agreement. The idea that produces it, that is acknowledged by so many different people to be true, and that proves its efficacy for so many different endeavors, evinces its own truth. . . .

[On the other hand] Social opinion, "union for truth," claims it brings men together, through discussion and voting, to obtain the collective verdict that real life is never intense enough to bring forth, nor real opinion mature, formed, and conscious enough to express. Instead of seeking consent *at the end* of actual development, of which it would be the climax, it is sought through verbal Work, of which association is *the principle* and the means—an undertaking on the same level as religious endeavor but in the opposite direction.

At first glance, nothing seems vainer, since this undertaking consists in simply denying the difficulty, and is proposed ever so modestly as a mere conversational game. But we must not stop at this discreet appearance, for the interest of the system resides in no way whatsoever in apparent attitudes and doctrines, but [rather] in the unwitting action it exerts on "Socialized" thought.

2. Social Opinion

The essential characteristic of the Social group in question is to exclude any real achievement. Within the group, opinion is elaborated verbally, by discussion— not actually, through endeavor and in achievement. The "Workshop" is a hot-bed of words, as in real life it is a place of labor, and the "Work" is a convergence of words, as elsewhere it is a production of objects.

Hence at the outset one condition is necessary for the members' thought: it must be readily and easily communicable; the members must be able to speak to one another easily. This [communicability] is as necessary [to the thought] as truth, for in this new world opinion replaces testing, and words replace achievement. A thought, an intellectual endeavor, has no other existence here than by consent. It is opinion that makes the being. What is real is only what the Society sees, true only what it understands, good only what it approves of, since everything stops after it is voted upon, and achievement is not present to reflect thought, nor testing to judge intention. Thus the natural order is reversed: the group's opinion is a necessary condition here, and not, as in real life, a negligible consequence. Appearing replaces being, and saying replaces doing.

"This is the city of the clouds," the outsiders will respond, interpreting Aristophanes' profound and charming myth mistakenly. When we speak of the city of clouds, we are only thinking of the clouds in order to mock those who claim they are building a city there. [But] Aristophanes, who lived in a century of "philosophers," and knew what free thinking was, does not mean the same thing. It is a city that he sees, no doubt built in the clouds, between heaven and earth, but with good quarry stone, populated by citizens in flesh and blood, driving humans crazy and starving the gods. The city of clouds is a dramatic device, not a pamphleteer's witticism. It is not utopia that the Greek poet is emphasizing, but reality and its fatal consequences.

We must do the same: observe the success and seek the reasons for it, instead of questioning the likelihood of it. Such research is worthwhile, for with this success acknowledged—and who would deny the fact today?—the new city makes real, before our eyes and within our reach, the most remote hypotheses of sociological and political theorists. This is Rousseau's "contract," Kant's *Reich der Zwecke*."[1] It is also primitive society, social fact in its purest state, which Durkheim seeks in Polynesia, a bit like eighteenth-century philosophers used to go to China to seek the free man, the natural man, who abounded in the Parisian lodges and salons. Indeed the distinctive characteristic of this Society is precisely to place union in itself before any principle of union, the Social fact before the moral fact, to make a principle not of conviction but of union. That, we shall see, is the necessary and sufficient law that determines both the object and the outcome of discussions in the Society's world. This law orients the [Masonic] Work and determines the whole economy of the "Great [Masonic] Achievement."

Indeed, to be communicable to a deliberating public, in the conditions of the Work, the ideas must be clear and objective enough to force conviction upon everyone, and simple enough to be within the reach of the whole audience. The first condition is necessary to the orator and determines the method of discussions. The second is forced upon the audience and determines the choice of subjects, the agenda.

The clearest ideas, the ones that are defined and expressed best—the best-made language, Condillac used to say—are the principles of the exact sciences, and actually it is from those sciences that free thought takes the type of truth it is seeking. The Work appeals to this Cartesian reason, which, being the same in everyone, therefore leads to the same truths. The Work also eliminates any unclear idea, and makes a principle of ignoring anything related to faith, political loyalty, or even the practical conduct of life. There is not a single Philosophical

Society that does not begin by making a very sincere declaration to this effect, not a single one that admits it has ever failed in its principle—nor a single member worthy of the name who does not use the most abstract and general terms, even in his personal quarrels. We know what odd examples of this can be found in the minutes of the Convention and the clubs: the game consists in ceaselessly exposing, but without ever naming.

Unfortunately, the domain of clear ideas only supplies free thinking with its method, but not with material to study—for the exact sciences would gain nothing by the Work. The expression of truth is too precise in science to lend itself to debate. It is precisely because reason is the same in everyone that the thinker does not need to consult it in others, but only to follow his own attentively. Hence the effort of Cartesian thought, essentially isolated—Descartes's stove, Malebranche's closed shutters, Spinoza's shop. However, the Work loses in this thought, for though the principles are clear, the developments are not simple. How can one get an ordinary audience to follow "these long chains of reasons" Descartes speaks of? Directing a lodge is not a course in advanced mathematics.

The natural sciences are less obvious in their principles, and less complicated in their development. Apparently the tested formulas of these sciences would have more to gain by verbal collaboration, the assistance of witnesses, than the obvious propositions of the exact sciences.

But we must distinguish here between previously established science, which falls ipso facto into the public domain, and the science to be established, the scientist's intuition, which is personal in essence and assumes a concurrence of ideas within the same individual's mind, certainly not a concurrence of individual minds around the same idea. As it is with judicial investigation, so it goes with scientific invention: it would be useless to assemble witnesses, as Locke's intellectual atomism requires, and leave them to themselves. Only confusion would result if each were to present and uphold his own version. A judge is necessary to piece the various testimonies together in his mind, see them as a whole, and by unique apperception discover the true hypothesis, the only one capable of conciliating diverse points of fact, already known or to be known, in order to connect them as a unit. Here thought works actively and personally. The mind is not a democracy of concepts, as Locke imagines, even regulated, as Kant wishes, by a constitution and laws. Order is maintained here not by impersonal laws or forms. The mind is, rather, a monarchy, in which reigns a supreme judge whose past decrees we can codify, but whose future decisions we cannot foresee with certainty—a living law, which keeps talking but never reveals its last secret, nor utters its last word.

In short, it is the same with scientific collaboration as with economic solidarity: is it not true that in the economic domain all the creation of wealth and energy benefits the whole? Yet shall we say there is solidarity here? I think not. The socialists object, and with reason, to this extension of the word. In order to have solidarity, reciprocity, the impact would have to be understood and desired, but this is not the case for industrial activity any more than it is for scientific thinking. Each activity forges ahead using, and serving, the force of others, but never thinking of anything but itself. Science is a sum of isolated endeavors, not the product of a collective endeavor. Here again the unity of results is a fact, a consequence—and not a [cooperative] achievement, a goal. The [Masonic] Work is as foreign to the physics laboratory as to mathematics professorships.

The simplest of all our ideas are those that guide our practical conduct in all the meanings of this term, from the religious order to material well-being. We pass from the domain of scientific experiment to that of personal experience and everyday life—from the law of things to the rule of minds. Thus it is indeed here that the society's Work finds the terrain that suits it, and the Philosophical Society finds its *raison d'être*. On one hand, henceforth each testimony no longer expresses an obvious or observed truth—i.e. a truth which is the same for everyone, and indifferent to the number who adhere to it—but its own point of view of the world and life, thus presenting a new fact, the result of its personal experience. This testimony has value and consistency in itself, however lowly and banal it may be. On the other hand, there is none that implies less intellectual effort, that finds itself within easier reach of anyone's thought. Thus there is no example of a Philosophical Society that does not fall sooner or later—despite its original resolutions—into political action. For the Society, this is a propensity as fatal as the one that imposes objective and abstract methods on its "orators": a necessity of situation rather than prejudice, a Social fact rather than a moral one.

Thus the force of things, the very conditions of the Work doom free thought to method, to the spirit of the exact sciences—to the object of morality. How can we solve this dilemma?

It would find no way out in the *real world*, where thought can only remain free by dedicating itself to Cartesian isolation, to intellectual asceticism. Nor can thought become efficient, penetrate concrete reality, and affect social life, without being submitted to the three constraints, divine, human, and personal, of faith, tradition, and experience. Constraints for speculative thinking, which seeks the clear idea; assistance for thought incarnate, the mind, which strives for real achievement; they are transcendental "givens" for both. It is certain that in the present state of mankind, and without making too hasty a judgment of basic reality, these givens are necessary for any real achievement. *Whatever the endeavors and hopes of reason, the moralist without faith, the citizen without tradition, and the man without experience remain pitiful people, exposed to every sort of defeat.*

But let's enter the "Social world," where everything will change. Here there is no Work to accomplish that would oblige thought to worry about reality. Nothing to do but talk to talkers. Then what good is the teaching of faith, the knowledge of tradition, and the lessons of personal experience? Though they are necessary in order to make a fair and honest judgment, they are only a nuisance to opining clearly. Though they are indispensable to real work and achievement, they interfere with verbal Work, expression.

And better still: while annoying for the orator, they are unpleasant for the audience, for they cannot reveal themselves without making themselves obnoxious or ridiculous, as sincere conviction never fails to become the moment it is asserted apart from the real endeavor it is made for. Is there anything as intolerable as faith that is preached without sacrifice, patriotism exalted without danger, personal interest displayed without endeavor and risk? Such, however, is the position they assume unwittingly, if they appear in a world where, by very definition, achievement and endeavor are out of the question. There they will be called clericalism, chauvinism, selfishness. Is this ill will, unfair prejudice? Of course not; on the contrary, nothing is more legitimate. The first person to notice—and consequently to remain silent—will be precisely the realist, warned by his sincere faith and conviction. He senses that if inadvertently he should raise his voice in their defense, he would expose himself to accusation. One is certainly free not to enter the new city, but if one enters, one is not allowed to opine otherwise than as a "philosopher."

[Translator's note: Cochin duplicates the following text here from The Precursors of the Revolution: The Philosophers, *pp. 17–19 in the Copernic edition, "Thus a whole order of motives . . . This orientation of thought towards the void is a fundamental fact," pages 40 to 42 in this translation.]*

The orientation of thought towards the void is a fundamental fact [of Philosophical Societies], and now we can distinguish the opposition between free thought and thought. They both start from the same point, and aim for the same goal, which is that of any activity: to accomplish their own law, to emancipate themselves—in this case, to attain truth. They both meet the same obstacle: their imperfection, their insufficiency when faced with the unfathomable resources of reality. But though their departure point is the same, their progression is in opposite directions.

Personal thought comprehends things and seeks to achieve its dominion over them, its freedom, but through an effort of conquest, a battle with reality and its mysteries, which presumes a whole deployment of knowledge, systems, and sciences—or higher still, through the growth of spiritual forces, of supernatural assistance, which only God can give, the [Catholic] Church dispense, and faith imagine. Is it a victorious battle? Not always, and in any case there is an endless, continually renewed struggle. But it is a fruitful struggle, for though it does not exhaust [the possibilities of] reality, it deploys the powers of the mind, and puts the creative capacity of the intelligence into play, from the intuition of philosophers and scientists to the faith of the apostles and the supernatural vision of the saints.

The Work of the [Philosophical] Society, on the contrary, passes from the offensive to the defensive in this battle with reality. Subordinating thought to expression, making the word the condition for the idea, the Work reverses intellectual effort and tends to achieve unwittingly, by elimination [of reality], this agreement between thought and reality that [the Work's] contrary [personal thought] deliberately seeks to attain by development [of its own effort.] The [Work's] solution is logically just as good, since the problem of agreement is solved just as well by the destruction as by the accomplishment of the two terms [thought and reality]—solved in nothingness as well as in existence. But finally this solution is really the reverse, in its means as well as in its outcome: Social rather than personal, unconscious and undesired, negative and not positive, and it finally culminates in the destruction of the intelligence, whereas the other [personal thought] creates the mind.

The [Society's] Work removes the mind from reality, instead of reducing what is unintelligible in reality. It deals with thoughts themselves, not things, and is a veritable "thinking exercise" whose interest is not in philosophical or scientific results—which always amount to nothing—but in its effect on the members' minds. Thanks to this Work the members do become socialized little by little, i.e. they are unconsciously subdued, diminished by the action of the law of reduction. The Work has never created a philosophy, but it makes philosophers.

II. THE LOGIC OF THE COLLECTIVE IDEA

C. The Idea as Mere Word[2]

Now we can judge the value of the third sort of collective idea, the one produced by the Work and the law of reduction.

In the case of the *idée-type* [or the idea as describing reality], the center of convergence of thoughts remains situated higher than their current ideas, and intuition extends beyond expression. In the case of the common idea, the idea and the word are equally balanced [on the same plane]: this is Condillac's well-made language, whose content adjusts to its form. *Socialized thought* completes the inversion: by founding union on the word [the idea as mere word] and not on reality—on verbal endeavor and not on actual achievement—it finally inverts the direction of convergence [of thoughts] that the *idée-type* had produced. The nature of the Work, as we have said, is to maintain union at the expense of the very reality which elsewhere [outside the Society] makes the bond of union. Thoughts keep working, but by striving for the void, as in real life they strive for an existence and a plenum. Hence, between real truth and Social truth, there is a constant contradiction, in identical forms—an inversion of signs more than a difference of forms. To the plenitude of the Word is opposed the nothingness of the Letter, to the Spirit of the Law is opposed the Letter of the Law....

We have seen how the word properly defined [i.e., not in the Masonic sense] bears witness to, and how the convergence of ideas reveals, the spirit of truth that creates, quickens, and transcends any idea in the mind, and any form in the world. We have also said how human intelligence might limit itself to these ideas and forms and stop at this actuality, instead of following the movement, the direction of the real—how it might define instead of understanding, photograph instead of painting. Now here is the third step. What intuition grasps, what science sets aside, free thought destroys. This is characteristic of the Social law of reduction whose mechanism we have described and whose consequences we should like to touch upon. This law no longer cares about form, neither in its spirit nor in its actual material shape. Delivering it to the scientist, as a corpse to the embalmer, the law disregards it and tackles the mind that made it. It is the mind alone that is in question here, and not such and such an organ, form, or apparent ability. Hence the extreme difficulty of our study, for the life of the mind cannot be defined any more than the life of the body can be touched. To say what the law of reduction makes the socialized mind lose is as difficult as to show what a body loses at the moment of death....

Nothing illustrates this unprecedented phenomenon better than the conception of the savage or ingenuous person that takes such a large place in the philosophical literature [of the eighteenth century]. . . .

This philosopher-savage is quite an unusual person. Imagine an eighteenth-century Frenchman who possesses all the material attainments of the civilization of his time — culture and sensibility, knowledge and taste — but without any of the actual incentives, the instincts and beliefs, that had created all that, had animated these forms, given their reason to these customs, their force to these habits, and their use to these resources. Drop him into this world of which he possesses everything except the essential — the spirit — and he will see and know everything, but understand nothing. That is Voltaire's Huron.

The uninitiated protest that this is absurd. They are mistaken. This savage exists, and they meet him every day. To tell the truth, he does not come from the forests of Ohio, but from much farther: the lodge across the street, the salon next door. It is the philosopher himself, such as the Work has made him: a paradoxical being, oriented towards the void as others seek reality. His thought is without enthusiasm or real curiosity, more concerned with regulating than with acquiring, with defining than with inventing; he is always anxious to display his intellectual attainments, and always impatient — so as to convert these attainments into words — to break his ties to the real life in which he had been working and growing thus far like invested capital or a living plant, in the bedrock of experience, under the rays of faith. . . .

That was the *Encyclopedia's* whole *raison d'être*, and this immense intellectual endeavor did not make science advance a single step. It consisted in considering all the knowledge of the time in the light of the new spirit, and "neutralizing" the human mind. It is a strange, almost inexplicable work, the most futile and most immense — and the most devoid of interest. It contains neither an idea, nor a new invention, and yet it is most enthusiastic. Its authors worked at it with apostolic zeal. We must not judge as outsiders. For a follower, the Encyclopedists' endeavor had an immense importance. . . . [The *Encyclopedia* contained] no controversy to speak of — no argument and no system — nothing but statement. This was a new and unusual way to tackle positive ideas, a way that aroused no one's suspicions. The victim was disarmed in advance. There were no arguments here, no doctrinal system that might give rise to discussion or anathema. . . .

The Encyclopedic endeavor's point of departure was the idea that objects of knowledge can be described, verbally defined. Now this was a novelty. The ancient world could not imagine that effective knowledge could be *acquired* without real effort; that the formula could dispense with the finished work.

But now this new approach was used for the highest order of knowledge, faith, but also for the humblest: the manual trades that philosophism was to exalt and kill so swiftly and surely. The immediate effect was the death of folk art, "style," which the academic teaching created by the Encyclopedists, from Diderot to Condorcet, killed in one generation, perhaps a unique phenomenon in history. To teach in a school rather than train in a workshop, to have a pupil learn rather than do, to explain rather than show and correct—this was the essence of the new method, conceived by the philosophers and imposed by the Revolution. Isolated people survived, but like rocks beaten by the sea of banality and ignorance, not like tall trees in the forest. . . .

Societies and Free Thought

The first effect of collective thinking, the Work, is to force us, whether we want to or not, to ignore any sort of sentiment. A sentiment is not *spoken*, at least not in public. The critical point of view does not deny ethics but, by its very definition, it knows nothing of beauty or love.

Henceforth collective thinking will be critical. Eventually no personal sentiment will enter in. Personal sentiment, considered in itself and not in its object, is indeed strictly individual. For the person who loves or hates or pities or respects, it is he and he alone who feels all that. These sentiments may have the same end, the same object, but they will never be identical. The words that designate them will not transmit them like ideas, but will only be signs, without significance if the corresponding reality is not found on the other side.

Sentiments are not oppressed, they are respected. But they are put out of the question. Now, by ignoring something repeatedly, we lose the habit of it and [eventually] forget it. . . .

Faith cannot exist without good works. It is the first to be affected, and even targeted. We have explained why: merely by showing up in a Philosophical Society it is distorted and dishonored. There it can only be prejudice, superstition, abomination for the Faithful themselves. This effect of the Work can be called the Social phenomenon of religious inversion. . . .

Faith is the affirmation that some assistance superior to man is necessary, and that consequently man must obey a will higher than his own. Affirmation and obedience are acknowledged necessary by real endeavor itself: it is to the degree that man wishes to grow and create that he feels the necessity for faith and calls upon God.

Philosophical Societies, having nothing to create, do not sense the obstacle, nor the powerlessness of man, nor the need for God.

The destruction of the spirit is manifested in two ways by its consequences.

The first of these consequences, the closest to the cause and the fact itself, is the tone, the *new nuance* taken on by the sentiments, doctrines, convictions that needed this spirit to exist—not, of course, that this change can be defined, since, as we have said, the exterior did not change, but the energy, the incentive is broken: *there is no life left*. The principle of growth, the will to achieve and progress have withdrawn.

Actually, this is the case from the very moment these sentiments or ideas are proposed for the Work and enter the lodge, which means they renounce achievement to seek *verbal* assent.

The first noticeable effect is outer reinforcement. Sentiments become stiff and fixed; they stand out. They lose their flexibility and transparency. This is when the formulas professed by the doctrinaires make their appearance. Superficial people proclaim victory and mistake for growth the reinforcement of the body, what is actually the end of the spirit. It seems that the intrinsic value of moral forces is acknowledged at last, those forces that hitherto had only been considered in their accomplishments. *Authority, Loyalty, Tradition*, etc., sport capital letters and rise onto the altar. But this apotheosis adds nothing to their effectiveness—on the contrary. It is not these abstractions that work; they dispense one with working. One believes he has served them by worshiping them, as the freethinker believes he makes *science* progress by raising altars to it, by deifying it. But when sentiment is set by formulas, it appears both sterile and demanding. . . .

Once doctrines and positive sentiments enter the lodge, they quickly lose their true wellspring, their life, in the new atmosphere, and then reveal themselves such as the followers had imagined them: tyrannical, demanding, and hollow. . . .

Now we understand why Social thought is called *free*, and why this freedom has a negative characteristic, and always finds itself on the *defensive*.

This thought is free or at least appears so to each of its champions, *because it is no longer put in the presence of reality*, in any way, i.e. forced to transcend itself, to seek its unity beyond an effort for growth and expansion that it must ask of something higher than itself. [This new thought] no longer bears anything, so it is much lighter. Nothing remains of [divine] assistance, now become useless, except the *constraint* and the *bond*: to uphold is to hold.

Unity, on the contrary, is accomplished *from below*, and unconsciously, with neither effort nor consciousness.

The *first step*, as we have seen, consists in *doing away with the conscience*. This step is a negative condition, the destruction of *faith*.

The *second step* consists in rejecting *endeavor,* declaring everything that requires it tyrannical and unnatural.

However, reality cannot disappear—the brothers do not lose sight of it—and we have seen in what form it necessarily appears, in the world of words where *faith* becomes an absurdity, *tradition* a constraint, *experience* an obstacle: a futility that is ignored. Thus it is in this world of reduction where lack of knowledge is strength, any [divine] assistance a constraint, any innate gift a theft.

On the other hand, *truth,* rather than a conquest to be made, is no longer anything but a possession to be kept: intuition disappears.

But, we repeat, though we may sound tedious, it is the Social fact of training and selection [imposed by the Society] that we are thinking of here, not the individual fact of *abstraction,* theoretical speculation.[3]

The Philosophical Society and Democracy

Lastly, the humblest Philosophical Society is a "furnace of light" and at the same time (whether it realizes it or not, and, whatever its members' beliefs and doctrines may be), a small city taking shape, a *strictly democratic city.* In its midst it institutes a sort of opinion that is remarkably particular and peculiar, an opinion that is formed by discussion and voting, *freely and consciously.* The only *truly free* society, i.e. the one that has only the *current* and *expressed* will of its members to consider and no need to accept from the outside external necessities, whether moral or material, is the Philosophical Society. In the same way, any free society in the strictest sense of *pure democracy,* which means any society whose members *govern themselves,* in which the *current will* of the collectivity is the law, is necessarily a Philosophical Society.

One can see at the same time what is restrictive in this condition. To be *free,* a Society, in its role as a Society, must *only* be *thought,* and seek only *opinion* and not *effect,* the truth and not the good, the notion and not the finished product. Otherwise it would have to take the reality being sought into consideration, theoretically and independently of its members' current opinion. There would be a Social goal or dogmatic discipline, i.e. theoretical morality, and a social experience or tradition, i.e. practical morality.

Some discipline, some object, would have to be imposed on its members from the outside, before any discussion, and in the name of a higher interest.

And this is the truth expressed by these different facts: the *temporary,* or *unofficial,* or *secretive* character of Philosophical Societies in their different conditions, when they wish to compromise with reality.

Philosophical Societies, like direct democracy, are contrary to life.

CHAPTER 2: THE REVOLUTIONARY PHENOMENON AND THE SOCIOLOGICAL METHOD

2. The Conception of the State

Let's continue our natural history of the Philosophical Societies in their first phase.

The law of reduction has shown us this hollow thought, words without soul, soul without life. Yet it attempts to construct, to reconstruct, society. How can nothingness create? And what positive ideal can intellectuals be oriented towards in order to stimulate their enthusiasm?

For crowds, words are sufficient, provided they arouse passions, but for philosophers of the common good, there has to be a plan for the common good, a conception of the State. What is it? Is it a spontaneous product of the Social Work? Is it a foreign idea introduced from the outside?

And first what is the theory, the political conception, that will germinate and bloom in the Philosophical Societies? Before discussing its value, we must specify its effects.

It starts from the principle that all men are equal, on account of their absolute independence. It will be called the regime of direct democracy, which is a plurality of powers all held in the same hands that never let go of them, not even for an instant. And this sovereign of unlimited powers with no appeal possible, this master of justice itself, is the people, the people acting in unison to decree as a single voice their common will, the general will. And this general will creates the law, rights, and duties and is only responsible to itself. Each person's life and possessions are thus at the disposal of the sovereign people.

Such is the idea of the democratic city that, from 1760 onward, was inculcated into the Philosophical Societies' followers, who are chosen, guided, cultivated, weeded out by continuous selection—shaped, in a word, and passionate in this artificial environment, eventually graduating as apostles of this new religion. Their catechism was the *Social Contract*, which Rousseau published in 1762.

The best way to understand the character of this doctrine is to see it at work in the details of its application. We shall not consider it in its triumph when it reigned indisputably during the year of the Terror—all tyrannies are alike—but rather during its two-year struggle to come to power, when direct democracy was pitted against the constitutional or parliamentary democracy represented by the Convention.

Direct democracy keeps sovereignty for the people, whereas the representative regime takes it on lease from the people, and the authoritarian regime takes it away from them.

Opposite the Convention, the representative regime of popular sovereignty, thus arises the amorphous regime of the sovereign people, acting and governing on its own. Where do we find these people? In the streets and the clubs or "popular Societies," which are none other than the Philosophical Societies. "The sovereign is directly in the popular Societies," say the Jacobins. That is where the sovereign people reside, speak, and act. The people in the street will only be solicited for the hard jobs and the executions.

The popular Societies must be imagined as an enormous network emanating from the mother Society, the club of Jacobins: a nervous system transmitting this brain's impulses to the extremities of the country.

Opposite these Societies was the other network, this one legal: the whole group of electoral districts or assemblies under the Convention's jurisdiction.

These were the two powers that were to confront each other—the secret power versus the real power.

The electoral districts were open and public, since the suffrage was universal.

The popular Societies were exclusive associations, from the first lodge to the last Jacobin club. They recruited among themselves and limited and purged themselves by elimination.

The electoral districts functioned temporarily, intermittently, like the elections.

The Societies functioned continuously, ceaselessly deliberating: the sovereign cannot abdicate.

In the former case the power was constituted, in the latter it was constituent, always "standing," ceaselessly watching and correcting the legal authorities—until it finally absorbed these authorities.

From the start, the Societies ran the electoral assemblies, scheming and meddling on the pretext of excluding traitors that they were the only ones to designate. Later they added surveillance committees to each assembly. Finally they simply shut them down: no longer were elected representatives necessary, since the people reigned and governed on their own.

And this is how the club of Jacobins thoroughly lectured, browbeat, and purged the Convention in the name of the sovereign people, until it finally adjourned the Convention's power.

Though the sovereign people had their authorized agents, these were no longer "representatives" with their powers guaranteed but limited by the law. They were now direct agents, identified with the people, "presidents" of the people who kept them on a leash—dismissed tomorrow perhaps, but gods today, perfectly certain of the people's unlimited, irrevocable rights. But these presidents, mere agents revocable at a nod, were not distinguishable from their "brothers." Robespierre protested to the Jacobins (January 2, 1792): "Realize I am not the defender of the people. Never have I claimed this ostentatious title. I am a member of the people; I have never been anything but that."

This idea does not come from the *ancien régime,* nor from ours; it is the cry of the English caucuses: no man is a "savior." The commissioner—we call him a delegate—is therefore merely the people's spokesman.

And at the Convention (August 25, 1794), the Jacobins defined this regime of absolute equality as "dictatorship without a dictator."

From these facts the social doctrine of the French Revolution stands out clear and limpid.

On one side of the coin, the principles: all men equal, all men free, all men emancipated of all authority.

On the opposite side, the facts: the sovereign people are the little people of the exclusive Societies, sorted, purged, reduced, the only authentic representatives of the people themselves and the general will.

And these little people have nothing in common with the great people of France, since the former oppress the latter and eventually tyrannize them. In number the little people are an infinitesimal minority. The practice is the opposite of the theory. *De facto* tyranny at the service of theoretical freedom: such is the outcome of the Revolution. The idea contradicts the reality. The meaning of the words is inverted.

Moral appellations change their meaning. The meaning of right is no longer defined by human morality but by the revolutionary idea. Every act or decree of the sovereign people is called *revolutionary* and is thereupon declared legitimate. The fanaticism of the killers, the murderous courts, are called "the people's justice," and odious vices are "civic virtues."

Misinterpretation of words, or should we say lies? No. This was neither a concerted lie, nor an organized conspiracy. A plot would not have been so powerful, nor so widespread, nor so long-lasting. These people were not lying; they were convinced and driven. They were subjected to the law of the regime and this law overwhelmed them.

3. The "Social Contract"

Where does this political conception we have just seen at work come from? It would be tempting to say it is Rousseau's invention, for the Revolution took the

Social Contract for its platform. But is it not just as correct to say that Rousseau took the Philosophical Societies for a model? Reading him, would you not imagine you were looking at a lodge, an order, a Society: absolute freedom of opinion, equality of the members, all decisions made by voting. Nothing is more democratic than that.

It is therefore useless to seek the model for Rousseau's republic in the antiquity of Rome or Lacédémone, so greatly admired by the patriots, or in the little state that Geneva was in Rousseau's time. The model is not the heaven of angels, it is the city of the clouds with its chattering birds, remote from things existing or possible. Jean-Jacques [Rousseau's] citizens are not new men devoid of prejudice or tradition; they are worn out, cunning men who forsake their prejudices and traditions in the artificial world of the Societies. Thus in a way the social contract is no fantasy. It was achieved in Paris in the republic of letters. It attempted to become the regime of France under the Terror. Therefore let us examine it with the respect it deserves, i.e. in the realm of reality and not merely in the realm of abstractions. And let us give it its rightful place.

"A generous but dangerous utopia." Such, we know, is the judgment real society and the uninitiated world make of the ideal of democracy. Its principles appear corrupt or fanciful: freedom is permitted — equality promised — virtue anticipated. It is a mistake to believe and dangerous to say that every freedom is good, every equality just, every virtue certain.

[But real society's judgment is false] in a Philosophical Society. And here it is Jean-Jacques who is right.

In this particular city Rousseau is right.

Nature is good, virtue is the rule, selfishness the exception. What can political interest gain by Platonic discussions in which only opinions are considered? One takes no personal interest in theory. And so long as there is an ideal to define, rather than a job to accomplish, personal interest, selfishness, is out of the question. If such interest enters, it can only be by misunderstanding, for "lack of light." "Enlightened," on the contrary, aware of what it is doing there, this interest must tend to opine towards virtue, and natural thought relates here to virtue as it relates elsewhere to vice. Thus there is no fantasy in the democrats' surprising faith in the virtue of mankind. They are right: virtue is the rule here. The "general will" must triumph, and their opinion merely proves they are judging as followers, as "philosophers." But why not? These so-called fantasies are at home here. Any Philosophical Society is a Society of virtuous, generous people, subordinating political motives to the general good.

We have turned our back on the real world. But ignoring the world does not mean conquering it.

In real society there is a job to do, a position to keep. A being only has social value to the extent that he *exists*. And this is why [human] nature is bad, always falling short of where it should be, never placed at the true point of view from which one could do good effortlessly. It is always weak, negative, and egocentric. Hence the necessity to keep rising above it, the necessity of self-restraint, of obeying better and wiser people, accepting suffering, making an effort, and accomplishing one's duty.

There is no such thing here [in the Philosophical Society]. Producing, creating, doing is not the question, but rather talking, asserting—which require neither strength nor effort. To talk according to what one is or wishes to be— proof in real life that one has a heart—would appear as duplicity and ambition in the Society's life.

On the other hand, though there is no question of producing, one shares what has been acquired. What is considered acquired is what remains of the truth after discussion. This is what in politics we call *the law*. This will become the basis of the social contract. The law is the opposite of custom: it is written first, custom, afterwards. The law, a product of the intellect, precedes life, whereas custom is life itself, informing and progressing, recorded only when it begins to weaken.

The Social truth puts man in a position of innocence, but this is the truth of reduction, which is opposed to the truth of progress, conquest, and creation, opposed to the truth of faith, as nothingness is opposed to existence.

Thus there is no faith here inasmuch as it requires sacrifice, no privileges inasmuch as they presuppose duties, no moral authority inasmuch as it implies real superiority.

We can see Jean-Jacques's citizen is not a fantasy.

A Philosophical Society, an entirely intellectual city of equals and ideas, this is for Rousseau and the philosophers of his time the only regular form of human society.

Indeed, Rousseau presents this society founded on individual will as the initial fact, anterior to justice and any doctrine. This is the primacy of social action over thought, thought only being derived from function.

It is the dream of an ideal city of sheer beauty. This city offers the most alluring purpose, "happiness";[4] the easiest means, freedom, in La Boétie's meaning of emancipation—emancipation from all authority, adds Rousseau; the noblest motive, "good"; and lastly this city offers the vastest social justification, since this happiness, this freedom, this good will be those of "man himself" such as every man desires them once he is enlightened. Thus the philosophical "patriotism" of 1789 is taken for a goal. Today, keeping the same meaning, we have improved on the expression, calling it "humanitarianism."[5]

Now, since society is virtually universal, the result is that it can only consider its members in a single way, as man in general. It can only take into account what its members have in common with all men. And this is only two points: on one hand, the perfected model of humanity, and on the other, primitive nature, preservation and reproduction. Angel and beast; in this way we can say without absurdity that all men resemble one another. They are equal, alike, only in these ways.

Which of these two conceptions will be imposed on [Rousseau's] society? Primitive nature, for the single reason that it confuses the two and considers men as *presently* equal: for the other equality is to be gained, it is not of this world. Primitive nature denies personal effort, deifies nature, establishes the relative and the contingent as absolutes. It considers men free by right, but freedom by right is appropriate only for a being who is considered finished and complete; it cannot be appropriate for a doctrine of endeavor and sacrifice.

And pushed to this limit, only the *Contract* contains the doctrine. The form implies the content. . . .

How can this virtuality become reality? By strictly intellectual work: "the Enlightenment," and certainly not by a real and moral task, endeavor, internal struggle. One "becomes aware" of this freedom, this equality, whereas Christian freedom or equality is not a starting point but an arrival point that is gained and deserved by one's works. A freedom or equality that only intellectual work can lead to is therefore necessarily negative. Political freedom, strictly speaking, is a social fiction.

And this "sovereign," as Rousseau calls the people of this perfect democracy, does it not seem as though it comes out of a fairy tale? The people keep all the powers, unlimited, for themselves and wield them alone, delegating none to anyone. Did Rousseau suspect, while writing his idyllic constitution, that one day people would want to accomplish it, and could he see his sweet dream ending in a bloody nightmare in a terrified France?

And yet the ideal Rousseau conceived of, a free people *par excellence*, direct democracy, does not cease to attract democrats of all sorts as if by an invincible fascination: fatally they are drawn to it and fall for it. The oracle is there. The voice of principles speaks there and only there.

But let's take a closer look. Rousseau's criticism of collective thinking or the general will is as little understood as it is profound. There is an a priori will of the people: principles. If the actual people, the "multitude," agree to these principles, this is fine. Otherwise it is the people who are wrong and there will be someone present to straighten them out—the people of the "Societies," who, thanks to their organization, are always on the right path. And even though there might be ten in this little city against a thousand, the "Society's" voice is indeed the people's voice. No one speaks more often about the people's will, and no one inquires less about it.[6]

One can imagine an absolute right of the majority that is only a relative absolute. But such is not the idea of the people's survival as it appears by 1789: there is a being who is good, virtuous, just, and wise *par excellence*, the people. The people are God. Not as a majority making decisions against a minority, but speaking absolutely.

For the regime's doctrinaires, philosophers or politicians from Rousseau and Mably to Brissot and Robespierre, the real people is an ideal being. The general will, civic will, transcends the current will of the greatest number, as grace rules over nature in Christian life. Rousseau said so: the general will—the real people—only exists virtually in the conscience or imagination of "free men," "patriots," what we would call today "conscious citizens."

Hence the idea of a *legitimate people*—which is very similar to that of a legitimate prince. On one hand there is a man, quite identical to other men, but often very inferior to them, and on the other hand a crowd, like other crowds, but often much less numerous and more contemptible. But there is an external characteristic to this man or this crowd that makes them *king* or *people*. For the former it is heredity. What is the talisman for the latter? The number? Nonsense! An "empirical means," says Jean-Jacques. As if we could say the king is the most intelligent man in his realm. The general will has other characteristics: *principles*, which is the will consistent with the principles. Here we have the real people. The rest is merely "a few petty details." Nothing is more amusing than this doctrine among the devout defenders of the people, for they are not any more willing to give up the law of quantity than the legitimists[7] are willing to give up the law of quality. . . .

But then actual history comes along and has no trouble revealing the fraud.

The fact is this: the action of the Societies on the people was not thought, but force. Such was the real truth before which the Social truth vanished like a phantom.

The colossal force of the regime that was to triumph in 1793 was none other than the force of inertia guided by the secret Societies' machination. The followers were only vaguely aware of it. Not because they understood. They were the last to understand, for entering the machine rid them of their subtle ability to discriminate, this sense of reality that rectifies the geometrical minds of ordinary men and prevents them from making foolish judgments of a logical order.

It was not the light of truth that philosophic Masonry represented; it was blind pressure on the people kept in ignorance by informed insiders.

The façade of truth was only a lie.

Thus a new conception of society was born that was to create a tremendous upheaval in human society. . . .

CHAPTER 3: THE PHILOSOPHICAL THEORY, THE PHASES OF THE SYSTEM

4. The Development of the Enlightenment

Happiness, reason, nature are words of very respectable meaning in the mouth of a High Court president [Montesquieu] speaking in the Bordeaux Parliament. Montesquieu used these words only for very noble ideas and instincts. No doubt the bond with the principles of Christianity had been broken. The mirage of the golden age had appeared on the horizon. It would come, naturally, through human science and morality all by themselves. Paradise had descended from heaven to earth, which made this philosophy no longer Christian, but it still kept this paradise so remote that it fooled many Christians.

Paradise remained well above the masses. Before emancipating the people, one had to educate them. Before proclaiming the Republic, its citizens had to be virtuous. Before laying the reins on everyone's neck, this would have to be done to Montesquieu. Only then would the Republic be possible.

The next generation of philosophers, economists, men of letters, or scientists had less ability. They came later, after the last glimmer of the age of Louis XIV had been extinguished. Manners and morals became corrupt, character less noble, magnanimous souls rare, all of which lowered ideals proportionately. The golden age was drawing nearer: between these men and the masses the objective appeared less distant.

These men no longer attacked manners and morals, but only errors, habits, prejudices: once the peasants learned to cultivate the land, and tradesmen understood the theory of free trade, people would be ready for freedom and happy. With a few good regulations and good education in the countryside, the golden age would arrive. And agricultural Societies full of lawyers were founded: the ministers made ordinances that were treatises.

After the economists came the politicians. This was the third transposition, that of the politicians. The level dropped still another degree. We descended from Turgot to Dupont de Nemours, much more a politician than an economist, and from Mirabeau the Elder to his son. The new generation was in more of a hurry.

In their eyes, evil did not come from man's corruption, nor even his ignorance, but only from the laws and the regimes. With privileges abolished, the
people's sovereignty established, and political equality achieved, mankind would
be happy. Such as people were already—not in a hundred years as the moralists
said, nor in ten according to the economists, but right now—they were good,
wise, and ready for freedom. Let the bonds that hamper them be broken, and
you would see the people achieve their own happiness themselves. This time we
were nearing the golden age.

For in this new system, evil was no longer anything but a misunderstanding.

Such were the three main phases of the "Development of the Enlightenment"
in the eighteenth century.

We can see the law of this Development. The doctrines are different, but
they proceed from the same principle, and the principle always agrees with the
last doctrine to come along, against the others. For each doctrine establishes the
triumph of a freedom over the preceding order, but at the same time it founds a
dogma opposing the next doctrine to come.

Montesquieu and his generation established the primacy of the decent man
(*"l'honnête homme"*) over religion. But in the realm that a refined, noble nature
like his was dreaming of, a citizen of Mirabeau's type would have felt quite
confined.

Mirabeau the Elder established the primacy of the useful man (*"l'homme
utile"*) over the law of honor and unbiased morals.

Mirabeau the Son established the primacy of man in general over any law of
religion, morals, or special interest. Man's will was [considered] good in itself.

This was the proposed theme: man, like all natural beings, is finished, complete, and consequently worthy and capable of happiness, i.e. of harmony between
his desires and his condition. His reason is sufficient, his nature good. There is
no harm in developing this argument in itself, provided it remains an ideal. But
one always makes the same mistake: it is transposed into reality, the game is taken
seriously.

If there is evil in the human world, it is because man considers himself an
imperfect being, opposes the moral law to the natural one, and submits to its
dogmas and discipline. To destroy this evil, all this dogma, discipline, authority,
and prejudice must be destroyed: *laissez faire, laissez passer* (do not interfere,
allow everything), and everything will be fine.

The first theorist of *laissez faire* (non-interference) is Fénelon, in quietism.
This is the rationalists' perpetual argument that mystical theology agrees with
them, because it rejects dogma and rules and lets grace operate. (*"Laissez faire*

la grâce.")

Then there is the whole school of moralists, atheistic but respectable, from Montesquieu to Turgot. They are unaware of grace, of the necessity for supernatural assistance. One arrives at perfection by natural means, but one is not there yet. Nature, for them, is something very noble. Do not interfere with decent people. *Laissez faire,* but [it is] only the decent people [that can be ignored]. [The others] need moral and intellectual training.

Applied to political economics, this is free trade, the freedom of commerce and work: do not interfere with competition. *Laissez faire,* and a commercial balance will be established. Do not interfere with greed. *Laissez faire.* Do not interfere with shoddy goods. *Laissez faire.* No more regulations, Colbert's[8] successors were told. The nature of things [will take care of itself].

Lastly, applied to politics, this is the government of citizens by themselves: no more authority. Let the people rule (*laissez faire*) and everything will be fine.

This is theoretical, radical liberalism, based on an absolute idea of the perfection of nature, and not on actual reality. And here we have the wellspring of the Development of the Enlightenment.

The doctrine is strictly negative: eliminate dogma in morals, eliminate morals in questions of personal interest, eliminate personal interest in politics. Let the people rule, and they will not harm themselves.

Hence the point of departure for the whole philosophy of the Enlightenment: *the goodness of human nature.*[9] There is only one sort of politics that can be made for such people. Public opinion can only develop in one direction, and the politics will be defined by a simple expression, which must not be reserved for the economics school alone: *laissez faire, laissez passer,* a formula that sums up the philosophers' method, whether it be in the domain of ethics, political economics, or plain politics.

Such is the "Development of the Enlightenment." We see it has led us from the most exalted doctrine to the law of numbers, "this empirical means," as Jean-Jacques says (*Lettres de la Montagne*).

But shall we stop here at the morality and the vulgar ideal, individualistic *par excellence,* that reduces the role of authority to its smallest portion and grants the most freedom possible to the most individuals possible, to the great "every man for himself" of 1789?

This is where the difference indicated above will appear in all its force, the difference between actual freedoms, gained as privileges, and freedom on principle, claimed as a right; the difference between artificial union based on common principles, theories, and opinion, and real, profound union based on a community of interests and real needs; the difference between the order of things established by the merchants and farmers associated in 1688, and the order that our philosophers thought they were founding in 1789, which lasted six months. Though the appearances, the letter, were exactly the same, the means and the spirit had nothing in common, and it is by the effects that one judges.

The letter of the law may be the same: Malouet and Mounier really believed, in 1789, that they were founding an English regime, according to Young's naive conception, but the spirit that was founding it was not the same.

Indeed, if a movement is founded on facts, if a union is founded on profound and durable material needs and interests, the resulting regime will be the strongest and its freedom the soundest that exists, for it will be founded on the interest and firm will of the greatest number.

For the same reason, this [form of union] is the rarest case, the most difficult to achieve: actual equality and a community of interests are rare in a great people. But in this case the principle of authority will be maintained and will sanction the conquest of force, which will be founded on an absolute principle: not only will this force not destroy the principle of authority, but it will request the consecration that the principle of authority does not deny to true, holy, and living force.

On the contrary, if the movement is founded on a general principle, on right and union, the more generous, i.e. general, the opinion is, the more it will adhere to a principle, and the frailer the regime will be. This phase will not be any more definitive than the others.

For the principle will turn against the regime: why indeed should one stop here? There exist reasons and natures inferior to this level. Why shouldn't they too be good, worthy of freedom and happiness? Because they are not the greatest number? But the number matters as little as the quality of morality. The new doctrine will no doubt have the number against it, but the very right that established the freedom of the number will be for it. The mob will curse the new philosophers, but as the priests used to curse their predecessors: in the name of morality and higher principles. Now, the mob has overturned these morals and principles, hypothetically, since we are under the influence of the Enlightenment, which only subsists by destruction, not of a certain faith, but of every faith, in the reign of freedom, which is opposed to any sort of dogma. The priests were consistent: they had their principle for them. But the mob is no longer consistent: their principle has turned against them. The mob has rejected the old principle and lost the new one.

Thus, founded on fact and sanctioned by authority, the parliamentary regime is the most stable of all. Founded on the principle of popular right, it is only an arbitrary and temporary phase in the indefinite development of Enlightenment.

So where are we headed? What is this new morality, inferior to nature, inferior to religion? It is Rousseau's morality. And what are these new politics? Again, it is Rousseau who gives us the principle, in his *Social Contract.* It is the doctrine of the general will, the will of "the people per se," opposed to the will of the greatest number, the "actual people." And was this doctrine applied? No doubt, by the one [Rousseau] who said there was only one free man in France: himself.

Rousseau had understood that the principle of philosophy led beyond liberalism, that the law of the greatest number, established in the name of an absolute principle, ceased to be an absolute law and became a special case. He had distinguished between the general will, always right, and the will of the greatest number, which can go astray; between absolute freedom, the only legitimate one, and relative freedom—"We shall force them to be free!"—which applies to those people whose traditions, habits, any sort of bond, might still make them superior to negative morality.[10]

And Rousseau was not the only one: the Illuminists would come after him.

But no one believed him. The obvious fact was denied. Rousseau was called crazy and Robespierre a monster. The Illuminists were denied, because no one understood how such a power could be established. No one believed him, and yet the principle of the evolution of opinion had not changed. The principle was still the same, after as well as before this intermediate phase of real, vulgar morality, set halfway between the highest morality and nothingness. But the principle no longer acted in the same conditions. Before this phase, it was drawing closer to the law of the greatest number: the general will and the will of the greatest number coincided. Thus it could hide itself behind this general will used as an excuse. It gave itself a *de facto* excuse, which was only an excuse—since the force of the movement was in the principle —but a necessary excuse, for it could not reveal itself in the open. Further on, however, this excuse would be lacking. So how would the principle sustain itself?

First, by this doctrine of the general will that incensed the philosophers against Rousseau, and later roused France against the Jacobins, the personification of the people per se.

Then, by the fact, the organization, certain processes that . . . already existed in the first period, but were concealed by the fiction of the general will. In the second period they appeared in the open: Free-Masonry and Illuminism, lodges and clubs.

All of this is very banal, satisfactory as far as ideas are concerned. Why were people not content with that? The reason is that, though one can see the logical relationship between the systems and how the latter can fight one another even though they start from the same principle and the same spirit, one cannot imagine the alliance between men. How can men who hold with the mind alone be *united* with those who adhere only to such or such a system? This perpetual criticism of Rousseau's followers is strangely contradictory: improvident weakness, clumsy precision. *Society*, that is what is lacking in the ordinary facts. Alongside the ideas there is a social state, with some established relationships among men, such that union is possible.

The process is the same, in all the periods of the Revolution and for all the philosophical, political, and social problems. And the same situation gives rise to the same quarrels between yesterday's ringleaders and today's victors. We can see all of them are right. Ungrateful individuals, say the former; if we were wrong, why didn't you say so in the past? Blind men, reply the latter, we are doing what you did: we are applying your method. It is the method and not us that you should be attacking.

The first ones are right: former heroes, praised to the heavens by their future enemies, they have done nothing since then that justifies the outrages they are accused of. But while the first are consistent, the second are logical, for nothing in the former principles was opposed to the later excesses. And it is the principle they are defending, not its application to such or such a doctrine, or "constitution." It is on this principle that union is founded; the principle is its bond. The principle is that the *present* decision has absolute value.

It does not matter where each man stops in [his] development of Enlightenment. If he stops, it is not because of a principle, but because of his individual temperament, an external cause: belief, interest, traveler's fatigue. In a word, he stops at individual interest. The question is not to know where one is, but what one's propensity is, and where one is headed. And that is why a suspect is never asked for a profession of faith, but whether or not he is a patriot and has "pure" principles.

Thus Union is not a sheer lie. It is real, legitimate in a way, and strong, but on one condition: that we remain on an abstract, intellectual plane, for it is founded only on the principle and perishes by being achieved. Acts, effects, consequences shatter it.

Hence in the world of Enlightenment and freedom of thought, the realists, the people of government, the progressives, the doctrinaires will always be united while the conservatives, the moderates, will be divided. The former will be united by the cement of the principle, the latter divided by the fermentation of discord in its application and in its reality. In the Revolutionary order, the advantage is thus ensured in advance for the violent and the theorists, over the realists and the moderates.

Another consequence is that the "development of Enlightenment," as the name itself indicates, will be less a real development than an intellectual one. It is less a question of living than of thinking. The history of the Revolution gives some striking examples of this. The Revolutionary constitutions were all voted into law, but never enforced. Why? Because they were all born of logic, intellectual necessity, more than of real necessity. They were the product of thinkers, and not the result of the people's instinct. The people judge reforms by making use of them, logicians by thinking about them. And in the intellectual domain, an idea need only find its formula to lose its power.

Thus there was a change not in the principles but in the processes. We evolve from Enlightenment to Illuminism, from positive to negative human morality, from associations to Societies, from the theory of the greatest number to the theory of the general will.

Can this will be established? It has God and men, law and force, against it, and outside the highest authority and the will of the greatest number, outside God and men, what else is there? What is doctrine, morality, or will that is established against both of them? And yet it is established, it triumphs over the number. The obvious fact was denied, because it could not be comprehended. But it can be explained, as we shall see farther on, when we speak of *organization*.[11]

It is of little importance here, though, as it is the ideas alone that interest us. Taking one of the propositions of eighteenth-century philosophy, we have briefly illustrated the various transpositions of the theme, the main phases of the "development of Enlightenment." Again, it is the law of this development that we wish to emphasize, and not the Enlightenment itself, which is already well-known.

ENDNOTES

[1] Translator's note: This expression designates a state of mankind in which people would be governed by reason alone.

[2] Translator's note: For Cochin there are three categories of ideas: the idea as describing reality, which he calls the *idée-type*, the idea that most people entertain about reality, which he calls the common idea, and lastly the Masonic notion, the idea as mere word.

[3] A sociological law, not a psychological one.

[4] cf. D'Holbach

[5] No fatherland when there is a master, says La Harpe (cf., I think, Rivarol's *Mémoires*, a speech by La Harpe in 1790).

[6] Cf. "Rousseau's Mysticism" in *Philosophical Societies and Democracy*, p. 27.

[7] Translator's note: The legitimists are the monarchists.

[8] Translator's note: Colbert held various strategic positions under Louis XIV, including Minister of Finance. He favored the development of commerce and industry.

[9] Did the philosophers think man was good? Of course not: they were not stupider than others, and much more cynical. But they nevertheless reasoned from this hypothesis, because they were reasoning for Philosophical Societies. They reasoned out of prejudice, and openly, as utopians and not as men responsible for souls. Jean-Jacques writes "for a people of gods."

[10] Morality inferior [and subservient] to selfishness; activity inferior [and subservient] to individual interest, rejecting vice, not because of virtue, but out of sheer laziness! Rousseau admits it in his first letter to Malesherbes (Montmorency, January 4, 1762): What is the cause of his disgust for Society? It is, he says, an indomitable spirit of freedom. "It is certain this spirit of freedom comes less to me from pride than from laziness. But this laziness is incredible: everything scares it away, the least duties of private life are unbearable to it. A word to utter, a visit to pay, the moment they become necessary, are torture to me . . . In a word, the kind of happiness I need is not so much to do what I want as not to do what I do not want." Second letter, January 12, 1762: "A lazy soul that is frightened at [the idea of] paying attention to anything, and an eager temperament, excessively testy and sensitive, don't seem able to be combined in the same character, and yet these two contrasts are the basis of mine."

[11] This is the object of the following part: Freedom.

PART TWO:
FREEDOM OR SOCIALIZED
WILL, 1789–1793

CHAPTER 1: THE ORGANIZATION

I. THE FACT, THE ENSLAVEMENT OF THE MANY

The Machine

We have reached the second stage of the development of the Enlightenment, the time when philosophy becomes politics, the lodge a club, and the philosopher a citizen.

And we observe the conquest of lay opinion by "philosophism,"[1] the conquest of the real city by the city of the clouds. Rousseau's ideal architecture starts being constructed. Let us recall its principle:

The sovereign power belongs to the people, but they cannot delegate it; they keep it for themselves, to wield it constantly. It is not in the assemblies elected by the people, not even in the primary assemblies [of voters]; it is in the standing popular Societies. In other words, it lies in the crowd, always standing, always ready to chastise or revoke its delegates.

It is pure democracy, or direct democracy as Taine says.

It is egalitarian society in its perfection, just as it is absolute freedom for every citizen.

Common opinion holds that the many reign when equality is established, and it is for this very reason that an egalitarian society is generally presented as the regime of chaos and anarchy, for can the many reign? Is this not diversity and incoherence? [In such a regime] there is no order, no unity, no coherence. There is no authority.

But in a way, this is a mistake.

It is a mistake that comes from paying too much attention to the principle, a mistake excusable before the Revolution, [but] no longer, now that pure democracy has revealed itself in the facts.

Actually, this experience of democracy demonstrates just the opposite of the theory, which expected freedom while fearing incoherence. Experience has proved that democracy's virtue is not freedom, nor is its vice incoherence or variation. Nothing is so uniform nor so regular as the Revolutionary phenomenon. Far from being unpredictable, it is on the contrary perhaps the only type of phenomenon in the social and moral order that is stable enough to permit an effective scientific study, the only one on which human will and calculations have no influence, that enters as an unconscious factor rather than a conscious agent. The phenomena, the development, the spirit and procedures of the philosopher and terrorism are identical from Paris to Odessa, and from Odessa to Teheran and Constantinople. If there is a constant, it is surely this.

Let's have a closer look at this phenomenon:

First, it is obvious that the regime of standing consultation can only be conceived of in the form of "standing Societies of free discussion." [Public] opinion must be "organized," and the people "standing," in order to "speak."

Now, the fact is that speech of this kind cannot be found without a Social network that instigates, receives, channels, and centralizes it. This is the Jacobin Society, the American machine, the English party as it has been constituted for [the past] forty years, our Masonry, our C.G.T.,[2] our trade unions. And this regime is unique in that, theoretically at least, it is only a form, a self-sufficient one that dispenses with any moral content. The *actual, current* will of the collectivity determines and creates the law. Its only discipline is freedom, its only master the collective will, its only dogma the opinion of the day.

Everywhere else there exists a principle of social union that the humblest will can recognize, accept, and call upon, that controls special interests and theoretically opposes selfishness. But here there is no such thing: the goal is everyone's good in the broadest sense of the term, and the means everyone's opinion in its strictest sense.

The general will, it is believed, must be that of the many. [But] such is not the case.

The law *under* this regime expresses rather that against which the many have not rebelled, that which has managed to occur without the many desiring the contrary. The myth of everyone's actual, active will being made manifest to each individual is nothing but a legal fiction, and does not correspond to any reality. What is meant by everyone's will is the will of a few men, shaped, imposed and reigning in certain specific circumstances by the nature of things and the nature of the regime—a definition which would suit the power in the most domineering of authoritarian regimes just as well.

It is never ever true, that in an organized social collectivity, the collective will, expressed and shaped at the center, is the will of the many in the common meaning of the term: the actual, real, positive will of each individual. The more one speaks in the name of the common will, the less it is this will that speaks. The common will here is not what each person wants, but what each lets some others—a very small number of people—want.

The fact that democracy is actually, and even legally, the reign of a minority, just like the old political regimes, is scarcely contested by anyone today. And this is already considerable progress over the political schools of the mid-nineteenth century that believed in the reign of the many, as witnessed by their constant concern for saving the minorities. The oppression of minorities is the basis and conclusion of the criticism formulated by people such as Tocqueville.

The fact that Revolutionary democracy subsists is an enigma, for it seems to be a living contradiction. For a society to last it must have unity of direction, but Revolutionary democracy has no men; and it must have unity of opinion, but Revolutionary democracy has no platform.

And yet this type of social form lives and lasts, growing stronger, more threatening and more terrifying.

Then just what is this general will? That is the problem. It is certainly not a new one, and the answers are easy to classify.

The general will is that of the inner circle of a few men, the ringleaders. This is the usual answer, and hence the various judgments made according to one's personal feelings: tyranny, protest the reactionaries; abuse, concede the democrats, theoreticians, and philosophers; victory, proclaim the militants, the victory of the conscious elite over the unconscious minorities. We shall ignore these evaluations and stick to the fact: is it true this elite can be identical to the reigning elite of an authoritarian regime?. . .

Whatever the answer to this question, the aforementioned fact [there is a reigning elite] is not usually contested, but one [still] cannot see what necessary law governs the Social world.

Rather than seeking personal causes—such as abuse, tyranny, despotism, plotting, machination, intrigue—"a handful of ringleaders have confiscated the will of everyone for their own benefit"—one should observe the laws of nature. In a word, the Jacobins are not men; they are the products of a Social law, the Philosophical Societies' law, which acts in the same way and with the same effect on everyone, an effect which varies first according to temperaments: brutal with Danton, sly with Robespierre, vile with Barrère.

In the political discussion clubs as in the Philosophical Societies, the same Social reactions will occur, eliminating and grouping, then finally bringing about this unexpected dual result: the Social body will spontaneously present a *discipline* and a *cohesion* that mindful intelligence would have been incapable of creating.

In its essence and principle this Work is unconscious, of a strictly Social nature. The law of reduction in both of its forms, *selection* and *training*, remains a Social fact that every one of its followers is unaware of.

With the frequency of meetings and discussions a movement will begin amidst the passive crowd whose inertia has gradually been contained by a few active, agitating units who will take control of this inertia.

Among these people will emerge new types of men, [including] the agent of the Revolution, the lodge secretary who makes his condition a *royal art*, the art of electoral manifestations. Let's follow the movement.

1. Unity of Direction: The Principle of Predetermined Decisions

Of course, all the members are not equally diligent, active, zealous, and suited for the task. A spontaneous selection is made in favor of those temperaments more gifted for the game in question. Out of one hundred registered members, fewer than five are effective, and these are the masters of the Society. They are the ones who choose the new members, appoint the board of directors, make the motions, guide the voting—smoothly, without affecting the principle, without reproaches from the others, for the absent ones are supposed to agree. And are there not a hundred honest ways to get rid of a troublemaker? It requires just a bit of mutual agreement and a few accomplices to make life hard for him and dissuade him from attending meetings. The worst an isolated, independent person can do is withdraw [voluntarily] in a dignified manner. If he insists, moreover, he is "weeded out" by vote: it is well-known that purging by ballot was frequent after every political crisis in the heyday of the Societies from 1780 to1795.

As an example we can take the literary Society of Rennes, which assembled most of the ringleaders of the Third Estate in 1789 and played a large role with its modest title of "reading room." Its statutes can be summed up in two words: a Society of equals, in which everything is determined by vote. A board of ten commissioners was elected every two years to determine the agenda and the dates for the meetings, and to manage the budget. Official assemblies took place four times a year. Correspondence and affiliations were maintained. Nothing was more perfectly democratic nor more banal than its regulations. They were the same for all the Philosophical Societies whatever their purpose: science or politics, charity or pleasure.

But this body was especially eager and active. The literary Society, or at least a portion of its members, was preoccupied with philosophy and patriotism—and one knows what those words meant in 1789—with the consequent result which common sense could foresee. This apparently innocuous machine, innocuous even from the start and as it would have remained in the hands of a few peaceful beings, became a formidable war machine, for it had the two necessary qualities: it was easy to control and it was united.

First, it was easy to control. Theoretically, it was composed of one hundred members. One hundred and one paid their dues in 1788, eighty-nine the following year. But it was only managed by the active members, of which there were not more than twenty on average, despite the statutes which set the quorum at thirty. These were the ones who chose the new members, thus shifting the majority at will. These were the ones who appointed the board, made the motions, controlled the votes—and they voted all the time about everything—for they held in their hands this marvelous instrument: the vote, which is the decree of the sovereign people.

This was the internal regime of all Philosophical Societies, Societies of equals, from that of the Holy Sacrament in 1650 to the Grand Lodge of France in 1780, from the Jacobin Society to Mr. Chamberlain's caucus. Everywhere it had the same effect: the formation of what our Masons call an *inner order*, and the English politicians call *inner circles*, i.e. a small Society acting in the midst of a larger one, secretly guiding the voting by the thousand "parallel" means available to the *gang* against the *crowd*: predetermined agendas and motions, hired clappers, imperceptible purges, surprise balloting, etc. The common characteristic of these means is that they are not perceived. The American professionals aptly call this the operation of the machine.[3] Whether it is a learned Society, or any Society—an order or a lodge as our Masons would call it—the machine always ends by putting the actual power in the hands of a hierarchy of *wire-pullers*, as the secretaries of the local Societies in Birmingham are called, who in turn take their orders from a "center" composed of a few individuals, such as the central association in London, the Correspondence Committee of the Jacobins in Paris, the center of the Grand Lodge, etc.

These facts are found wherever pure democracy reigns, i.e. wherever public opinion is "organized," fixed and established by discussion and voting in standing Societies.

Thus in the heart of the large Society another smaller, more active and more united one necessarily and naturally takes shape and will have no trouble directing the larger one behind its back. It is composed of the most enthusiastic and least scrupulous members, those who know best how to manipulate voting. Every time the Society meets, these people have [already] met in the morning, contacted their friends, established their plan, given their orders, stirred up the unenthusiastic, brought pressure to bear on the reticent. As they have long been in agreement, they have all the trump cards in their hands. They have subdued the board, removed the troublemakers, set the agenda and the date [for the meeting]. Of course discussion is free, but the risk in this freedom is minimal and the "sovereign's" opposition little to be feared. The "general will" is free—like a locomotive on its tracks.

This process relies on the law of Social practice according to which every official vote is preceded and determined by an unofficial deliberation. Every Social group is uninformed in comparison with the group of initiates, who are more restricted, united, and trained. This can be called the *principle of previous decision*. It includes a whole development of applications which Mr. Ostrogorski has attempted to inventory.[4] They are the "royal art" of our Masons or the "science of electoral manipulations" of the American practitioners, practices that share in common the fact they act upon the "electoral matter" in a mechanical, unconscious way, always influencing men without their realizing it, acting on their passive, inert side dominated by ignorance, indolence, fear, or passion. Hence the terms of *machine*, machinism, attributed to the Society and its techniques by American practitioners, and the term *wire-puller*, attributed to the effective "agents" in the inner circle. These terms could have been used by our first theoreticians of democracy: Rousseau, Diderot, Condorcet.

Thus every egalitarian Society fatally finds itself at one time or another in the hands of a few men. Such is the nature of things. This cannot be called a plot, but a law, what might be called the law of automatic selection: a Society that is the least bit active, by its speech-making and voting alone, is in a state of perpetual purging for the benefit of a certain type of person: the English wire-puller, the American politician, the patriot of 1790; in a word, the machine.

And if the inner circle's secret and anonymous power can and must be established, it is because *the principles* exclude any other personal or public power, from the highest to the lowest, including demagogical authority, which still has an image to defend, be it by money, fear, or the most blatant publicity. This would still be "domination."

2. Discipline: The Principle of Conformity

Easily managed by the action of the inner circle, the Society is also united. This is due to the clause essential to the Social pact—that the decision of the majority on the inside will be admitted by everyone on the outside. This is called conformity. Free in the midst of the Society, the member is "bound" (this is the accepted term) outside of it. It is a question of life or death for the Society, since union is not based on any positive force—the influence of any man, or the power of a doctrine—but rather on the single fact of union. "Voluntary Society," Taine called the clubs—for where is the power of a Society that is known to be disunited?—and this is what distinguishes the [Philosophical] Society from open assemblies. In the latter the dissident might be called an imbecile, but nothing more. In a [Philosophical] Society, on the contrary, whoever maintains his [dissident] opinion outside of it is a traitor, for he breaks the "bloc," he "secedes," he reveals dissent within the group, which deprives it of all value and action in the eyes of outsiders. For its whole force resides in its unanimity.

This is the reason for the *oath*, another characteristic of the Society's life that surprises people unjustly. Every member is obliged to be obedient and discreet by the very fact that he has been admitted. And the guarantee of his loyalty resides in his fear of the group more than in his oaths. Fear more than honor: the Society swears to punish much more than the follower swears to be worthy.

The Society submits wills and reasons to the common decision, not because it is just and legitimate, but because it is common. Thus this *fraternity* is the weightiest of the Society's burdens. Every Society of equals is fraternal, i.e. united to the extreme: a strictly legal bond, need one add, and which in no way diminishes moral isolation, but, on the other hand, eliminates independence.

Hence, lastly, there is the mutual and universal espionage, called "surveillance," the Jacobin's only function and *raison d'être*. Fraternity makes policemen necessary, just as union increases the need for public law, and since all acts emanate from the Society, all the brothers become policemen.

Thus, just as the workings of the inner orders ensure its *unity of direction*, the *discipline* of the Society is based on the great principle of Social interest. This is called "regularity" by American politicians, "conformity" by the English, "patriotism" by the democrats from 1770 to 1794. We can see the importance of this principle and how felicitously it complements the first one [the principle of unity of direction].

The discreet and persistent action of the inner circle puts the majority at the mercy of a few "wire-pullers"—but it is an artificial, haphazard majority. The principle of conformity strengthens this fragile structure. The mass of members, directed unawares by the inner circle, votes too quickly—on a preconcerted motion, with incomplete information—to approve a decree drawn up in advance by the ringleaders. If the voters were free, they would change their minds. But then arise two powerful reasons not to do anything about it. These reasons are always the same, always at hand, and they maintain the isolated individual's belief that the decision he voted for *en masse* was the right one. They are weighty arguments, certain of their effect: *the general will has spoken*. This is the reason of the "*fait accompli*" that imposes itself upon uninitiated or blind, poorly educated, and unorganized majorities that do not agree with one another. *The interest of Union requires it*. This is the argument of Social interest, which, once a vote has been approved, eliminates the problem of recalcitrant minorities.

Hence this famous *rule of secrecy*, which is a law of the regime—and not a plot fomented by a few zealous men. Is it not vain to wonder whether such and such a Society has or does not have a secret? What would the inner circle do if it did not prepare the votes, "pull the wires?" And how can it pull them if the public can see them or even know who is holding them? A Social ringleader can only control a crowd on the condition that he be invisible in its midst. The motion will be proposed by a "citizen." If a motion is to pass, people must believe it to be approved by everyone, and it will only be everyone's if its promoter remains anonymous.

To do away with secrecy would be to kill the Society. For example:

Does one wish to kill the Society's life in 1791? There are two means: requiring the signatures that expose the inner circle's members, or public posting of the [entire] membership list which exposes the [whole] Society.

On the contrary, does one wish to give the Societies the advantage over the public authorities? One forces the authorities, and not the Societies, to sign individually and to deliberate in public.

Does the center of the Society wish to ensure its hegemony over its affiliates? It asks for their membership lists.[5] Having obtained the members' signatures there is no longer any secrecy, nor any machinism possible, since "the troublemakers, knowing they will have to sign, will fear to become known" [to the public].[6] For "when the leaders are known, the revolt stops on the spot."[7] Corresponding by "president or secretary," "corporately," is abuse, says Rewell,[8] for (as Bentabolle observes), "when the people hear a decree signed by the president or the secretary of a Society, they think it is the wish of the whole Society, whereas it is the work of five or six schemers who dominate the Society."[9] "In every Society, it is those who hide behind the scenes who do everything."[10]

We know with what energy the Grand Lodge naturally refused to register its Bulletin with the National Library. No doubt this bulletin was merely an adjusted summary, but made by the majority of the brothers, who nevertheless formed an inner circle with respect to the uninitiated public. Surrendering their bulletin would have been tantamount to giving up the first rampart of the machine.

Even the mother Society of Jacobins, at the height of its power in the spring of 1794, when it was directing the Convention and governing France, had only one fear: that it would be "incorporated"—that it would be "acknowledged" to have authority and actual rights. The same concern exists with our trade unions [nowadays]. We know with what obstinacy they refuse the right to possess: they dread ownership and its obligations as Jacobin Societies dreaded acknowledged authority and its duties.

We can see it is quite useless to wonder whether a Society is secret: every inner circle is secret by its very definition. And every Society is secret inasmuch as it wants to act upon uninitiated opinion as an inner circle does, mechanically. It goes without saying that this secrecy does not have the goal its members lend it in order to excuse it in the eyes of the public. The persecutions of the authorities are feared much less than the clairvoyance of the masses, the pastor's anger feared much less than the suspicion of the flock.

Moreover all degrees of secrecy can be found, and what is ordinary discretion in a small Society becomes a whole apparatus of rites, vows, and formulas in large ones, or may become a new Society which, too, has its inner circle. The machine is built like a feudal castle of the Middle Ages with a double or triple surrounding wall, where the lord had a first rampart against the enemy outside, and a second against his unreliable allies.

But banal or mystical, the *raison d'être* of secrecy does not change. Secrecy is nothing more than the necessary condition and the natural characteristic of machinism and the royal art.

Secrecy is found in all societies which people join to think together, but it is the characteristic resource of the philosophical and intellectual Society *par excellence* that Freemasonry represents.[11]

3. A Society of Societies

It is evident that everything we have just said about a society of individuals is applicable to a *Society of Societies*, an "order" as our Freemasons would call it. The proportions change, but not the relationships, and the propensity is the same.

The Societies of one order are theoretically equal, as the brothers of a Society are equal to one other, but in fact both are unequal. The Societies unite, form a "federation," establish "correspondence." And as soon as they do that, doesn't the richest and most active fatally dominate the others? It gets the news first and has the most able and numerous agents, the most widespread correspondence [or connections], the most effective protection. It would be contrary to its principles for this hegemony to be sanctioned by law, but it is all the better guaranteed in reality. All sorts of minor means are employed. For instance, the main Society will require its affiliates to send it the list of their members, and will do away with any intermediary between itself and the local, provincial Societies. It will jealously supervise the correspondence between individual Societies and will manage to be the only connection to the whole machine, by having all communication pass through itself. Thus is established what is called the "center" in the Society's jargon, i.e. an inner circle, formed within the most powerful of the federated Societies, setting the whole machine into motion. This will be the mother Society. Banal correspondence becomes affiliation. If the Jacobin center was almost instantly established, it was because the Masonic hierarchy supplied the ready-made elements.

This actual power is not established without a struggle.

The local Societies resist the center as the members resist the inner circle. The center is always in a state of latent or open struggle with the "federalism" of the "circumference," but the dissidents always give in, for they are isolated against a single adversary. It took sixty years for the Grand Lodge to be constituted (1720–1780), twenty years for the central association of London (1860–1880), three years for the mother Society of the Rue Saint-Honoré to kill its rivals and purge its "daughters." The "Union of Sharpshooters of the Five Powers," an old and powerful sharpshooters' Society that played a role in 1789, only had its center constituted in 1787.

With the center reigning exclusively, unity is established, and the machine is completed. Such is the mother Society of the Jacobins in 1794, with its 25,000 daughters; the Grand Lodge in 1785, with its 800 lodges; the machine of the American state, with its hundreds of "primaries."

This is surely the most centralized instrument of pressure that exists. The actual power is in the hands of a few irresponsible people. The whole machine is just a hierarchy of *wire-pullers*.

It is also the most comprehensive [instrument], for this strange regime, contrary to ordinary law, has the privilege of gaining strength as it spreads. The more remote and numerous the Societies are, the less they resist the action of the center, for this real action, performed in the name and with the resources of the entire Society, grows with the Society, while the power of individual resistance does not increase. We can say the dream of humanitarian unity, which was born in the Philosophical Societies, in this case at least is not so vain. Such a regime is not cut out to impose itself on only one nation: if ever the government of all mankind is to fall into the same hands, it will be those of Social ringleaders.[12]

It is the strongest instrument, too. The power of the center, in a well-controlled Society, is incalculable, for it supports, directs, and unifies the action of the inner circles in the entire Society. The inner circles depend on this instrument and its support against their followers still more than this instrument depends on the inner circles. Hence the power of its impulses.

It is obeyed without delay. Its proposed decrees are approved by vote and returned unaltered. As an example we can cite the agendas of the central committee: *cut and dried*, the English say, i.e. ready to serve like slices of ham. Such are the Jacobin communications sent out discreetly from the center to their local agents and returned from the circumference with much ado, in the name of the people. Such are the motions imposed by the American machine on the *voting cattle*. Our more unctuous politicians of 1788 used to call this the communication of the center's means to the circumference.

With a mere phone call, the Birmingham caucus sets hundreds of *wire-pullers* into motion, and through them [other] loud, disciplined groups. Within three days, "the nation speaks" throughout the country.

Such is this spirit of public opinion—"electric" vigor as it was called in 1793, galvanized by Social action—that stuns outsiders and arouses the admiration of its initiates. On All Saints' Day [November 1st], 1789, a pamphlet in Brittany naively declared that not a single inhabitant imagined doing away with the privileged orders and obtaining individual suffrage in the Estates General, but by Christmas hundreds of the common people's petitions were clamoring for individual suffrage or death. What was the origin of this sudden discovery that people had been living in shame and slavery for the past thousand years? Why was there this imperious, immediate need for a reform that could not wait a minute longer? Was some enormous crime of the "aristocracy" the cause? No, on the contrary: six months earlier the "generous nobility" had been borne in triumph on the people's shoulders for having resisted the kings.

Such abrupt reversals of attitude are easily explained—as we shall see below— by Social opinion, which is not at all the greater public's opinion, and such abrupt reversals are sufficient in themselves to detect the action of a machine.

The conclusion to these very banal ideas is that in a strictly democratic society, just as in an authoritarian one, there can be no question of freedom for the masses, no actual, real sovereignty. This ideal [of real sovereignty] remains at the end of a society's evolution, [but] in fact, the power is in the hands of the few in the reign of freedom, as it is in the reign of authority. And the masses follow, obey, and believe.

However, what have we added to the two very simple principles acknowledged above? Like the cat in the fable, the Social regime has only one trick. A national order is governed like the humblest Society. Here again the whole movement is reduced to the two essential processes defined above, the *preliminary vote* and the *fait accompli*. It is reduced to the two times when the center acts.

The *first phase* is unofficial and secret. The center prompts the nearest inner circles, which gradually transmit the message all the way out to the circumference, to the last local Societies made up of poorly informed people. The majority offers no resistance to the preliminary decision and the machine's operation.

This is the secret portion of the Work: it goes without saying that the motions, discourses, etc., are prearranged among the initiates within the inner circles. Then they are presented ingenuously and respectfully to the other members, who are free, but whose inertia and ignorance are expected to make them accept these ideas.

The *second phase* is official. Once the vote is cast, conformity is established. The affiliated Societies vote in their majority according to the prompting of the center's agents. Indeed, despite whatever resistance there may have been, the secret prompting and the thousand little means are certain to carry the majority.

The powers come back from the circumference to the center. The center acts again, but openly this time, no longer by means of the inner circles, but rather through the instrument of a Committee. It is a *central Committee* elected according to the inner circles' views and provided with official powers, or elected by virtue of a decision made at the same time by all the Societies and secretly circulated by the center. The Committee has only one argument: it speaks in the name of the general will and commands in the name of Social interest, the highest of authorities. The few potential dissidents yield, not because a few energetic men may have destroyed one of their social habits—were it by criminal action—but because there exists the theory of *absolute freedom*, according to which all the voters are emancipated, i.e. dissociated, isolated, and finally overwhelmed.

The effect of a "Work" of this prolonged, widespread, and centralized type is to produce an opinion that has body and substance, which reveals a continuity, cohesion, and vigor that stuns the enemies of Jacobinism.

Thus anarchy is not disorder: it is just the absence of authority. It is, on the contrary, order itself.

One cannot say the regime of absolute freedom in which the people decide on everything, all the time, is the regime of independence: it is only the absence of obedience. The machine is there to maintain the harshest kind of discipline, for it is unconscious discipline.

The regulating power of the machine is born out of the members' actual inequality, as surely as anarchistic Society is born out of their legal equality. Once freedom is conceived, a Society's members have to be equal, free, and so forth. Once freedom is established, it is fatal that an inner circle should take shape and rule. Wherever freedom reigns, it is the machine that governs—the former exists by the nature of principles, the latter by the nature of things.

As you see, we are not observing a utopia, nor a plot, nor an abuse, but a Social regime as viable and tangible as an authoritarian one or a representative one.

This Social regime has its prototype, the Philosophical Society, just as the regime of divine right has its own, the family. This regime is aptly called *Social*, since the *manner of association*, anarchy, is the only one to play a role here. All other regimes are forms that assume *given* moral realities: the ascendancy of the representative, the prestige of the prince, the nature of the race, the spirit of the doctrine, the presence of some material interest. Here there is nothing to assume other than the existence and form of the voluntary Societies and the inertia or ignorance of their members. There is no consideration of time, race, or milieu; the contracting parties are thinkers in the vaguest, most general meaning of the term. It is the mere reality of the Society, the existence of the voluntary Society alone that produces a whole series of phenomena characteristic of the regime: unification, secrecy, initiation, etc.; the irresponsible character of power, the negative character of freedom.

But I have come back to the starting point: machine and Society, servitude and freedom do not contradict each other, nor exclude each other, for one remains secret, while the other remains theoretical.

II. THE MEANS: IDEAL LIBERTY

We have seen how the machine can act without affecting the Society's principles. Let's go further: the principles serve the machine. Equality and freedom are bound up with its tyranny.

And we shall see by what means the machine reigns, i.e. gains followers and votes.

To understand the means one must consider the process of the inner circle.

One can imagine three sorts of votes:

1. Vote by conviction, loyalty, or reason. Such votes are out of the question since the inner circle is secret by its very definition, and the delegate is the valet of the power: he neither commands nor instructs.
2. Vote by self-interest. Here the machine has the advantage over an authority or parties, for a man has fewer scruples about selling himself to an unscrupulous organization than to a person. Moreover, the machine offers more guarantees: the necessity for the existence of the machine is reassuring to the point of making any formal contract useless.
3. Vote by passive adhesion, because everyone adheres, no one objects, and everyone watches the others, thus following like sheep. Here the fait

accompli triumphs. The inner circle, because of its standing existence and its secrecy, is particularly well equipped to obtain pre-arranged votes.

This process of the *fait accompli* that the machine erects as a system consists in this: whereas an authority presents titles, and a party presents a group of well-known, recognizable politicians, the machine offers votes: 100,000 approvals without any reason [given for them]. Instead of speaking to [public] opinion, the machine makes the opinion speak. The vote is the point of departure, the means, and not the end or goal.

This process may be found in many forms.

The classic form is to *influence and carry* the vote of one body after the other by the example of several similar bodies by unofficial preliminary consultation, and to win over social groups by [allowing them] the right to petition.

Another way to gain approval is to have the masses vote, and by acclamation, which is very favorable to the machine. Indeed, it has been observed[13] that crowds submit almost mechanically to movements of enthusiasm or hatred. There is a chemistry of crowd [reaction] that has nothing to do with reason. And this is what the wire-pullers know in a very objective way, and what the machine is particularly equipped to exploit by means of expressive eloquence, hired clappers dispersed throughout the crowd, and demonstrations. The machine mobilizes all of its followers and all of its resources. . . .

All of this depends on one condition: the degree of inertia must be increased and independence, the sovereign's authority, diminished. And this is what the machine strives to accomplish in all the measures it adopts. They are easy to classify. The idea is to dismember, confuse, and dissolve the mass of voters by any conceivable agitation, while at the same time jumbling ideas and preventing any discussion:

1. Constant, frequent voting. This is the only way to eliminate busy people. Serious decisions are made in the Philosophical Societies after eleven o'clock at night, when family men and everyone else are in bed. Only a few dozen fanatics still remain in the room.
2. Multiple polling places. This is a good way to lower the level, by separating and dispersing the independents. In Paris there were 48 places to vote and in addition Societies were split in half, which meant 96 different polls. And nowadays Paris is five times larger, which would mean 450 to 500 standing discussion rooms (today there are twenty *arrondissements* [administrative districts] and forty or so subdivisions).

3. The vote extended to everyone: foreigners, women, criminals (whereupon shady bars, slums, etc. are created).
4. Or, on the other hand, voting by acclamation, *"en masse,"* to submerge the independents instead of dispersing them as mentioned above.

I shall not dwell on these methods of which an entire catalog could be made. There is a whole technique for the machine's Work. But simply observe the power of these methods. After a certain point it is no longer on inertia, ignorance, or the individual's spirit of imitation that they are founded, but on the natural limits of human forces. For example:

Unless one is omniscient, how can one scorn or even be wary of similar news arriving from several different sources? What is a better guarantee of truth than the concurrence of various testimonies? And the Society, through the operation of its correspondence and inner circles, is able to give an illusion of this guarantee, thereby lending credit and force to any useful lies. Better still (and needless to say), the guarantee of truth comes about automatically without resorting to impossible plotting—just as the Society purchases consciences without resorting to useless perversity or formal contracts—[simply] through the operation and automatic selection of its correspondence. That goes without saying.

As examples we have the Great Fear [of 1789] and the famine, stupendous panics due to unbelievable lies.

Now what is the key to all these methods? What is the argument, the only method? *Freedom!* Continual voting, everyone voting, without regulations, all the time, about everything—why, this is freedom itself! Or rather the Social principle defined. "Freedom," that is the only secret.

The more things there are in question, the more people there are who have neither doctrine nor leader, the more easily the inner circle will operate.

Here we grasp the practical utility of the great principles of 1789 and what was positive and useful in their negative theories. Leaving ideals aside, this rhetoric is meaningful and efficacious, this logic is practical, and the Social groups that directed everything and astonished the world with their unity of action are the ones that applied it. Their whole secret was union in freedom.

Thus the Society is composed of "half-men"[14] who would not survive alone, who survive by relying on one another, or rather by replenishing their deficiencies with forces "drawn from the mass." Each man has two faces, his own and the machine's. Here there is an exchange, an intricate operation that must be understood—the "Social transaction" that attaches the individual to the impersonal machine.

But this is no ordinary contract.

The machine utilizes selfishness in both of its forms: the desire for gain and the fear of loss, *self-interest, fear* with *denunciation* as an incentive, and finally mere *passivity*.

1. Self-interest

Self-interest first: electoral corruption has always existed all over the world.

The country with the most shameful political corruption is indisputably America, as we shall explain presently. From the start, America was delivered into the hands of standing political Societies born of the [Masonic] lodges.

Corruption was [already] advanced far enough in England by the old parliamentary parties, and yet with the arrival of the machine it made such incredible progress that the Parliament, blasé though it was, was obliged to pass the strict but useless law of 1881. The "Caucus" was presented precisely as the great remedy for corruption, which (it was claimed) was rendered impossible by grouping the previously isolated voters and retaining, by loyalty to their Society, those whose self-respect did not save them from temptations.

So what is the origin of this strange coincidence between the discovery of the remedy for the evil and its multiplication?

Mr. Ostrogorski has clearly shown that this so-called remedy is the very cause of the evil, and far from destroying abuse, the machine makes an institution of it, for the machine makes corruption acceptable, giving it an excuse. A man who would have hesitated in the past to sell himself to a candidate or a party that would purchase him for its own interest, no longer hesitates to sell himself to a Society that purchases him for the people's interest. Such a noble cause ennobles everything, including the service one performs for it that makes a virtuous act out of a contemptible one, and the price one receives for it that makes a well-deserved reward out of a bribe. Corruption takes on the appearance of a duty, and many indulgent consciences are fooled.

But we find the same objection here. What right has the machine to speak for the general good? Do not all the parties do so? Why should one believe the machine more than them? The answer is always the same: one believes the machine because it is the spokesman, not of unofficial advisors, like the old leaders, but of the sovereign judge of all good: the people. The machine has consulted the people. Therein lies its strength, its only response to everything and for everything; and it can say it consults the people because it is a Society of equals, strictly speaking.

In the reign of absolute freedom or equality, in a popular Society of 1793, in the assemblies of the Caucus or those of the American machines, one can say all trace of free discussion has vanished. Nevertheless the principles remain undamaged. The more powerful the governing power actually is, the more secretive and more careful it is to deny any liability and place everything in the name of the people. Thus is born spontaneously, without fraud or concurrence, this phantom of the people that hovers over any democracy.

2. Fear

Everything I have said about self-interest applies to *fear*. The two sentiments are equally played upon. Only the moment differs. The spirit of lucre and ambition are used by the machine at its inception, while it is still shy and discreet and has few members, for it has fewer appetites to satisfy and more enemies to treat tactfully.

Later, when it triumphs, fear supplies it with a resource that is more economical and just as certain to keep its troops in line. It is no longer necessary to offer jobs and money unsparingly to those who lack them: it is sufficient to threaten to take them from those who have them. One passes from the reign of corruption to the reign of *Terror*. This is the principle of the so-called "spoils" system in America, and the principle of the Terror of 1793 established during the triumph of the Jacobin machine.

We can see how to account for this apparent contradiction that the Revolutionary party is all the more violent as its power is less contested. The party is not free to maintain itself by corruption and leniency when it is in power, because its followers have then become too numerous and there are no longer enough favors and jobs to satisfy everyone. Terror is all the more necessary as the people are more submissive.[15]

3. Denunciation

The only drawback to this resource is the practical complication. Terror assumes surveillance, and surveillance gives rise to *denunciation*. How does the machine find so many informers, and such reliable and inexpensive ones, when one man or party would find it difficult to buy just a few? It is thanks to the same moral fallacy that allowed the machine to buy so many consciences at its inception: one would not act as an informer for an individual, but one does so for a powerful Society, for the good of the people.

Here we must answer two questions, one very simple, the other difficult. These acts of corruption and denunciation increase, because, thanks to a certain fallacy, the Society finds an excuse for them. Does it not follow:

1. that their effect is less serious where public affairs are concerned?
2. that their perpetrators are really less guilty?

The answer to the first question is easy: from the point of view of public interest, only the act matters, not the intention. The evil is as great, the effect of the sin the same, whether it is due to the casuist's fallacy or the penitent's malice.

But how does one attribute the responsibility? Is it true the machine's informer or minion is less odious than the one from an ordinary party?

No doubt a steadfast conscience will not agree that the noblest ends justify such means. But weak or simple consciences may be partly excused, if the person sincerely believes in the Society's mission and intention. But can he believe in the presence of such maneuvers? This is a moral dilemma. It all depends on the subject's clairvoyance, the Society's reputation, and its agents' tact. Let's stick to the general case.

The most natural and no doubt most frequent transaction is that of the tacit agreement: the informer is not paid immediately, nor the deal confirmed in due form.

4. Inertia

Self-interest and fear still imply a state of mind or some [mental] activity. These resources are used at the start to win over followers, but once the machine is assembled, it has a more convenient resource: the *passivity* of the sovereign people.

Indeed, the strength of this strange regime lies precisely in that which would characterize the weakness of others. This regime manages to take advantage of the force of inertia as other regimes would take advantage of enthusiasm. It relies on its reserve, its particular asset, this *caput mortuum*, the "dead weight" of opinion that it organizes, disciplines, and augments—to heave it in one solid mass at anything that retains the notion of independence.

This regime is partial to lame ducks, people with all sorts of defects, theoreticians, failures, discontents, the dregs of humanity, anyone who cares for nothing and finds his place nowhere. The laziness of some, the stupidity, ignorance, or timidity of others, the material isolation of people who neither know nor understand one another, the moral isolation of people who possess neither faith nor conviction—in a word, inertia—these are the guarantees of Social orthodoxy, prepared to change its doctrine with successive leaders. All of this is what the Revolutionary agents aptly call the dead weight of [public] opinion.

Observe the Society at work, in a neighborhood meeting in England or in one of the people's branches in 1793. Where is its promise of success?

First, there is the absence of educated people of comfortable circumstances, who would make objections to the motions of the machine's personnel, who would argue about the cut-and-dried agendas—and that is why the assemblies are set at all hours of the night in shady bars. In 1793 all the "patriotic" decisions were made after ten o'clock [at night]. And whose decisions were they? . . . Then there is the isolation and timidity of the objectors: a wire-puller's first concern, in England, America, and France, is to assemble a group of clappers, "boys" or "workers," "heelers," the last term indicating their job of following at the heel. They never miss a meeting and understand how to bring the hothead, the "kicker" or "bolter," into line. They are the mustachioed men of our local branches, whose role is to oppress the objectors.

[The promise of the Society's success lies in] the ignorance of the voter, the absence of any feeling or idea that might oppose the machine's suggestions. Hence the preference for foreigners, the haste in naturalizing them, such as the Irish in America, for example. In France many foreigners were used: Carrier had Germans to do the drowning, while others used men from Marseilles, Normandy, Brittany, or the Girondins, to do the dirty work. These people were not disturbed by the moral bonds that would have stopped a fellow countryman.[16]

Indeed, what is necessary for a Society to be perfectly malleable? Is it not good wire-pullers and good voters?

Disintegrate or pulverize the voting matter to make it inert—that is what is meant by the expression *liberate* man.

And it is this isolation that is ostentatiously called his *freedom*. I mean not only material isolation, the absence of any sort of bond or party, but moral isolation, the absence of any idea or feeling that might form a bond. There must not be religious people among the voters, for faith makes one conscious and independent; there must only be isolated, unadulterated reasons. There must not be faith among the wire-pullers either; that encourages domination, playing the apostle or at least the chief, [whereas] the only thing that is sought is activity without any goal, and reason without any character.

Such is the machine. It is, we can see, the natural effect of Social organization, the inevitable reverse side of this handsome medal.

We should add that the machine is necessary, and the Society would perish without it. Indeed, one must not forget the Society possesses none of those supports of a moral order that other regimes have and that imply conscious adhesion: a lord has his right, a representative his influence, a party its platform and its leaders. The Society rejects all of this on principle, in the name of freedom. It establishes standing discussions, absolute equality; it is terrified of "dominators" and avoids platforms. Thus it is inevitable for the unthinking machine to take the place of all these well-known and accepted influences that are no longer desirable.

III. THE CONDITION

Freedom: Individualism

We have seen: *I. The Fact* and *II. The Means*. There remains: *III. The Condition*.

Freedom is the means, but it is also the indispensable condition.

Not only do the principles not oppose the existence of the machine, not only do they serve its tyranny, but they are coercive, and it is *freedom* itself, when it is made an absolute principle—as it is in pure democracy—that makes this servitude necessary.

The cause of freedom is that of the Society.

It is a question of life or death for the Society.

Indeed, let us return to the principle. This "freedom" assumes, as we have seen, that there is standing discussion—no men, no platform. Is this what preserves the dignity and the independence of the citizens? No doubt in a way, but this is precisely what obliges the *machine* to remove what little portion of dignity and independence the *parties* had left them.

Thus freedom is a Social necessity, the absolute condition for exercising Social coercion.

But what, then, is this freedom that is the foundation of the new Social regime? Whether we stick to the idea or take the facts, we arrive at the same definition: the freedom of the Socialized man is *individualism*.

It is very important to distinguish the opposition between the individual, the product of the negative Society, and the *person*, the condition for real society.

Considered in their relationship to the Society, *individuals* are identical. This is the consequence of their training, which is negative in character, resulting from the elimination of the mind's positive forces. An individual is a creature emancipated from all moral authority, any bond of this sort being considered as strictly *voluntary*. There is nothing more to the word, and it is clear that this strictly negative definition does not admit of any difference: individuals are equal.

Such is the essence of Rousseau's citizen. His will is isolated from natural tendencies on one hand, and from moral influence on the other; it is severed by abstraction from the impulse from below and the attraction from above. The will is "emancipated," the philosophers say. In a word, this is the "individual," a new and odd conception imagined by the Philosophical Societies and sanctioned by their Work—for in reality the will never functions in such a void. The notion of *person*, of personal bond, has no place in their world.

Our natural being only takes on a personal value to the extent that it has a moral one. It is only in the dynamic sense that the notion of person can be understood.

In the real world personal autonomy is the last effect of moral development. We are only persons, with personal rights, to varying degrees and with relative meaning. There is only one being who is worthy of absolute rights, the Divine Being. If we appreciate a man for being himself and his personal type emerges, that certainly does not mean he is obeying his nature, but starting from his nature he is heading towards a perfection that I am seeking, too, and whose reflection I find in him. It is through this ideal, and by it, that his nature—which otherwise would be a blind force like the others—takes on a personal value.

The intellectual individualism of Philosophical Societies is a doctrine of containment, of immediate completion. It determines the human being arbitrarily, proclaiming that he has arrived when he is still on the way.

Individuals among themselves are perfectly isolated from one another; no bond results from a formal agreement or contract.

The individual will be defined as a morally isolated, materially federated man.

The bond of union will be impersonal and compulsory *solidarity*.

Thus individual freedom has only a negative character in this conception. It is not an activity that creates, that achieves something, be it at the price of sacrifice. It consists in refusing endeavor, in declaring everything that demands such endeavor unnatural and tyrannical, in rebelling against any moral force or any form of duty or respect. In the same way this freedom ignores natural affinities, the family and human feelings. Theoretically, man is a slave when he does not obey himself alone. Do we not go so far nowadays as to speak of a *child's rights*, the right a child has to be emancipated, i.e. to answer only to himself? To be emancipated from those who are his responsible and natural educators, whose duty and mission it is to help him develop his moral being and shape his personality?

Individualism undermines the family just as it does other social edifices. The dream city will only be made of human atoms directly massed together.

The facts will confirm these inferences. This individualism is the characteristic achievement of the Revolution, the Jacobin spirit, for the rest would have occurred as it did elsewhere without them. From them we get the mania for "emancipating" that is rampant today—emancipating people against their wills—and also the mania for egalitarianism, the foe of any elite, and the passion for leveling that dreams of the same upbringing, education, and function for all, since all are decreed equally capable.

All the Revolutionary laws are laws of emancipation: the law [creating] the departments, the laws against religious congregations, against professional corporations, against public bodies [such as] the Sorbonne and the Parliament, against provincial bodies. It is Revolutionary individualism, we see, that is the first condition for the proper functioning of the machine. [This means] the destruction of every political organization, public body, or professional corporation; the destruction of every faith, common idea, *esprit de corps*, and especially the religious ideal.

Thus the doctrine is in agreement with the political form: one is the soul of the other.

The condition for the voters' docility is that they be divested of any attachment. Only on this condition can passive force come into play: the spirit of imitation that places a man thus divested at the mercy of the first impulse to come along and makes him spin with the wind. For we shall see the final goal is to hold all the voters at the mercy of every proposal without examining it. Material isolation is the condition for this—and especially moral isolation.

What a marvelous means of ensuring isolation and docility this Revolutionary freedom is!

This notion [of freedom] presupposes this organization, and vice versa.

And when they are united, they develop: the form becomes a natural force, the idea becomes fanaticism.

We arrive at the absurdity of having for leaders, not talented revolutionaries, not even spirited demagogues, but lackluster misfits like Collot, Marat, Chalier, Hanriot, or stupid pundits like Petion, Bailly, or Roland.[17]

And for gospel [we get] such wretched phraseology as that found in the columns of the *Moniteur*.[18]

THE RESULTS

Jacobin Orthodoxy

Then a new kind of orthodoxy appears, what English politicians call conformity, Americans regularity, and our Jacobins of 1793 patriotism—an odd conception peculiar to the regime. It is not constant adhesion to a doctrine or a platform—

moral constraints from which the Society declares it will emancipate minds—but rather implicit obedience to all the successive watchwords from the Social center. Adhesion to the organization, and not to the doctrines, is the severest of actual constraints. In England people are enrolled instead of being convinced.

This variable orthodoxy has become the law of the parties in England: the party henceforth takes precedence over the principles. It is the party, rather than the principles, that one adheres to. This is the work of the wire-pullers, who have hired clappers permanently at their disposal and make any independent and henceforth isolated intervention impossible (Ostrogorski, I, p. 206). As the Americans say, "There is no politics in politics." And the watchword for the voters is, "Vote as you are told."

Here is dogmatism of a new type, *conformity*. The old one gives reasons, preaches, harangues, convinces; the new one has only one reason: the general will has spoken. Ostrogorski is correct to emphasize this.

As Durkheim[19] has rightly observed, it is conformity that replaces the old arguments of reason, feeling, or self-interest. Such is the will of the people. This is the new and only argument. No more preaching; people are just asked to vote. A favorable decree is presented—a mere question of skill, the "cut and dried" [technique]—using the argument of the *fait accompli*.

On one hand, indeed, conformity has the rigid appearance of an orthodoxy, which makes the English artisans of the Caucus say, "We now think in battalions," while the Americans say the machine's discipline is stricter than that of the Catholic Church, a comparison which was familiar to the eighteenth-century philosophers and their Jacobin heirs, and which is found in Roustan's *Critiques de Grimm* as frequently as in articles by Desmoulins or Hébert.

But orthodoxy relies on dogma. It implies a creed. The Society has none, since it replaces faith and loyalty precisely by a contract and solidarity. It does not owe its unity to such and such an article in its platform but to surveillance and the argument of solidarity. It has all the rigidity of orthodoxy without faith to found it on. It has outer material unity without inner moral unity, coercion and hatred without appeal and love. The difference can be felt in the very terms that are employed to designate the actual power. In multi-party democracy the terms are already quite degrading. The words "whip" in England or "sheepdog" in our old Estates are good indications. But in the Social regime the terms are still more brutal: the secretaries of the English Societies are "wire-pullers," the American Social organization is the "machine," a term already familiar to our eighteenth-century theoreticians. The sovereign people become "voting cattle" or "electoral matter," and their delegates "merchandise" to be "delivered" on the day agreed upon. [Our vocabulary] evolves from pack to machine, from whip to wires.

These terms can be justified. However degrading it may be, *party* discipline still retains a doctrine, men, and a goal to present to its members' hearts and reason. Obviously these resources are prohibited to the anonymous power of the inner circle and to Social democracy.

Specially organized anarchy—it cannot be durable otherwise—is therefore not disorder. The regime of absolute freedom and equality is on the contrary the most powerful one that can exist, the most extensive, most hierarchical, most stable, and most demanding as well. There is no other regime in which dogma is less discussed, just as there is no other in which the authorities are less elected.

The Social Order of the Revolution Compared to That of the Ancien Régime

The new order only resembles the old one in its apparent, material effects. In all other ways they are opposed and their foundations are not the same. The old regime relies on acknowledged authority; the new one on anonymous power. The old one is the product of men and ideas; the new one of the nature of things. The old one is moral, founded on enthusiasm, fanaticism, or faith, as one likes; the new one is mechanical, founded on inertia.

Loyalty is the natural form of all acquired devotion. The personal, voluntary act is strictly individual and cannot be made reciprocal, and that is why military service has kept this characteristic.

Solidarity,[20] on the contrary, is the natural form of passive service and profits, those which do not apply to our personal being—taxes, for example.

Another aspect of the same fact: whereas loyalty unites, i.e. brings together people who think the same way and have the same faith, solidarity mutualizes,[21] i.e. equalizes the burden by dividing it.

Solidarity makes risks, burdens, profits, advantages reciprocal. There is only one thing that is not made reciprocal—the personal act, the freely consented act, the personal feeling, under penalty of denying it by making a debt or an obligation of it. Reciprocity applies to everything passive in ourselves: profits or losses. Better still, it removes the moral characteristic from everything it touches; a reciprocal burden loses its moral characteristic, [which is the case for] taxes, for example. Will one's charitable gift not lose its moral characteristic the minute it becomes a tax?

Such is, on either hand, the nature of the bond of union. What are its guarantees of solidarity?

In the case of *loyalty*, there is only one guarantee: the strength of the feeling itself. The power of authority is determined by opinion. When respect vanishes, force cannot save it. Respect will last a while by habit, but will collapse at the first breath of wind. "A nation is free as soon as it wishes to be," that is the refrain of all the foes of authority from La Boétie to Desmoulins, and this, it seems to me, is both the honor and the danger of the regime.

How astonished the defenders of the republic, the free order, would be if they knew the monarchy, the tyrannical order, had no material means of maintaining itself! The army in the old days was much more accustomed to waging war on the outside than to maintaining order on the inside. Marseilles, [for instance], had no garrison.

The *Social* bond is of another order.

The theoretical basis of solidarity is what Montesquieu called *conscience, virtue*, the spirit of justice that prompts each man to pay his debt. But I only mention it as a reminder. First, because conscience is the exception: "Virtue is in the minority on the earth," Robespierre replied to Montesquieu. Secondly, because conscience can speak here only if it is the rule. Other people's offenses release me from my obligation. And my obedience without theirs is gratuitous idiocy, a lost cause.

But every debt is something owed, and it is as something owed that solidarity becomes real. It is urgent to watch one's neighbor so as not to have to bear his burden, and easy, in case of fraud, to set off the whole weight of collective resentment against him: the outcry against the selfishness "that thrives on the people's sweat" is always noticed. The motive for this union is *self-interest*, rather than each man's duty; *surveillance*, rather than conscience; coercion and *fear*, rather than enthusiasm and love.

This is what experience proves to us, and this rule was verified to the point of giving its name to one Society's eighteen-month reign: the *Terror*. It can be said that "Terror" is the normal state of *Social* life. It is always by mutual spying and fear that a Society holds together—at least to the extent that this political form is applied to the real world and emerges from its natural domain that is the world of Philosophical Thought.

Terror reigned over France in 1793, but was already reigning over letters at the time when philosophism ... closed the Académie [Française] to "heretics." Before the bloody Terror of 1793, the Republic of letters, from 1765 to 1780, experienced a bloodless Terror whose Committee of Public Safety was the *Encyclopedia* and whose Robespierre was d'Alembert. This bloodless Terror destroyed reputations as the other [later] sliced off heads. Its guillotine was slander, "infamy" as it was called then. . . .

We have seen how the machine establishes an impersonal people: Social solidarity founds an *impersonal* government. Now we shall see in what way and how.

The contractual regime does away with the *State*, since everything is decided among associates. Supporters of solidarity are proud of this. Is the State not the pet aversion of liberal opinion? What a pleasure to show this opinion that so-called Social tyranny [solidarity] begins by killing the tyrant [the State]! This joy, I fear, is premature and a distinction must be made here between the State: 1. as a legal entity, the source of authority and object of loyalty and respect, an actual person under the *ancien régime*; 2. the State that was still a legal entity under another regime (the parliamentary one), which does indeed disappear; and 3. the State as a power of collective coercion that gives us orders in the name of the contract and the general will. This last type of State remains, and, unlike the others, has won public favor.

Now, I do not believe we have gained anything by destroying the first one; on the contrary. The first one is the only guarantee and alleviation of the last one's power; it is the only principle of conscious attachment, the only principle of responsibility.

It is because the State is a *legal entity*, distinct and superior, that one can still criticize it, discuss it, call it to account. And for the same reason the contract is limited. The very real power that aimed to overthrow the State when the power spoke in its own name under the *ancien régime*, and that, as we know, is no longer scarcely anything but platonic under the parliamentary regime since the latter has been speaking in the name of the people, will disappear entirely when it is no longer distinguishable from the people and becomes the people themselves. Can one argue against the State today, as one used to argue against the king?

On the other hand, we now know towards what universal bondage are borne the free people, the "emancipated," as today's philosophers say.

It is a necessary, unavoidable state of bondage. There where the people reign, the people—the participants—are slaves, enslaved in their very freedom to the cause of freedom of thought.

And it has to be so. Opinion could not reign if it were not organized, and it must serve as soon as it is: *no freedom without organization, no freedom with organization.*

Hence this odd result: the disappearance of [public] opinion in demagogic regimes, and these orgies of power among the ruling minorities—for example, in 1793, the reconsideration of the Edict of Nantes, not aimed at two thousand philosophers, but at twenty-five million Catholics. What Louis XIV would ever have done that?

In brief, in the "Social" conception of the State all the social relationships are inverted, all personal freedom is destroyed, even that of the ringleader who must remain invisible.

Words change their meanings. The changeable will of the inner circle is called "Social conformity" and its right "solidarity"; its force is reduced to a process, to focusing the weight of general inertia on every isolated resistance.

It is the decision of others, "the law," that replaces the conviction of each person; it is the interest of others, "the public good," that replaces one's will, and it is the fear of others and surveillance that will determine effort. [Thus] we have, in all the force of the term, government by the foreigner.

And the conclusion was to be the terrifying year of 1793–94.

[Translator's note: Chapter 2 is omitted.]

CHAPTER 3: THE ACTIVE TYPES OF MEN

I. The Machinists

Disintegrating the voting matter and isolating the individuals to make them inorganic (which is called *freedom*), and to make them indifferent and homogeneous (which is called *equality*), nevertheless imposing mutual adherence on them (which is called *fraternity*), in a word reducing them to a docile, perishable magma, such is the effect of machinism.

Thus there can be no question of freedom, real independence, for the masses.

This peculiar conception of freedom makes it reside entirely in a few uncompromising people.

And so there remain these "pure,"[22] uncompromising ones. Are these men free, at least, and the others because of them? That remains to be seen.

What can be said about these leaders, made masters of this powerful machine by slow, undetectable purging? Are they superior men whose worth has made them indispensable to others? Do they represent strength at least?

The public believes so . . . The oppression is too obvious, the little people [in the Societies] too reduced in number and quality, too visibly prompted from the center. Hence the great chorus of Thermidor against the "conspiracy." It resounded, one might say, throughout the century. And just as the history of republican Defense makes the Revolution the work of the people, factual history makes it a plot, the scheme of a few ambitious men—the latter theory as false as the former, I think. The mistake always comes from the same source: one makes a psychological problem of a Social problem. The fraud of machinism is not at the service of personal ambition any more than lying is at the service of the [Masonic] correspondence. These are collective Social facts.

If there is an elite in this regime, it is due to the inertia of everyone and not the superiority of a few. But doesn't this amount to the same thing? Yes, of course, theoretically—or let us say relatively, [but] certainly not in reality. Whether order results from a few men who dominate the rest, or from many who abstain and allow themselves to be dominated, obviously it is not the same thing.

And this law is not only true on the whole, but can be verified even in the details of the selection that produces this elite.

We have seen that just as the ideas of free thought have nothing transcendent, so the people, the automatic product of the Social Work, have none of the eminent qualities that make them leaders of men. They, too, bear the stamp of the machine that produces them. Their qualities are of a special nature that is due neither to the worth of the ideas nor the worth of the person.

It is this type of Social handler that we still have to study.

The Societies are in a continual state of sifting and sorting, mechanical elimination in favor of the same type of people, the best wire-pullers, who are good machinists because they possess perseverance, love of intrigue, unscrupulousness, glibness, etc., and are skillful at increasing the "dead weight" in the Societies. The machine draws its force from the inertia of the unconscious, as the party does from self-interest, and the sect[23] from enthusiasm.

Does this mean the citizen of the new city must forgo thinking and acting in general? Certainly not. He forgoes any personal idea, desire, or attachment; [but] he must have ideas and activity that are impersonal.

Passive when uninitiated, he becomes active when initiated. The machine actually needs a lot of zeal and intelligence, "virtues" and "talents," as the orators of 1789 used to say. The stronger and more precise the cogs are, the more powerful the machine.

But here the machine makes a subtle distinction that only it can make: the intelligence and activity it asks of its members will be as developed as possible, but neutral and impersonal. That is the suitable sort of positive qualities required of the good partner.

[Let's examine] activity first. The work of the inner circles, the service of correspondence, and the management of assemblies require a lot of it. The machine, as its name indicates, is an organization as much as a system. It cannot manage without skilled agents.

But what is this energy of the will as an impersonal power? To understand it properly we must study the new Social type created by the machine, or rather the triple personage:

1. the politician
2. the worshipful master [of the Masonic lodge].
3. the orator.

They are the three kingpins.

1. The politician

And first the American "politician" type, the English wire-puller, the "agent" of Revolutionary Societies, the professional agitator of 1789, Volney or Mangourit, Target or the Knight de Guer.

Let's study this type in its purest form, among those initiated into the last of the secrets.

Nothing is so strange as such a career. On one hand the center's leader, the "boss," as he is called in America, is omnipotent. Holding the cogs of the machine in his hands, he controls [public] opinion. If the Society has credit, he speaks loudly in official bureaus and directs popular assemblies without their realizing it.

No office, electoral or not, civil or military, is obtained without his approval. There is no despot or czar whose power compares with his, since [public] opinion itself can do nothing against him.

And yet this despot remains merely a private individual. This leading man stays backstage. The boss, Mr. Ostrogorski stresses, never assumes any of the offices that he distributes as he pleases. From power he only takes the means to command it. All the rest—titles, honors, popularity even, responsibility, too—is no longer his domain. It is for the persons he has had appointed by either the people or the established government.

This strange moderation is in reality quite natural. The boss cannot do otherwise, and the new republic has nothing to fear from 18 Brumaire. The republic is preserved by this great principle of the Society's practice: the reality and the appearance of power must not be joined in the same hands, and the orders must never [appear to] come from the one who is responsible for them.[24]

Here is the explanation:

In the past a public man needed two types of opposing qualities: enough practical sense, enough experience of men and life—no disparagement intended—to obtain his office, and enough specialized knowledge to perform it well. One can say each of these qualities counterbalances the other and prevents abuse. The ideologue, who is too abstract, lacks the necessary resilience and tact to succeed, while the popular orator or scheming courtier do not always have enough depth to maintain their positions.

But here the machine applies the principle of division of labor, and the two types of talent required of the same man in the old order become two distinct professions in the new one. There is the politician, in the American meaning of the term—or machinist, as we would call the secret Society's agent—and then there is the civil servant, elective or not, of the new republic. The former person will find jobs, and the latter will fill them. This is the alliance of a blind man and a cripple, and we can see its advantages. To the former man, skilled and active but cynical and crude, it gives the reality of power and relieves him of the problems of responsibility and State duties. For the latter, shy and indolent but educated and vain, it ensures titles, jobs, medals, and "honorability," which spares him the difficulties of competition and the anguish of conflict. This is an ingenious transaction between two types of incapable men. It is both a means for them to succeed and a guarantee for the machine's safety, for the machine will have nothing to fear from the official pundit who has too little energy, nor from the omnipotent wire-puller who lacks the necessary "personality" to appear in public. Neither man can do without this transaction, nor be his own master; the activity of one and the credit of the other are impersonal. This [type of] activity has no specific goal; it does not have the incentive of personal ambition. It goes into the [machine's] mass. And [this type of] honor, not attached to a specific person, does not originate in personal talent. It is taken from the [machine's] mass.

The country in which political corruption is most shameless is unquestionably America. It is in America that the type of man we call a politician is revealed in all his brutality. Now, from its beginning, America has been consigned to political Societies born of the [Masonic] lodges. Mr. Ostrogorski has drawn a striking portrait of the [American] politician: the boss, the machinist-in-chief, is a self-made man. He has dynamism and energy, but of the basest quality. He comes from below and has no education beyond the primary level at most—not even the most common eloquence. One boss, for example, the sovereign master of a large city, has a vocabulary of less than three hundred words.[25]

[These men have] no ethics: the politicians are all corrupt. [They have] still fewer ideas or doctrines: that "there are no politics in politics" is the principle of the machine's agents. And in America the chiefs of the two enemy machines, Democratic and Republican, have been known to agree in order to defend their common interest, the Society's regime, against the exasperated masses. Eloquence, manners, honor, knowledge, what would they do with all that? Never will they have to hold office or perform duties.

The politician needs only one skill, the one Mr. Ostrogorski calls the "science of electoral manipulations," the "royal art" of our Freemasons. It is a difficult skill, moreover, and one which is enough to make a career. While quite young, the politician learns its technique, thoroughly studying the machine's mechanism and standard procedures for obtaining votes. Then he ascends through all the ranks of the trade: a mere "boy" first, or "heeler," i.e. the bodyguard of a well-known machinist; then a "repeater" (an electoral agent who votes several times); then a "leader" (a secondary machinist); then a "henchman" (a boss's trusted assistant); and finally a boss himself. In this long career of scheming, he has studied men—but from the machine's point of view, in their ignorance, corruption, and fear; and he has handled ideas—but without seeking anything more in them than clichés for the "stump" or means of publicity. He governs at last, but nothing he does bears his imprint. He does not rule; he crushes others' will, but not to impose his own. He answers to no one, but is not there for his own account. He is omnipotent, but on the condition he is only an instrument, not a man. His will determines everything, but belongs to the machine, without which he would be nothing. He is condemned to remain underground, like the spirit of evil.

He is the master only on the condition he is not his own master; he only wields tyranny for others.

The only passions he can satisfy are negative (i.e. impersonal) ones: vengeance, envy, hatred, or crude orgies. Anything that might enhance them—the delight of attacking one's enemies face to face in one's own name, of spending what one has amassed, of converting all this power into a bit of authority—is denied him.

He is powerful precisely to the extent he practices self-denial. Robespierre is a striking example: what potentate could have allowed all those massacres? He had overwhelming power, and yet he yearned for a particle of authority—a bit of the respect the least of village squires enjoyed among his peasants. But he could not obtain it. He was not the master of his will, not independent. He did not rule over individual wills.

And yet he was still a man, and he desired what every man desires—respect, men's love—and secretly tried to obtain it. But this he was not allowed: nothing is so dramatic, so striking as the scene [of Robespierre] before the supreme Being[26]—[like] Cromwell's struggle before the crown. On that day Cromwell was much higher than a king, as far as his power was concerned. But he was on the opposite slope [from the king], separated by a gulf from that grandeur he could see on his level but which diverged all the more the higher he went. . . . It was by committing crimes that [Robespierre] wanted to make himself loved, centralizing the system of Terror in his hands before bringing peace back to France, breaking the yoke he would be the only one to impose, thus making himself an authority by giving up all his former power.

We see and pity the suffering of those outlawed by the Terror, [but] we do not see the dreadful yoke borne by the terrorists themselves, a moral burden that saved them from material dangers only at the price of an incomparably deeper and more agonizing servitude. Let's take the example of Hérault de Séchelles, who we can say was forced to follow in the Revolution's footsteps until 1794, even though at first he did not agree to any of the great acts of the Revolution except perhaps the princes' rupture with the king. He agreed neither to the abolition of the first two orders [the clergy and the nobility], nor to the fall of the monarchy, nor to the proclamation of the Republic, nor to the death of the king, nor to the coup d'état of May 31, nor to the terrorism, nor to the cult of Robespierre. [But] he accepted it all! He had to give up the very great pride he had in his caste, his pride as a man of letters and a philosopher, his tastes, his pleasures, his comforts—without complaint or merit—to end up guillotined by the machine to which he had sacrificed all of this.

Robespierre had the whole odious aspect of tyranny without having its wretched advantage of at least ensuring the triumph of a will and an intelligence, however contemptible they might be. This tyranny knocks everything down but erects nothing. It is an anonymous, impersonal tyranny. But isn't this Choderlos de Laclos[27] a boss too? His name has only recently been exhumed; yet he held the fate and the government of France in his hands for several months. For a long time he had sought his way, trying and failing everything. He wanted to be a nobleman, [so] he purchased an office and altered his name [to make it sound noble], but people found him pedantic. He was a gallant but boring husband, a poet whose verse was banal, a soldier whose unfortunate fate kept him hanging about the garrison rather than going to war, and an inventor whose ideas were judged unfeasible. Driven by an anxious personality and deceived by his partial talents, more crafty than intelligent, more restless than active, he had failed his life when the world of the Societies offered him a way to a career. He had found his vocation: this failure of a man became the Jacobin Society's secretary of correspondence, which made him the master of France for six months. Then he was purged and dropped back into the crowd, ending up in the Quartermaster Corps.

What we have said about the characteristics of the machinist-in-chief can just as well be applied to the little ones, the least of the wire-pullers.

The machine prefers negative passions—envy and hatred. It adjusts to the others—resentment, ambition, greed, avarice—so long as they remain impersonal: it only forbids that something be taken to be kept, or destroyed to be founded. The machine's agent has the right to steal and loot, but the minute he wants to save something, the machine rejects him, for then the goal of his ambition would be to prepare his future, or, worse still, his family's future. This would be a personal ambition, of "individual interest."

And this is why to all other activities the machine prefers the unsound, feverish, or sterile ones, unfit, by nature and in themselves, for normal life. Only these cannot be but impersonal. [The machine's agent is] a pleasure-seeker who squanders what he steals, and this is the definition of extortion.

2. The Worshipful Master

The politician is only half a man. Reduced to such agents, the machine would be only an energy with neither head nor conscience, a gang of schemers known as such, and possessing few resources as a result. The machine therefore needs a good reputation, "respectability," as the English say, an honorable façade. It asks this of the man who is the politician's counterpart. He is the official pundit, the honorable man of the English Societies, the "worshipful master"[28] of ours, the high-ranking civil servant of Social democracy, what the English call a "figure-head," after the sculpture that used to adorn the bows of sailing ships.

This new type of man is a complement to the politician. The worshipful master is the Society's honor as the politician is the machine's engine. He is made to be shown; one refers to him as one denies the other. He is strict integrity—all affability and liberalism. This is his function; he lives onstage. It is true he never goes into the wings—that would be dangerous. This Ormuzd[29] must be unaware of his Ahriman's[30] maneuvers, to be able to deny them ingenuously.

He denies [the machine's] anonymous calumny, which nevertheless produces its effect; he aids victims, who suffer none the less; he deplores abuse, which continues to exist. If he were better informed, he would at least have scruples, and would lose the confident look and the whiff of honor that give him all his value. But to tell the truth, he does not care to understand, and looks no farther than the explanations he is given. He does not have the resentment against the machine's practices that would have been given him by a feeling of personal offense, for some good fairy seems to keep clearing the road before him of the violence or calumny that strike so many upright people around him. Still better, honors, positions, and popularity seem to befall him naturally. The most venomous pamphlets have nothing but praise to shower on him. So he is indulgent: excesses are unfortunate, he moans. But the people suffer. What a sensitive, generous soul! sings the "opinion" or the "public," as people said in

1789, i.e. the anonymous chorus of the brothers, with Ahriman to set the tune.

Two kinds of men are particularly suited to this role, because they are well removed from the real world. There is the scholar whose works are respected but who is ignorant of the world. The machine will take him into its laboratory to cast him into its politics. He approaches affairs with an entirely new logic that has never been used before. And there is the degenerate gentleman, noble by ancestry and instinct, but with a bourgeois soul, vain about a name whose responsibilities he no longer understands. Only such men can and must suffice for the regime's jobs.

These men can do the job: the Society seeks honorable names but can dispense with the rest—energy, talent, and experience—for the machine is there, silent and active, to supply these. It watches over the naive scholar who without it would attack every windmill and drown in the well. It supports the weak-willed gentleman, astonished by his unsolicited popularity and unforeseen favor—so great is the force of virtue, he thinks, as if his virtue were of a different nature than the mere absence of vice.

These men, and only these, must do the job; the interest of the machine requires it, for if one [the scholar] had judgment and the other [the gentleman] will power, they would be men in the full meaning of the term. They would owe their authority to themselves and not to the one's particular studies, and the other's ancestry. Their credit would be personal, and this is what the machine cannot allow, for then they would be able to dispense with it, [since] their apparent force would be a reality. They would not let themselves be protected or led.

And they yield to temptation and take themselves for what [the machine] makes of them. Pride destroys one: the pride of advising experienced professional people with his plain logic that he takes for conscience because it does not compromise, and for genius because events prove him right. Vanity destroys the other: worshiped in the Societies, flattered to discover a world in which the name can bear the man, he who is so weary of bearing it himself.

But then the scholar's ingenuousness, touching in his laboratory, and the gentleman's unconcern, that had its grace in the idleness of a fine retreat, become a plague and a crime. For neither ingenuousness nor unconcern was made for life and action, and thanks to the machine's care and secret work, these false powers gain influence in the counsels of the prince and ascendancy over the opinion of the common people. For the machine is master of [public] opinion and looks after the glory of its great men. It only presents them in their best light, to their advantage; it keeps them in favor and surrounds them with solicitude. The public is deceived, and these men first of all; it is an unnatural situation in which weak minds are destroyed. It is a time of giddiness and intoxication, unmerited reputations that are tremendous in the morning and ruined in the evening; false wise men, false scholars, false victims, false heroes, a time for lies and dreams. Wasn't Louis XVI's reign a long nightmare of this type?

It is then, in the midst of general destruction, on a ship that is no longer steered, that we see our people discoursing, complimenting one another, presiding over parties, toasting one another. They cannot scoff enough at the dismayed looks of the crew, nor protest indignantly enough at the shipmaster's desperate decisions—until the dreadful day of catastrophe.

When the machine does not need them, it does not kill them; it simply drops them, and then they discover that nature is not good. They learn the true weight of a name without a noble soul and the true price of logic without judgment, for the machine's invisible charm is no longer there to spare them these bitter lessons.

It lets them perish, but when they have died, one crushed by the scorn of his class, the other losing his mind alone in some attic, it remembers them. The Society comes back and seeks out these souls it destroyed, and this will be their last punishment. The Society takes credit for the forgotten glories it made, it makes speeches over their graves, it records their names on its "lists" where they will forever remain what they once were during an hour of weakness and inexperience—a name on a façade, the machine's decoy.

Is this not in its essence, stripped of its accidental variants, the whole story of the Rolands, the Baillys, the Liancourts? It is quite a banal story. It has been related by many historians and related again for many worshipful masters. And if we too refer to it here, it is to show that this criminal weakness, this unforgivable blindness, was not the doing of individuals, as it seems, but of a certain situation that has not been properly understood. Human foolishness and conceit cannot, in themselves, explain such obliviousness. This is so true that other, secret feelings—fear and hatred—have been gratuitously resorted to [as explanations].

But then might these fine men have been real demons of cowardice and hypocrisy? Everything we know about their private lives and their pasts would prove this supposition unfounded.

Isn't it much more natural to blame the situation for that which no literary or psychological sleight-of-hand can fairly attribute to individuals? To acknowledge it is merely the mechanical working of the machine—without any conspiracy or any action prepared in advance with these individuals' [cooperation]—that accounts for this conduct? What destroyed these men was their success, an unnatural success, not due to their merits but to Social notoriety—to their adoption by the machine. Now, this adoption is not an act of personal calculation, and it is not without reason that we speak of the machine and its necessary laws here: every constituted democratic society needs a façade.

These men's conduct only appears monstrous because we do not know the working of the machine, the Social practice. It is the Society that is responsible here, the Society that must be blamed for acts of excessive ferocity or cowardice committed by mediocre, decent, bourgeois men. These men were not to blame, and far from making demons of them, on the contrary one must admit that only near heroic firmness and the acumen of genius could have extricated them.

Only heroism and genius could have resisted the unnatural situation the Society put them in.

Such are the first two roles of the Social comedy, a very monotonous comedy whose characters are few and whose plot is always the same, because it is not a "human" comedy and it unfolds according to fatal laws. These roles are represented in our [Masonic] lodges by the secretary or chancellor and the worshipful master.

3. The Orator

There exists a role, or rather a series of intermediate roles, less passive than the latter and more honest and "enlightened" than the former. It is the role of the orator in the Societies and lodges. The orator is like a link between the machine and the Society. He personifies the association's heart and head, as the others personify its appetites and its conscience. For the Society needs enthusiasm and ideas. The orator's characteristic is to possess the qualities common to all the members to the highest degree, being "patriotic," "enlightened," as people used to say in 1789, possessing "virtues" and "talents" or enlightenment. But these virtues and talents are always impersonal, and it is thus that these vague words take on a new and precise meaning, designating, in a member's mouth, the type of feelings and ideas that can only be found within the Society, and only understood by it. Here again it is the situation and not individual character that explains the acts.

Perhaps no feeling is better known, if not more common, than fanaticism, revolutionary enthusiasm, and none has been judged more diversely. We know what the word designates, [but] we cannot agree on our judgment of the thing.

It does seem that the grandiloquence of their speeches and the rigidity of their principles only left the "patriots" (of 1788, like those of 1794) with the alternative of being either apostles or actors. Otherwise they could not have tackled a whole regime, ostracizing entire classes [of people], posing as official champions of "virtue," "reason," "nature" in general. Whether this means immutable nature, as with the Jacobins of 1783, or, as with those of today, nature varying according to the moment of one's existence; [whether] realistic and dogmatic Jacobinism or an evolutionist's idealism, Helvetius or Mr. Lévy-Bruhl—to guillotine them, it is the same thing, and there is even more satisfaction to be had, it seems to me, to tell oneself that one is guillotined for eternal truth, rather than for a variable truth which is here today and gone tomorrow.

These men are not heroes. For many of them this is easy to prove by their own brothers-in-arms' accusations in the name of these same principles; for others by the recantations of their own careers; and finally, for most of them, by the dearth of talent and will that clashes with the immensity of the principles and the violence of the acts.

So the Revolution's enemies triumph, [for] if these men are not heroes, they are wretched creatures, decapitating so many in the name of virtues they themselves did not possess, in the name of an ideal they betrayed in order to save their own heads. They are theatrical Catons standing before a captive and compliant king; lackeys at the tyrant's boot, sacrificing everything except their own interests to their system; so prodigal with the blood, money, and interests of others and so sparing with their own.

But here the defense regains the advantage, and [though] beaten at the grand finale, manages to preserve these men from dishonor. We know its arguments: first the mediocrity itself that served as the basis for the accusation, because the disarmed Jacobin, so bourgeois in his feelings and tastes, had the qualities of his defects, at least. He was as little a Borgia as a Brutus. Time-honored arguments add support to this first impression: the argument of "generous illusions"—the argument of [being trapped and led astray by the Society's ceaseless] training[31]—and then the lack of material evidence. For the first Revolutionary teams, who still acted under cover of anonymity in the manner of the secret Societies, "veiling their own crimes as a mistake imputed insultingly to the people, [these arguments] obtained and restored a sort of amnesty," (speech by Edme Petit at the national Convention, 28 Fructidor, Year II, *Moniteur*, p. 1479). "Such is the fate of revolutions that crime prepares them, and the people regularize them" (Cambon's speech at the Convention, 1 Brumaire, Year III, *Moniteur*, p. 151).

The vilest terrorists [are accused of] madness. A tender smile [is reserved] for the most ridiculous. The most odious [are declared] monstrosities. For all of them, there is the great argument of Revolutionary solidarity: if one patriot is guilty, they all are—and the whole country was patriotic.

Finally, if gaps remain [in this defense], one resorts to flexible causes impossible to evaluate, such as the reaction's power (which was ineffectual) or its presumed plans. Or one resorts to the people's enthusiasm or, when this was too obviously lacking, their true interest—both of which precisely are to be ascertained.

And each [defender] sticks to his argument. For the sake of peace, they finally even give up quarreling, as there is no way out. They resign themselves to a false yet stable situation, referring to this grandiloquence, these murders, these contradictions, these betrayals, as a hideous, universal evil of the time — some speaking mildly, gravely, impassively, as if it were a question of physical contagion and not moral failing; the others with furious but helpless irony. Little by little, amnesty is tacitly acknowledged, and *de facto* privilege is granted to Revolutionary crimes. It is admitted these crimes are not answerable to ordinary conscience, like common cowardice, contemptible acts, and betrayals—and thus, by a strange contradiction, a sort of moral fatalism appears in history, precisely at the dawn of "self-conscious democracy" and in favor of its first champions. The first acts of the "virile age," the "age of reason" and "humanity," to read its own worshipers, were acts of irresponsible people.

There is a general cause [for these acts]: the explanation is not in the men at all, and not entirely in the principles. One always forgets to include the Society.

Isn't it, again, the working of the machine that will extricate us from this quandary? The point of view is correct, [but] the explanation is not.

The problem is insoluble because one addresses it wrongly and one forgets, when judging the conduct of the "patriot," what this word actually means: that he belongs to a Society. Now, one cannot judge the member's acts without considering the Society. And it is unfair to judge these people as if they were independent individuals, when they act as if they were no longer anything but the unwitting and irresponsible cogs of the machine. They are not Tartufes[32] and hypocrites [by nature, but] the working of the machine makes the trade much more accessible [to them]. Tartufe was a poor devil forced to ply two trades at once, to serve his honor with his right hand and his interest with his left. The Society's man is dispensed from this arduous and perilous plurality of tasks. The machine takes entire charge of it, to the great relief of the individuals.

Let's take a look at the orator at work, the "mover of a proposal" in a critical situation, [such as] Petion or Bailly, or later Robespierre speaking to the Jacobins.

Danton (on September 2, 1792) mounts a club podium and gives a speech "analogous to the circulars," to cite the awful expression already in use around that period. At that time, in the Societies, the orator—eloquent, sensitive, generalizing, and particularly logical—would give a certain direction to the "public mind" against blunderers and traitors who wished to deceive the patriots, or against the treachery of the court, the authority. But this speech would always remain vague and the direction general, without a precise conclusion. No one would be named, no precise act even suggested. No one would be addressed in particular. Nothing would be said that could not be said by an honorable man — dignified, sensitive, calm, respectful of all the freedoms.

It is the outburst of a generous and honest soul, the voice of the nominal Society speaking. But the people have heard it, the anonymous machine acts, giving a precise meaning to these vague declarations. The audience is suitable, selected in advance by the Society to represent the more-or-less "uninitiated." The machine's agents are there with their gang scattered among the crowd. They encourage the crowd's enthusiasm, applauding frantically, emphasizing the allusions. They designate traitors by causing [certain] names to run through the crowd.

With perfect timing, decrees on the same subject and with the desired objective arrive from other clubs, and a rumor, opportunely spread, will provoke an outburst. [Thus] the "people" speak, i.e. the anonymous, disorderly crowd of followers, machine ringleaders, and mere bystanders surrounded and guided by the machine's men. If this occurs in 1788, a perfectly-timed, ready-made petition is signed that will henceforth "bind" the individuals to the party's cause. For how can the consequences be distinguished and rejected? There would be only one way: consult the people again and have them speak. But who is capable of doing this against or even without the Society?

Later, people march to Versailles to fetch the king, or to the Bastille to deliver the victims of despotism, or to the Convention to demand heads and expose the Girondins, or the Abbaye [Prison] to slaughter the captives. The effects vary with the sort of public, the time, etc. The sin is similar whether it emanates from moderate members, reading rooms, an assembly of peasants, or the public of a popular Society.

We have taken our example from the patriotic Societies of the Revolution. [But] obviously all of this is applicable *mutatis mutandis* to any motion to be voted upon in the most bourgeois and peaceful of the patriotic Societies of 1788.

The historians' mistake is to apply the methods and points of view of ordinary history to the history of the Revolution's men, to judge individuals as if they were independent. But one is forgetting in all these existences a common factor, which is the general cause of their downfall as it is of their grandeur: the machine, the Society. Indeed the Society, if one studies not its theoretical principles but its practical conditions of existence, plays a greater role in the lives of its members than their interests or individual passions; it is through the Society that they are so great and so wretched. Men do still have a role, but a secondary one. It is the impersonal Society that plays the main part.

It is the Society's action that made them unwittingly violent—with impunity for some, the brutes and the bandits, [while] others were forced to be cowardly, for one must talk, demonstrate, agitate, or else be suspected. They [later] bowed to the [Napoleonic] Empire, but they were just as much slaves to freedom. And, as Linquet so rightly said, "It is fear that made them so proud." The imperial tyranny [of the Napoleonic period] would not have been possible if the era of freedom had not dissolved the public bodies and crushed character.

The machinist can plead unawareness, the worshipful master ignorance, the orator the cult of principles and ignorance of the facts. The orator is not necessarily informed about what is being prepared: what he says is suggested to him. Robespierre does not speak to the Jacobins himself, and he takes even less a part in what is done.

The people have done everything: where is the orator's crime? Need he know the procedures, the means, the plan, or even who the machinist is?

No doubt it is necessary for him to want the people to rise up and do justice to the priests, [but] it is not necessary for him to know what is behind this dummy of the people, and what the doers' means are. He washes his hands of all that; this is his role. He has expressed his feeling; the people are the best judge. He can indulge in his enthusiasm without qualms, something that the doer, for example, is not able to do, as he has prepared his public and holds their strings. Bailly knew nothing. It is sufficient that he suspected it, and let no one be mistaken: there is a whole world of difference between knowing in detail and knowing in general.

There must no doubt be some correlation between one person's preparations and another's discourse. But doesn't the situation suffice? A third party can handle this, suggesting reasons to one, giving orders to the other, getting them to act in unison without their realizing it and without doing anything himself. This is the role of the American boss and more than one Revolutionary ringleader (Choderlos).

But when the machine takes charge of the risks, it demands the benefit. Tartufe remains master of his benefits, works for himself, and retains his personality. [But] not the orator, nor the worshipful master: he who ventures nothing gains nothing, and the benefits are impersonal.

In the well-organized machines, where there is a complete division of labor, the function of orator [or] writer is reserved not only for individuals but for special groups. The liberal caucus has founded a club in London where it keeps the ebullient phalanx of its orators in reserve, sending them out to various districts to speak according to the needs of the moment. Similarly, in 1788 the Societies had a poetico-political "phalanx" of men of letters that supplied the machine with what the circumstances required: songs, lampoons, etc.

These people are enthusiastic; this is their condition. They took care not to soil their hands with the doers, and knew nothing of them. They can be almost as easily deceived by the machine that uses them as the general public, and only have eyes for the Society and its general suggestions.

Thus enthusiasm is possible since there is not really hypocrisy, and hence inevitable. The Society's orator is not a cynic. He can look away from the wrong he does, head for the goal, and wash his hands of the means; he can be intoxicated with the principles and ignorant of the machine's schemes.

The characteristic of the boss is obliviousness, the characteristic of the worshipful master is ignorance, the characteristic of the orator is inconsequential reasoning, imprudence. Steeped in theoretical spirit, he cannot help seeking opportunities to display it, always with enthusiasm. Enthusiasm is appropriate in this case; the democratic principle requires it. On the morrow he will see; he will understand the abuses and attempt to oppose them bravely, ridiculously, all by himself. And the day after that he will start all over again. This is La Fayette, for example, refusing to do away with the Societies in 1791—and especially in 1830, when he repeats what he had done in 1789; he was incorrigible.

So how could these provincial men of law, who formed the greater part of the Social phalanx, not be enthusiastic?

What emotion for a "philosopher" of the shops or law offices to see his petty logic set the "people" in motion, and such great things as the State, the crown, the king, and the nobility shaken by his voice? What faith in the ideas, the principles of theoretical democracy, when one accomplishes the great Work by their means? He does not know and does not want to know that he is but a cog, an instrument, himself, and the people an organized gang. In a way, he is right, for he is a necessary cog . . . If he is a cog, the machine can no doubt replace him, it does not need him personally, but it cannot dispense with the role he plays—and so long as he plays it better than others, he can make himself indispensable.

This power is not *personal,* however. The orator, the writer, the necessary cogs, are never anything but cogs. It is not for their talents and characters alone—for themselves, in a word—that they are appreciated and heeded, but inasmuch as they serve patriotism. The machine does not submit to their influence, but most generously rewards their good will.

Their talent, their glory is not theirs; it is in the role they have agreed to play. But they do not know this. Hence the incredible obliviousness of the Revolutionary and [also] his astonishing clairvoyance.

Desmoulins, in 1792, is always six months ahead of [public] opinion. Once he is purged and fallen from his perch, he is as blind and obtuse about the

Revolution as the most benighted of the émigrés.

II. RESPONSIBILITY

We forget that the world of Philosophical Societies creates a new condition, in which eventually one no longer knows whether one is guilty or innocent, and in which Christian morality no longer exists. Of course, one is free to leave this condition, but so long as one remains, moral freedom, which no undisguised tyranny can touch, is destroyed. One renounces one's personality, one's own being. Here one can do wrong without remorse or responsibility, and good without effort or merit.

Thus the working of the machine has as its condition and effect the creation of special moral situations that are new, previously unknown and still not understood. They are impossible to understand and judge if one abides by natural relationships between men, normal living conditions and moral conscience. The patriot submits to a Work of moral dissociation that makes him lose, in fact and by right, all autonomy, all personal independence, and any chance of ever retrieving it if his training [by the Society] is completed. For the machine can only put up with impersonal instruments, and the moral dissociation we have tried to describe is the guarantee of this impersonality and the means by which to obtain it.

Indeed we must realize that these causes, these situations we have described, are permanent. It is not just once, but for years, that the orator, the ringleader, and the worshipful master, are placed in unnatural situations. They are submitted to veritable training which keeps their Social beings, the citizens in them, constantly growing, while their real characters and personalities wither. And thus Social life[33] moves proportionately farther and farther away from real life, the world and society of the real world, as one gradually penetrates into the governing inner circles.

Thus one must not hasten to accuse the least guilty. Those who know the machine know there exist mitigating circumstances, unknown to ordinary life, and the popular curse that weighed on the last Jacobins' old age may be as unfair as the enthusiasm that had acclaimed their elders. But conversely, inside the machine, though crimes are defensible, enthusiasm and the apparently purest virtues become ambiguous and sound hollow. Enthusiasm: let us not forget Linguet's phrase, "It is fear that makes them so bold." Virtues: let us not forget the tacit contract, which leaves no trace—scarcely even a memory—and which is concluded without a word or even a glance, and yet is there and gives secret, renewed interest to the most austere republican virtues. There are no true virtues, no total crimes inside the Society—for one does not conceive of either great virtues or great crimes without great character, and the machine's object, or rather its effect, is to do away with character and individuals. . . . Great virtues and great crimes are the works of men, personal works.

Shakespeare would have found nothing to inspire him [in the machine] despite the dramatic appearance of the situations, which is actually closer to the psychology of Alexandre Dumas, the elder.[34]

We see where the orator's role is positioned, between that of the worshipful master and that of the secretary or executor [the doer]. Actually, these roles are connected by masses of intermediate ones placed on a graduated scale. Nothing is more difficult than to ascertain a Revolutionary actor's precise position on this scale, and his responsibility. They are nevertheless very distinct, and it is useful to distinguish them in order to understand the machine's action. The hierarchy of symbolic Free Masonry rests on this distinction.

The worshipful master's role is the least odious and the most ridiculous; the executor's is just the opposite; the orator's is in between: his speeches are just generalizations. One must not be mistaken: these speeches of Robespierre's, full of pomposity and nonsense, which appear so mortally dull today and suitable to any situation, were timely works prepared for the occasion, with a specific goal in mind. That does not mean they required precise knowledge of the executors' plans, for this could only have been harmful, and anyway the working of the machine allowed this to be avoided.

This moral scale of Social roles terminates at the top in intellectual obliviousness, and at the bottom in moral obliviousness. The worshipful master is the nominal head of the Society; he keeps his honor intact, but on the condition that he knows nothing and understands nothing. The executor is the actual master of the machine, actually responsible, but morally irresponsible—for he can be sincere, he sees the machine's ideal from the outside and is too narrow-minded and unrefined to have the slightest personal consciousness of moral good, the good that bad methods dishonor. Thus one can imagine that such a man could put great generosity, even a certain disinterest, into the worst betrayals, when, [although] his instinct shows him the goal as the triumph of his appetites, he [also] sees it hailed by so many respected and honorable men as the advent of justice and happiness.

Put together Petion, who knew nothing, with Danton, who saw nothing, and Panis, who thought he was doing the right thing, and you have the September massacres. Danton acted as Panis's conscience, and Panis saved the Republic while Petion cleansed its virtue.

But where is the responsibility, and who should be blamed? The association.

One can at least imagine that such an example and such [Masonic] training took a great load off the conscience, or what was left of it, and in the atmosphere of some lodge's back room could eventually produce veritable moral monsters, inverted consciences, guided by hatred and death rather than life and love.

What this all amounts to is the destruction of the individual by means of moral dissolution.

CONCLUSION

The Effects of the Machine

The machine creates the kind of men that are necessary to it. It develops this new breed, nurturing it secretly in its bosom first, then gradually bringing it into the light as it gathers strength, encouraging it, sheltering it, protecting it, ensuring its victory over all other social types. The impersonal man, the man without attachments that the ideologues of 1789 dreamt of, is born. He is multiplying before our eyes, and soon there will be none other. This is the colorless bureaucrat, just educated enough to be a "philosopher," just active enough to be a schemer, good for everything, because everywhere one can obey an order, collect a salary, and do nothing. He is a civil servant of the official government, or better, a slave of the unofficial government, the enormous secret administration that may have more agents and creates more paperwork and red tape than the official one.

To be sure, this homunculus has disappointed the expectations of the great geniuses who once entertained him, and Rousseau would refuse to recognize him as a citizen of his republic, but the puny freak would have the right to reply, "What's wrong with me? I am what you made me." And the philosopher would have nothing to say, for the Social contract only asks one thing of its adherents: that they have neither by their education, nor by their families, nor by their circumstances, any feelings, any special attachments. Now, our man corresponds point by point to this definition. He believes neither in God nor the devil; he has no family, no attachment, either in the past or in the future. His mind is perfectly free, mocking everything except the Society to which he owes everything. As for pride, dignity, intelligence, independence, what right has anyone to ask him for these? There is no question of them in the contract.

As for the effects of the machine's triumph, I shall only cite one: the decadence of the arts. It is in the arts that the character of a race or an individual used to be best distinguished, and this is where the new regime was to do the most damage. Indeed, the victory of the Caucus coincides with the disappearance of popular art, style, which for six centuries had followed and attested to transformations in the character of this people. In the following century, there were still great artists in France, [but] no longer any French art. There are still great painters (Delacroix, Manet, Corot, Cézanne), but no longer as painters used to be, surrounded, protected, sustained by the national art and taste, like large trees by the forest. If a comparison must be made, these painters would appear rather like those rocks in the middle of the sea, that are isolated, misunderstood, persecuted throughout their lives, beaten by waves of Philistines. The sea, a monotonous and sterile sea, flat and bleak, that only finds motion, rage, and foam around these last witnesses to the grandeur of the race—a sea without a name or homeland has spread over this beautiful country, and this is the effect of the Caucus, the achievement of the Society.

Fragmented Character

To sum up: must the good Caucus member be a man without energy or resilience? No. An imbecile? No. He can keep his intelligence and his activity, but not for himself. On entering the Society, he gives up his personality. The working of the machine manages to dissociate two elements that no one had separated before, nor perhaps even distinguished: a man's activity and his personality, his abilities or resources and his soul. It is his soul he is asked for, and to be sure to possess the soul, the machine isolates the abilities.

It is a fine present. And what right does the Caucus have to ask for it? We need only remember the theory: the Society asks the citizen to abandon himself in the name of the general good. And what right does the Society have to speak in the name of the general good? Because the Society has consulted the people and is the veritable spokesman of their general will, not their servant and advisor like a parliamentary party, [not] their protector like an aristocracy.

Here is what the machine requires: no more personality, and it proceeds by splitting human abilities apart. What is the bond? The machine itself? But is this nothing? It is in the machine's interest, since all the men owe it, not their talents, but their credit.

Thus the Society is composed not of men, individuals, but of human qualities, human fragments, unequally developed minds, whose talents, activities, or credit the machine uses.

But these talents obey collective and anonymous impulses. It is not the relationship of one will to another, as an officer to a soldier, or God Himself to a monk, for example; it is not an individual who gives orders, and it is not to an individual the orders are addressed—there is nothing of personal service here.

Personally, the follower only obeys his own reason, or the general will, i.e. the contract apparently signed once and for all. And in reality he obeys the contract against himself: for the general will and his own are, theoretically, one and the same.

As for will, the free gift of oneself, the Social theory asks nothing of him, since the Society is only founded to ensure the abstract independence of this will . . . pure democracy asks nothing of the people.

The gift of oneself, this is what cannot be contemplated, since the goal of the Social theory is precisely to ensure each person's ownership of himself.

From everything we have said above, we can draw general conclusions. It is not necessary for the executive agent, the boss, to be educated and have general views; nor for the worshipful master to have specific knowledge of what is taking place; nor for the orator to have anything but logic, enthusiasm, and general information about the orthodoxy of the moment. The first can content himself with activity, the second with logic, the third with fervor.

It is desirable they do not have anything else. [For] if they had everything, they would be *rare*—such perverse malice is not human—and *dangerous*: for being masters of everything, informed about everything, they would be tempted to turn everything to their individual profit. There is certainly something of this in Robespierre's case.

In short, the Society is satisfied with, and the machine needs, "fragmented characters," as Father Guillon so aptly puts it. Incomplete men are necessary, with gaps either as far as their consciences or reason or common sense are concerned, which makes them unfit for sufficing unto themselves, for they must not serve themselves. On the other hand [they must have] a quality sufficiently developed: eloquence, or practical intelligence, or honor and respectability—for they must serve. As for the aspect to be developed, the Society takes charge of that by the training only it can give: coaching orators in the semi-secret Societies and wire-pullers in the back rooms.

But this very necessity really shows what these men are and what is even positive about them: they are *impersonal*, in their roles as patriots, of course. These are little men rigged out with an enormous quality, which when isolated is of no use to them and is rather a hindrance in real life—their petty little private lives—but which finds its use in the Society that is seeking activity, not energy;

respectability, I do not say conscience; logic, not reason: impersonal qualities; human qualities without men.

Let's sum this all up:

The machinist, the man of action, is attached or forced to submit to the machine. He is not his own master, because he is compromised and could not maintain himself alone, nor bear the responsibility of what he is doing for the machine and himself. He knows he is serving the machine, and he wants to inasmuch as he has surrendered to base passions. His better side suffers under this yoke and disapproves of it. How many Jacobins were known to moan over what they were forced to vote for! This begins with ambition—the wrong kind, the kind that wants material power, not moral authority; [material power] for itself, without risk or responsibility. This begins with hatred, the wrong kind too, the kind that is content to crush the enemy without being on an equal footing with him and acting face to face. And this ends with fear: it is conscious servitude, the most despicable role.

The man who acts as the window-dressing, the worshipful master, is attached to the machine unwittingly and he maintains himself insofar as he is unaware and vain: it is unconscious servitude, the most ridiculous role.

The orator is between these two men. His is the most odious role.

If there is a milieu in which men are not responsible for their acts, either because of unawareness or pressure, it is the machine.

Put a fine man into the machine and he will do dreadful damage, conscientiously even, if he has a weak mind. Take the most bloodthirsty members out of it and they become peaceable civil servants, as they proved to be during the [Napoleonic] Empire.

Evil comes from the regime, which is the first condition for its existence; it does not come from men. It is like those retirement funds into which the individual puts one [share] and his company [or "society"] ten.

It can be said that in ordinary life, great virtues are held up by little defects that allow those of average courage to rise above life step by step: the conscience rests on some concern, [such as] concern for [public] opinion or for legitimate vanity. It is this combination that is called honor.

It is not the same way in the Society, where, on the contrary, the same little defects become as harmful [as they were harmless in ordinary life], and lead to great crimes: the most legitimate vanity suffices to make a worshipful master.

The effect of the [Masonic] Work of dissociating the individual's elements is that the faculties themselves, thus dissociated, first wax enthusiastic, then falter and waste away.

But what about the division of labor? It is good, no doubt, but on the condition that in each individual the person remains superior to the instrument and the society is a society of men, human wills and not human faculties.

Thus the historical misunderstanding concerning these three types [of men] in the Social drama is always the same. It consists in attributing to individuals and character what was due to situations. It comes from our persistence in considering the men of the Revolution in the state of moral freedom in which Christianity had placed the generations preceding theirs. In that state of freedom, evil was only attributable to men, each person made his moral being and was responsible for his mistakes, and religion gave the man himself, personally, and not his race on the whole, the means of salvation. The Christian religion is the first and only one that addresses individuals, that founds a personal morality.

ENDNOTES

[1] Translator's note: This word, which first appeared in the eighteenth century, was used by Cochin in a derogatory sense.

[2] Translator's note: The *Confédération Générale du Travail,* a French trade union founded in 1895.

[3] Translator's note: "Machinism," says Cochin.

[4] Ostrogorski, *la Démocratie et l'organisation des partis politiques*, 1903, a study of the American political process.

[5] Decrees of May 10 and 18–22, 1791, which were not respected by the Societies, and of Sept. 2, 1792.

[6] This, for example, is what was done by the Parisian center of the arms manufacturers of the five provinces or the mother Society of Jacobins.

[7] Bourdon de l'Oise at the Convention, Oct. 19, 1794.

[8] *Moniteur*, p. 205.

[9] *Moniteur*, p. 127.

[10] *Moniteur*, p. 307.

[11] Masonic secrecy is a means of training and progressive initiation. By a whole apparatus of rites, vows, and formulas, a whole hierarchy of ranks and powers, by the repeated promise of emancipation, enlightenment, and freedom, the follower is solicited step by step. He always thinks he has finally grasped the whole truth; he behaves as if he has: he has rejected

every faith, dogma, or personal authority. But other steps, new initiations are promised him. As long as he retains habits and vestiges of his former condition — normal life — he will not be qualified for the higher ranks and the revelation of the last secrets. Religious mysteries are nothing in comparison with the mysteries Freemasonry takes pride in.

[12] See "Humanitarian Patriotism" in *The Philosophical Societies*.

[13] Le Bon, *Psychologie des Foules* (*Psychology of Crowds*).

[14] Translator's note: "*demi-hommes*" in the text.

[15] Cf. Part Three.

[16] In the history of Bolshevism this remark about the preference for foreigners is verified once again.

[17] Translator's note: These men were all extremist leaders during a particularly bloody phase of the Revolution.

[18] Translator's note: The leading political newspaper of the time.

[19] Translator's note: Durkheim was a French sociologist whose prevailing idea was that individuals are essentially molded by society.

[20] Translator's note: "*Solidarisme*" in the French text, one of Cochin's neologisms.

[21] Translator's note: Another of Cochin's neologisms.

[22] Translator's note: Cochin uses the term "pure" to signify "uncompromising, strict," and/or "pure, unadulterated."

[23] Translator's note: Cochin refers to the Freemasons as a "sect."

[24] To the naive voters who address him as though he were a true sovereign, the boss modestly replies: "You're right, and I agree with you, but what can I, a simple citizen, do?" And they have no answer to that. (Ostrogorski, *Democracy*, vol. II, p. 380.)

[25] Ostrogorski, vol. II, p. 379.

[26] Translator's note: the "supreme Being" was the Revolutionary substitute for God.

[27] Translator's note: author of the famous novel, *Les Liaisons Dangereuses*, 1782.

[28] "*le vénérable*" in French..

[29] Translator's note: The supreme deity of Mazdeism.

[30] Translator's note: The evil spirit opposed to Ormuzd.

[31] Translator's interpretation of Cochin's favorite term, "*entraînement,*" used to describe the Masonic Society's manner of continuous mechanical persuasion and indoctrination.

[32] Translator's note: Tartufe is the infamous hypocrite of Molière's comedy by the same name.

[33] Translator's note: i.e., the Society's life.

[34] Translator's note: Dumas *père* [1802–1870] was a prolific author of historical novels, including *The Three Musketeers.*

PART THREE: JUSTICE OR SOCIALIZED PROPERTY, 1793–1794

CHAPTER 1: SOCIALIZED PROPERTY[1]

INTRODUCTION

Now we have arrived at the last act of the drama that unfolds with the logic of a theorem. Men are overwhelmed. The history of Jacobinism is not the history of the Jacobins. The men in the machine are like steam in a locomotive: there will be more or less, no doubt, but that is not what matters. It is the form, the mechanism, that we must examine.

The development of the idea, the "development of Enlightenment," presented us with three goals: Truth, Freedom, and Justice. And by a fatal inversion, what was to emancipate man enslaved him. The Society that was to enrich man annihilated him.

Behind the word Truth (1750–1789), we have discovered the *socialization of thought*, and at the same time intellectual servitude. Not only does the Work of the Philosophical Societies lose contact with life and stray into the unreal and inhuman, but it presents us with the tyrannical reign of a few members over the ignorant and unaware crowd: the uninitiated man does not know where he is being led; he must go there blindfolded. Passions and great empty words, such will be the people's share in the distribution of truth by free thought.

Behind the word Freedom (1789–1793) we have discovered the *socialization of the will*, and at the same time the moral enslavement of the person. The sovereign people can only want things collectively, with a single will by which individual wills will be absorbed. And the Social will thus obtained is nothing other, as we have seen, than the will of a few to which all the individual wills, after being disintegrated and isolated, will be led by coercion, their inertia borne along by the argument of conformity and *"fait accompli."*

Lastly, behind the word Justice (1793–1794), we shall see the *socialization of property*. It is a consequence of the socialization of the person.

For everyone justice means the respect of other people's rights, respect for the person first and for his individual freedom and property, an extension of his activity. But these notions cannot enter the categories of the socialized man. Respect is a moral element that implies a moral law and a conscience. In our [Philosophical] Society's world there remains only nature with its appetites. The philosophy of free thought has reduced life to a calculation of appetites.

"Society" is simply a large, well-balanced structure comprised of selfish individuals, each holding the others in check according to the rules of a "distributive justice" that gives equal shares and treatment to all. That is the theory, and if, in practice, a man does not see his interest this way and takes advantage, too bad for him: society coerces and condemns him — in the name of his own interest, it is true, not that of a higher principle. He is [considered] "unaware." Ever since the peasant uprisings[2] and the trade unions it has been like this.

Social duty may be understood as a sacrifice to a higher reality, not as a sacrifice of oneself for the sake of oneself. Rousseau himself acknowledged the fact and that is why he founded his civil religion. This is a makeshift resource, a necessary symbol, intended to help corrupt or weak men elevate themselves to the *Social state*. This resource is a religion, but a religion that has nothing to attach people and everything to coerce them. It is an expedient, a legislator's subterfuge, not an apostle's teaching.

Rousseau, despite his utopian *Social Contract*, remains a son of tradition. He speaks like a believer in God, and his disciple Robespierre indignantly spurns the goddess nature and the goddess reason. This mystique of Rousseau's would be utterly disdained by our free thinkers, the Durkheims or the Lévy-Bruhls, for whom morality and religion are aimless mistakes and illusions.

And if there is neither duty nor obligation, there only remains coercion. So think the Jacobins and our socialists. Society is a conflict between covetous desires. But here again, thanks to organization, instead of anarchy and domestic warfare, we find order — a monstrous, forced order, the product not of love but of hatred.

Historically, this third and last phase of the Revolution, when Rousseau's idea of direct democracy was finally achieved, was the year of the Terror or Revolutionary government (August 1793-August 1794). It was a vast collectivist experiment encompassing the entire country of France.

This new Revolution, as profound as that of 1789, was imposed by the law of democracy on the Jacobins themselves, who followed along under duress, without seeing where they were going. The Committee of Public Safety, the center of the socialized bloc, became the regime of arbitrariness and skirmishes.

The philosophism of 1770 was the dogmatism of freedom; the patriotism of 1793 was the despotism of freedom.

I. THE REVOLUTIONARY GOVERNMENT

The date August 23, 1793, saw the finishing touch of the regime with the decree of levy *en masse*, which placed all the French people in standing requisition, body and soul, for the common safety. Thus was achieved the Social fiction of a single collective will, substituted not only rightfully, morally, but legally and in fact, for each individual will. This was the essential act of the new regime, an act of socialization; the laws of the Terror would only be its development, and the Revolutionary government its instrument. This was the official advent of direct democracy.

On one hand, ceasing to be the secret inspiration of the power, the hidden action of the Philosophical Societies was revealed and became the normal regime of public order.

On the other hand, carrying the consequences of socialist theory to their conclusion, this regime, after the socialization of the individual, undertook the communization of possessions.

The affliction it would cause and the violence it represented is remembered by its name: the Terror.

At any rate, we have here the oddest political and social experiment of this type that has ever been attempted so far.[3]

Direct democracy does not invalidate the will of each person; it sanctions this will by automatically attributing the only object to it that makes it absolute and that it cannot deny: the good of all. The new power's expression was never "I want," but "you cannot help wanting." It was not one man's convenience that dictated the law; it was reason, the *people*, whose current masters were merely their servants and spokesmen. It was in the name of this common good, this "Public Safety," that the new power would henceforth command. One did not admit that opinions could vary or intentions hesitate about this, for the people were reasonable and virtuous, which was why no one commanded. However, this consciousness lay dormant in most people; it was only conscious among those politicians who were democrats, the only people worthy of the name, though they were one in a hundred.

More serious was the fact that this consciousness that talked in the clubs and Philosophical Societies did nothing but talk—it was the real people who acted, suffered, and worked. Hence for *democracy* there could be a great deployment of virtue: it cost nothing. But for the [common] people the additional affliction was appalling, for they were the ones to pay for this virtue. [So] between the little people [of the Societies] who talked and the great people who worked there was more conflict.

There were people and people, depending on whether one legislated, speechified, and moralized on the rostrum [of the Chamber of Deputies], or one toiled, worked, and lived. Though denied in theory, the gap widened between the two precisely because it was denied, and the legislating logic lost the counterbalance of reality. The whole nation eventually submitted.

And likewise there was power and power: one in name, the Convention, which was nothing; and the other which was everything indeed, the Committee of Public Safety, or more exactly its Bureau of Enforcement, whose name the most qualified historians of the Revolution still know. Enforcement of the law, such is indeed the big problem in a regime. The problem of enforcing the laws was the only one the Social regime had to deny under penalty of disavowing itself, and it was what fettered the regime more than anything else, precisely for the same reason that made the regime deny the problem: faith in the agreement of the general will with the individual will.

When a question was proposed, each person was free to give an opinion. But once the Society had made a decision, one was "bound," i.e. obliged to adopt the Social verdict outside [the Society], whether or not one had approved it inside. There lay the essential reason for all the Philosophical Societies' statutes. And it was understandable. In any other society, union has a guarantee: the power of self-interest, instinct, conviction, and of the leader. [But] this Society had no power, only respect for the verdict of the majority. The law, that was the only cohesive bond, and he who broke the bond betrayed the others' interests.

And here was the peculiar characteristic of the new *power*. In theory there was no longer any power, since there was no longer any gap between the people and the prince, between the general will and the individual will. [But] in practice there was never any [power] more intrusive, since the gap was at its maximum, and increasing every day, and the two terms declared to be identical were not only different but divergent.

This consciousness of the general will was dormant in most people—for lack of enlightenment, it was believed at first, so reason was deified; for lack of virtue, it was finally acknowledged, so the perfect and sovereign will was proclaimed the Supreme Being, and was imposed on human weakness by the terrifying police laws of April to July 1794. This is not the place to study these two Revolutionary deities.

But this consciousness remained alert among the "pure." The "pure" were the people who talked, from the humblest people's Society to the Convention or the tribune of the Jacobins; they were democracy, those for whom virtue cost nothing. The others were everyone whose labor and anguish bore the cost of the virtue whose glory and profits were reaped by the oratorical tribe.

The democrats were, in brief, the ones who claimed to be interested in the public good, those who talked, i.e. the clientele, not numerous but well-organized and well-distributed, of the popular Societies, the vast political movement that was headed by the Society of Jacobins.

To speak like Jean-Jacques [Rousseau]: the gap appeared enormous, impassable, and irreducible between the general will, that of democracy, and the will of the great number, the people.

II. TRAINING

So there had to be preparation, training, to give consistency in people's minds to Rousseau's social myth, to give body to this fiction of sovereign people governing themselves by themselves. This myth had to take hold of people's imaginations. Some had to be urged to make reality of it, and others had to consent to submit to it.

The Masonic, philosophical, and literary Societies had worked for thirty years to familiarize minds with the democratic argument.

But another difficulty arose when it came time to act. One was confronted with living reality, deep-seated obstacles. The existing rational social framework, reinforced by long use, had to be replaced by an improvised structure, a dream State that no experiment had ever justified before.

Thus for four years, from 1789 to 1793, there was a series of assaults of Social opinion on real opinion, of the Revolutionary order on the normal order.

For the latter resisted and defended itself. It was only through a series of demolitions and successive encroachments that the "sovereign people," the people per se — represented by the people in the street, the shapeless mass of the crowd, but personified by the little people in the clubs and Societies — would substitute their unauthorized force for the constituted power of the Convention.

First, they [the "sovereign people"] used the assemblies themselves to destroy the existing bodies.

The great achievement of this doctrine, the preparatory act for the whole system, had been the immense political destruction of the Constituent Assembly (1789). Killed were all the social or political bodies that had a soul, a life, a spirit of their own, to be replaced with inert mechanisms. For it was necessary to clear the site before construction.

The historian's task is modified by the novelty of the conditions he has to describe. Local history managed well so long as the question concerned the old order, a *personal* order for the subjects even more than for the master. This was a diverse order in its essence, governing provinces, cities, and bodies, each according to its spirit, its past, and its law; an order comprised of as many different constitutions as there were towns, and never mentioning freedom and the people except in the plural. But democracy cannot allow itself such variety. It is by nature the regime of *uniformity*, standardization.

Uniformity, for democracy, is a necessity of a material order first, since democracy no longer commands, it administers. And there is no administration possible without uniformity. Uniformity is the first law of the Work that began with the division [of France] into departments[4] and ended with the radical socialization of Year II, this triumph of administration that substitutes collective force for personal incentive (the legal phrase for initiative), even in economic and private life. Subjected to its impersonal administrators, the human crowd truly appears to be *matter*, i.e. a homogeneous and indeterminate motive power, taking its appearance, direction, and use only from the machine it propels.

It is clear such a regime cannot enjoy the luxury of varying its means and measures according to people and places. The more complicated the mechanism is, the more the electoral or taxpaying matter has to be dissociated, pliable, and homogeneous. The great zeal for equality of Year II no doubt stemmed much less from the resentments of the crowd than from the necessities of the power. . . .

And at the same time, for the regime this is a necessity of a moral order, imposed on the workings of democracy from the very beginning of its philosophical origins. The secret of a democratic center's power is [its ability] to bring the supposed will of all to bear on each person, whether it be called reason, [public] opinion, or general interest. From the *Bureau of Enforcement* in the Committee of Public Safety to the least national agent, the decisive argument for dealing with one rebellious will was the submission of the other wills, and it was not rare to see circulars addressed [individually] to sixty recalcitrant towns in this form: "You are the only ones to resist." Such was the constant procedure for handling [public] opinion, from the "royal art" of the first Masonic centers, to the methods of Year II. In the heyday of the Bureau of Enforcement, starting in Nivôse,[5] its clerks spent their days making charts, recording, tallying, which allowed the center to focus all the weight of its [newly] acquired partisans on each dissident, "federalist" [town]. Now, it is obvious such a task assumes the terrain has been leveled and all the elements are the same. On the thousand diverse physiognomies of the former France that the personal power knew each by name, an administrative uniform had to be imposed, so that the confinement to barracks of Year II might be made possible. The towns had to be numbered, the provinces divided into lots, the nation chopped up.

Thus the historian can no longer restrict himself on such subjects to the literary methods that are well suited to the unexpected occurrences and variety of the personal order, but so little suited to the rigor and symmetry of the Social regime. It is not a pencil and a paintbrush he needs here, but a square and a compass . . .

[But] the center's plan, everywhere the same, was everywhere deformed by local resistance, revolt, or inertia, and the proportions of this alloy varied infinitely. To draw out the common element in its purity, the historian must broaden his field of research to grasp the frequently concealed characteristics. Then only will it become possible when studying each fact to distinguish the dosage—between collective action and personal resistance—of the alloy, ridding it of the ambiguous characteristic that no material precision can make it lose. Indeed the same act, for example the levy *en masse* of some village in order to treat ground with saltpeter in May 1794, or the "voluntary donation" of shirts and shoes by some popular Society, attested by the same witnesses in the same emphatic terms, may have been prompted by either extreme terror or extreme enthusiasm, depending on whether it was the action of the center or personal initiative that prevailed.

III. COMMUNIST AUTOCRACY

The communism of property is the last application of the Social contract. Since every *right* derives from the People-Sovereign, possessions as well as individuals are in the people's hands.

The decree of August 23, 1793, marks the advent of the new reign: the socialism of property will simply be the counterpart of the socialization of wills. No more intermediary between the governor and the governed.

Serfs under the king in 1789, free men by the law of 1791, the people become the masters in 1793. Becoming the governors themselves, they abolish the public freedoms that had been their only guarantees against those who governed them. The right to vote is suspended, since the people reign; the right to defend oneself, since they judge; the freedom of the press, since they write; the freedom of expression, since they speak—a limpid doctrine on which the terrorist proclamations and laws are merely one long commentary.

In the economic order, the collectivity henceforth manages its own affairs and dispenses with individuals. By abolishing the cereal trade (September 3–11, 1793), it socializes the agricultural reserves. By creating price ceilings (laws of September 29, 1793, and February 24, 1794), it abolishes commercial activity. With the universal requisition of labor and skills (April 16, 1794), productive effort itself is abolished. This is the end of the personal regime for the people as for the prince, in the fields and shops as in the Louvre.[6]

All industry: metals, mines, arms, saltpeter, devolve upon the State.

When the people are on the throne, it is the State that keeps shop.

This unnatural system required such a prodigious deployment of coercion that it received its name: the Terror. The reign of the impersonal is a hell: democracy, the impersonal prince, governs backwards, and the State, the impersonal people, works at a loss. These are the two great truths that the Revolution's doctrine denies and its history proves. How can this paradox assert itself against common sense, first, then rights and interests; last ten months and continue for two years?

It is because the Work of the Philosophical Societies, through their intellectual coaching and Social selection, had created a moral state of mind. On all the great problems of public interest there existed an opinion of the Societies that was the opposite of real [public] opinion. The terrorist legislation is not the concerted work of politicians, but just the echo of the Societies' opinion—to such an extent that the Convention's decrees are prepared and sometimes voted on or enforced in advance by the Societies.[7]

And the Societies—since they are the people—appropriate and exercise unchecked the rights of which the new regime deprives the voters. The people have lost the right to elect their magistrates according to legal procedure, and the Societies take the right to purge them continually and arbitrarily. The people have been disarmed systematically, down to the last shotgun, and the Societies take up arms. They train, purge, and direct special bodies as they please—the "Revolutionary armies" that they oversee in the war against the "domestic enemy." Thus the Societies had never been so numerous (nearly 1900 in January 1794) nor so "unified" since the defeat of the Girondin schism, nor so prevalent since the "fear" of September and the arrests of suspects.

However, the substitution of the Society's life for real life did not run smoothly. At the first contact with [real] things, the reason of the "legislators" was contradicted, often within less than a week.

The markets are poorly stocked, so the Convention decrees on September 11, 1793, that grain will no longer be sold anywhere but there. Immediately the markets empty, and provisions become rare and expensive. The Convention, by the decree of September 29th, lowers retail prices, imagining the wholesale will follow rather than not sell anything at all. [But] wholesale prices are maintained, and in less than a week the shops are empty and the shopkeepers on their knees. The same law decreeing a ceiling on meat prices decrees one on cattle, whereupon stockbreeding ceases, and the cattle are slaughtered. The Convention hastily repeals its decree in order to save stockbreeding (October 23). But then the butchers, who still have ceilings, stop purchasing and slaughtering, which triggers shortages in one industry after the other: tanneries, shoemaking, troop-outfitting, ending with a scarcity of meat and bread (February 1794). On April 11, 1794, the Committee of Public Safety, bolstered by its census-taking, requisitions for Paris and the armies every eighth year-old pig, which it leaves with its master until delivery time. The latter, instead of feeding it, lets it waste away and die.

All attempts at socialization lead to impasses of this type. If these attempts addressed men, these brutal lessons would make them stop and think, but a Social phenomenon does not think. This phenomenon pushes on from one disaster to another, producing a forest of unnatural laws whose success in the Societies and approval by the Convention were as fatal as their enforcement in the country was absurd or impossible.

IV. THE MEANS

So was socialization a failure? Was the Social machine going to shatter on contact with the real world? Not yet. Quite to the contrary: we shall see it, using its own means, achieve order through anarchy.

As long as Social opinion was confined to the Philosophical Societies, it reigned and developed at ease.

When, after 1789, this opinion undertook to act upon real life and the masses, it first did so indirectly, by means of the people in place, its creatures, then through the government itself, which was becoming more and more its instrument. At this point the impossibility [of it all] became glaringly apparent, resistance increased and brought on one crisis after another throughout the year 1793. The old ministry was not equipped for such a task and succumbed between the two contrary necessities, the constitutional regime and the Social regime.

The anarchistic crisis of the summer of 1793 put the country itself in danger: in the party conflict the Jacobin Commune of Paris in insurrection dominated and humiliated the Convention (May 31-June 2), while in the provinces each department, each town, each interest acted for itself alone, deriding a power that was no longer a moral authority and not yet Social despotism.

Following this federalist revolt, the old government was rejected. However, the institutions—in the absence of men—still impeded the process of socialization. To accomplish this, the revolutionary impulse was put into the government itself—a desperate course, a new revolution as profound as that of 1789, but imposed on the Jacobins themselves by the law of the democratic movement.

The Jacobins followed the movement that carried them onward, for in their Social customs they would find the means, the remedy, the process that would allow anarchy to hold up and deviate, passing from a state of emergency to a state of regime.

This means, this process, we know. It is what the Philosophical Societies had always used to acquire followers and gain approval mechanically. We shall see the peculiar effects it produced in this case in the government of France.

So we are still in the realm of the impersonal: the automatism is the same, whether it be the intellectual socialization of the "philosopher" of 1789 or the material socialization of the "citizen" of 1793. There is neither commandment nor obedience. The people reign: as a whole they decide, as a whole they follow through. The people's soul resides in the Committee of Public Safety and the Jacobin club.

But this is the game, analogous to that of voting in the Societies. There the vote is carried by the argument of the *fait accompli*, bringing the approval of others, the "dead weight" of [public] opinion, to bear on the hesitant or uninformed. It is the principle of "conformity" that does not imply that the voter is convinced or even aware of what he is approving. Mechanical action replaces thought. Here in the Committee of Public Safety it is the same thing. In the Committee there is a *Bureau of Surveillance of Law Enforcement* that will be the kingpin of the system. It no longer acts; it ascertains and compares. It will stress the argument of the submission of "others." Established in July 1793, it will be omnipotent by February 1794, at the Revolutionary government's apogee. Weekly[8] correspondence keeps it informed about all the districts of France. It is the eye of the indivisible. Merely ascertaining and listing states of "enforcement" and non-enforcement, it applies the argument of the *fait accompli* automatically to every [attempt at] dissent.

And here coercion will be added to the argument of conformity, for this was the result: without any interference from either the Committee or the Bureau, the decrees were spontaneously enforced through mutual surveillance and coercion.

Indeed, every violation of these Social laws not only benefits the guilty party but burdens the innocent one. When a price ceiling is poorly applied in one district and products are sold more expensively, provisions pour in from neighboring districts, where shortages increase accordingly. It is the same thing for general requisitions, censuses, distributions: fraud in one place increases the burden for another. The nature of things makes every citizen the natural enemy and overseer of his neighbor. All the laws of socialization have this same characteristic: binding citizens materially to one another, the laws divide them morally.

Now public force to uphold the law becomes superfluous. The Revolutionary army, so necessary in November to seize the peasants' grain, is useless in March

1794 and is disbanded. This is because every district, panic-stricken by famine, organizes its own raids on its neighbors in order to enforce the laws on basic provisions; the government has nothing to do but adopt a *laissez-faire* attitude. Other people's misfortune is sufficient to prevent individual rebellion. And by March the Committee of Public Safety even starts to have one district's grain inventoried by another; to one department it only sends representatives from another.

This is a whole system of government by self-interest and hatred of others. Something need only be denounced to unleash the selfishness of all against that of the individual. It is precisely this passion curbed by fear that is called virtue in Social democracy.

There is no example in history of a more profound and complete social disintegration. Free thought killed society because it had killed the human person. Dissociating man and isolating him from every natural or moral attachment, it cast him like flotsam into the social torrent. In his soul the only thing it allowed to subsist was this ruin, selfishness, which it called reason and which would [in fact] be hatred or fear.

Normal society presupposes personal bonds: authority in the chief, competence in the administration, and among the members devotion to the common cause, confidence, respect, a sense of duty, and a conscience. It is love that has founded this society, not fear nor hatred.

In France the Revolutionary catastrophe has made national sentiment descend step by step—from the old sentiment of personal loyalty that used to give unstintingly and served itself without denouncing others, to legal solidarity and Social syndicalism that by principle goes to the highest bidder, offers nothing without getting something in return, always calculates and demands and never gives, and makes France a society of shareholders, a socialism of economic interests, and the nation a syndicate of selfish entities. It is the reign of the *citizen*, the Social man by definition, the reign of unity, indivisibility, as the Jacobins used to say.

In this organized anarchy of 1794 universal suspicion made every Frenchman his neighbor's enemy, tattling and informing on him, and the natural bond was—not a metaphor—the "iron circle" of foreign war and fear and hatred of the foreigner, not love of one's country. Without this negative reason, the brutal, external bond of Europe's cannons pointed at Paris, France would have been liquefied and spread all over Europe as it had started to do in 1789 under the disintegrating action of Jacobinism.

Such is Revolutionary justice, an astonishing edifice: *de facto* collectivism, continuous, universal sharing, established by the law of price ceilings and the principle of requisition, and forced commerce and industry, maintained by the surveillance of Revolutionary and freethinking committees. And this peculiar power, a tyranny without tyrants, pitting one village against another, one district against another, one canton against another, maintained, through universal division, the unity that the old order founded on the union of everyone: universal hatred has its equilibrium as love its harmony.

All the laws of nature and life were found violated in this adventure of a great civilized people that seemed seized by a fit of madness, with their mass executions, their shooting, drowning, guillotining, and, worse still, cold-blooded killing—by the hundreds—of women and children for a "principle of humanity." In reality there are two people. The patriot of the clubs, who denounces and harangues but does not fight, in no way resembles and scarcely pleases the patriot of the [military] camps, who does not guillotine but fights. Moreover, though circumstances made allies of them, they were never friends. They were wary of each other from the start. Each labored on his own side, one with phrases and pikes against poor Frenchmen piled into the prisons, the other with guns against the Imperial forces and the English. And though the oppression of the little people in the Societies was endured for a while by the terrified country, the reign of the impersonal could not last. The great people were too much alive to let themselves be thus subdued or reduced to inertia. The clubs were not the nation. The latter, which had reacted to every undertaking of communism,[9] started to straighten up after Thermidor. This was not the end of the crisis, but the specter was exorcised, and common sense gradually took possession of minds again. France could breathe [once more], as if awakened from a nightmare.

ENDNOTES

[1] Translator's note: This section is a single chapter.

[2] Translator's note: The most famous uprising took place in 1358.

[3] Translator's note: the original publisher, Plon, observes this was written in 1916.

[4] Translator's reminder: These are administrative subdivisions, like counties or little states.

[5] Translator's note: January-February, the fourth month of the Republican calendar.

[6] Translator's note: The King's residence.

[7] For example, the Law of Suspects (September 17, 1793), [already] enforced by the Societies

of Pontarlier, Limoges, and Montpellier from the 10th to the 17th, had been requested on the 3rd by the one in Valence. Laws on price ceilings were passed more than a year ahead in all the Societies. The law of November 1793, socializing basic provisions, was simply the copy of a plan outlined by the Societies of the Midi [the South] on October 9th.

[8] Translator's note: Actually every ten days, since the Republican week lasted ten days.

[9] Translator's note: This is Cochin's term in the text.

AFTERWORD, 1908–1909

During the past ten years our generation has seen the establishment of a new regime, in reality as in law. It has seen the tyranny of a "Society" succeed the conflicts of "parties" and the public habits of the machine replace parliamentary habits. It has seen the Philosophical Societies' verbal morality in the press and the [French] Chamber of Deputies: justice, truth, and conscience, grappling with real morality. Such is the fact everyone knows but no one mentions, the immense network of the Philosophical Societies, the true and actual—though not official—wellspring of our whole social regime whose vast administrative fabric would sag of its own weight, were it not for this invisible, extra-light support.

And our parliamentary regime appears like those caterpillars that feed their substance to a foreign larva that respects their central nervous system, which is the strict minimum [necessary] to keep these victims alive and feeding themselves, or rather feeding the larva. Then, when the larva has attained maturity, out of the cocoon comes a hornet.

This parasite that is neither seen nor named is tomorrow's official regime, today's actual regime, having finally completed its growth and ready to hatch, while many people are still unaware of its existence. It is pure democracy—whose parliamentary form is just an intermediate and degenerate one. It is universal statism, not a limited one like ours. It is socialism, collectivism, syndicalism, the name matters little: these are just diverse paths converging more or less directly towards the same end.

A generous fantasy, many an honest reactionary used to call it. Today it is no longer a fantasy. The fantasy, on the contrary, is the official regime, which is no longer anything but an accumulation of laws and fictions that are all distorted and driven by a new spirit. How can one call "fantasy" a social reality that killed the old France and has just killed again—for the benefit of Mankind—the France of today? When the young lay generation will have shoved the last old servants out, the old morality will just be a burden and the *ancien régime* in ruins.

A "city in the clouds" if you like, but built of solid stone, and that is no doubt exactly what Aristophanes meant.

ABOUT THE AUTHOR

Augustin Cochin

Augustin Cochin (1876-1916) has been acknowledged by François Furet as one of two indispensable historians who have written about the French Revolution. (The other is Alexis de Tocqueville.) Born to a prominent liberal Catholic family, he was able to be remarkably impartial on the historical subject to which he devoted his life. Inspired by the work of Émile Durkheim, Cochin undertook a minute analysis of provincial clubs and societies. Not only have the results provided the data for a sociological analysis of the revolution but, even more important, his work shows clearly how the revolution was organized long before the events of 1789. Wounded four times in World War I, Cochin died before he was able to complete or revise his work. This translation is an attempt to present his unfinished writings in a clear and coherent form.

BIOGRAPHICAL NOTES

Claude Polin

Born in Paris, France, in 1937, Claude Polin was educated in Paris in the French public school system—at the famous Lyçée Henri IV from first grade through high school, and then at the Sorbonne, where he accomplished the whole curriculum of philosophical studies, ending with a grueling and highly competitive exam called the *agrégation*, and, a few years later, a doctorate in philosophy on the subject of totalitarianism.

Professor Polin has been teaching political philosophy at the original Sorbonne (the University of Paris IV) since 1966, gradually moving up the hierarchy to full professorship in 1976. His specialty is communism.

A consultant for the Renault automobile company for ten years, Professor Polin is also a member of the Institut de Hautes Etudes de Défense Nationale, and was for seven years vice president of the jury for admission to the French military academy, Saint Cyr.

A corresponding editor for *Chronicles: A Magazine of American Culture*, Professor Polin is the author of countless articles, some in English, and many books in French, including *L'Esprit Totalitaire, Les Illusions de l'Occident*, and *La Cité Dénaturée*.

Nancy Derr Polin

Born in Boston, Massachusetts, in 1939, Nancy Derr Polin was educated in the Newton public school system, acquiring a solid foundation in French grammar, thanks to two excellent teachers. She attended Smith College for two years. She went to Paris for her junior year in the fall of 1959, met Claude Polin, and married him the following fall.

While bringing up two bilingual daughters, Mrs. Polin acquired a series of diplomas in English literature and translation, ending with the *agrégation* in English (which gives French civil-servant status and tenure as a teacher in French high schools and universities).

For 27 years, Mrs. Polin taught English as a foreign language to French high schoolers at the prestigious semi-private Ecole Alsacienne in Paris.

CPSIA information can be obtained
at www.ICGtesting.com
Printed in the USA
LVHW042356230222
711805LV00003B/262